Urban Tales Publications, Inc

Presents:

T0148044

Money &
The Power

Maurice Hawthorne & Jason D. Brantley

Urban Tales Publications, Inc
www.urbantalespublications.net
utp_inc@yahoo.com

Money & The Power

Money &
The Power

Maurice Hawthorne & Jason D. Brantley

authorHOUSE®

AuthorHouse™
1663 Liberty Drive
Bloomington, IN 47403
www.authorhouse.com
Phone: 1-800-839-8640

First published by AuthorHouse   07/07/2011

ISBN: 978-1-4634-0455-0 (sc)
ISBN: 978-1-4634-0456-7 (dj)
ISBN: 978-1-4634-1332-3 (ebk)

Library of Congress Control Number: 2011908100

Printed in the United States of America

Money &
The Power

Money & The Power

ACKNOWLEDGEMENT

Jason D. Brantley

First of all, I have to acknowledge my higher power, (which is God of course) who gave me the strength to over come those obstacles that I've faced in my past and also for the ones I know I will face in my future. I thank you for walking with me.

Secondly, to all of my beautiful children for just hanging in there with me when I was gon' on my long term vacation. Thank you Jaidion Brantley, Michelle Brantley, Camille Brantley, Brenden Brantley and Aniyah Brantley. Daddy love ya'll with all his heart and soul.

I give much love to my partner in books Maurice 'Moe' Hawthorne for helping a playa bust down these bricks! Yeah, I mean 'BRICKS'. Much love. I give thanks to my father Tyrone Simmons and my mother Brenda Brantley. Without ya'll I wouldn't even exist!!! Lol. To my sisters Keela Simmons, Tiffany Simmons and Tammy Barnett. To my brothers Tyrone 'Fat Dog' Simmons, Jr. and Keith 'Butter' Smith and Kenneth 'Flavor' Smith, Jr. I thank and love ya'll for ya'll support. To Kenneth 'Pops' Smith, Sr. may he rest in peace. Love you Pops. Also to Ronnye Beamon, Sr. R.I.P. and to Ronnye Beamon, Jr., keep up the good work baby brother. The N.B.A. making room for ya!!!

To my baby mothers Yvonne Echols, Loretta Gray, Kina Ferguson and Amina Goodwin. Thank ya'll for putting up with my bullshit.

I also like to thank the Federal Government . . . FUCK YA'LL . . . send another informant if ya like . . . .

Now, to all my fallin' soldier's in the belly of the beast, (Oxford F.C.I) Chi Towns Alexander Cooper a.k.a. Ghost, what's up play boy. Green Eyes out of Indiana, Tada and Jerome off of 40th, Lil Kev, Money, Lil E off Cherry, Magic off Center, Tydis, thanks for the shoes playa, C.P. and all the Mil town and Minnesota playas.

To my Milan playas, Paul 'Smalls' Moore, thanks for the knowledge and wisdom you shared wit' a playa, Perris Cannaday, can you see me now?? Lil Greg a.k.a. Gee, thanks for the advice on business, I needed that. To my brother from a different mother Shamari 'Twin' Hooper, Sherod, Lil Bro, Snoop, Quo, Lil Dog, TA, Lee-Lee, Charles Crick, Lil Dee Bo, Cash, Gutter, Stoval, Big Moe from Battle Creek, Adoff, Richard Woods, Antiono Washington, Pat, R.P., Sterlin, J.R.(H-Unit). Mike with the one gold tooth!! Lol, James Alponse, a real true friend, A.D., Red, Muff, Lil Mike, Bam, Nina Ross the Boss, Tim a.k.a. Timothy, Billy B.J. Chambers from the Chamber Brothers, whats up playa, Doug, the biggest nigga on the pound, McCray, Don Wan, T-Mack, Money grandiose ass!! Lol,

To my hood niggas, Larnell 'Fat Mack' Lindem, Taz, Lil Tone, Baseball fool ass, Amanda thick ass, Cash (R.I.P.), Peggy, Jeffery, Rico, Chris, Ponytail, Free my Nigga Antonio 'Chem' Williams, Torry Fisher, Cash Ball and Rolla Boy, Paper Chase, Cousin Corey, Deaky, Stevie, Chris, Tahee, Lil Mark, Irene, Gerald, Joesph and James, Black Mack, Lil Earnie, Sodie, Paulina, Rebecca, Take It Easy, Shake, Black (my sister baby daddy), L.A. a.k.a Lacey Smith, Drew, Greg Pitts, Keith Saunders, Tiffany Chiles, A.D. out of the Haute, Dwight Morgan and More 2 Gain, and if I forgot you, my bad . . . .

ACKNOWLEDGEMENT

Maurice Hawthorne

First and foremost, I would like to thank my higher power for walking me through all of my adversities and for blessing me with wisdom, knowledge, understanding and my intellectual ability. I couldn't have walk through this formidable journey by myself. During this crisis a lot of relationships with my family and so-called friends depreciated and became diluted over the years.

Although I've encountered many generic individuals who were false advertising, I've learned that people come into your life unexpectedly for a reason. When time comes, they are put of your life for a reason too. In between, they answer a specific need, help you through a difficult time, or teach you an unforgettable lesson. So I would like to give a special thanks to the generic individuals and the authentic individuals, because if it weren't for them I would never elevate. I also learned that the secret of success is not how much you know, but how much you know about yourself. Knowing myself is the key to overcoming all the obstacles and opening all the doors in my life. Vision has lifted me beyond the ordinary and revealed to me the extraordinary. I shape my circumstances and my destiny. Determination and dedication led me to manifestation. A man can never become bigger than his imagination. In order for me to get something that I never had, I have to do something that I never done.

Second of all I would like to give a special thanks to all my haters! Those are the ones that give me that extra motivation and inspiration. Every brick that they throw at me, I use them to lay a firm and solid foundation. A lot of people didn't believe in me, but I came, I saw and I conquered. My superior blessed me with a gift and I utilized that gift productively. Sometimes what we think is the worse situation in the world turns out to be an unexpected blessing. I took advantage of my circumstances and turned a lemon into lemonade. Sometimes a man has to be placed in the darkness's in order to reinvent himself. Everything in this world evolved from darkness before it was exposed to the light.

Third, I would like to thank these following individuals for keepin' it 100 with their input and believing in my writing skills. Anthony Harp (Kalamazoo) Koo Koo(Cleveland) My Spanish homey Jimmy 'Kilo' Aragonez (Kansas City, MO), David Rounsaville (Chi-Town) Jerome Jackson (Chi-Town), Young Hij (Det.), William 'Duke Wally' Barns (Maryland) O.G. (Gray) Archie Powell (Flint, MI) Wayne Saffore (Grand Rapids, MI) Shawn Gipson (Det) James 'C-Hustle' Mannings (Memphis) Derick Harrell (Det) Phil 'C.P.' Spivey (Toldeo) Jamar 'G.O.' Gage (D.C.) Chef (N.Y.) Mark Anthony Byndom (Chi-Town) Clearance 'C-Low' Bell (Det.) Sticks (Chi-Town) Billy 'B.J.' Chambers (Ark) Magyk (Chi-Town/Rockweil Projects) Maurice Buckley (Omaha) Gailyn. X 'Bass' (Ark) C-Low CEO of L.P.F. Ent. (Det.) Sherod (Mil) William McCray (Cincinnati) My old school homey Mr. John Bell (Rockford, IL) Clay (Cleveland) E. Walker (Det.) T. Hamilton (Cali) Bo (Cali) Freeman (Indiana) Will Powell (Det.) Dex (Det.) Vic (Grand Rapids, MI) Henderson EL (Chi-Town) L.T. (Chi-Town) Bam Hudson & Mike Hudson (Mil) Gregory Hayes (Mil) Black (Chi-Town) and my man Derick 'Big D' Jackson (Rockford, IL) Gavina. V (Atl) Kee-Kee (Mil) Keith Saunders from Marion Designs (Stockbridge, GA) Timothy Robinson my main man (Mil) Tweek, my main man of Keefe (Mil) Ponce Earle stay strong (MI) Mario Dickens Creations.com I have to say this, it was a blessing to receive your unconditional support. (Mil) My sister Cynthia Hawthorne, I want to say I love you unconditional although we had our ups and downs you still proved to be true. Thanks so much for embracing your little brother and for representing me to the fullest. I don't know what I would have did without you. My father Larry Hopson, you will always be in my heart. If it wasn't for you, your true support and love I don't know what I would have did. You was always there for me through the thick and thin. No matter if I was right or wrong. You are the best father in the world!

Last, I would like to thank the Federal Government, y'all created a mutha fuckin' beast!!!!!!!!! And oh! That RAT! Christopher Rogers REST IN PISS!!!!! If I forgot about anybody, just read the book, it's an exclusive shot out. And I can't forget my co-author/brother/family Jason D. Brantley, we did it baby boy. You played a big part in this!

Much love! It's are time to blossom. I also want to thank all of my fans for supporting my work. Be on the look out for our up coming movie 'Money & The Power'. We are working on 7 other novels that are scheduled to hit the store real soon. We are about to open the doors for those who want to help themselves.

Also I want to send a shot out to all the up and coming struggling authors out there and all the soldiers trapped behind these walls. Don't allow the storms to stop your growth. Also I can't forget all the strong queens out there that are holding their strong men down through these trials and tribulations stay strong . . . .

Money & The Power

INTRODUCTION

Life is full of so many surprises,
And the haters come in many different disguises,
For the love of money a man is quick to sell his soul,
And fails to realize that you reap what you sow,
The root of all evil is not money . . . it is men,
Money can't walk or talk or commit a sin,
Living the fast lane who can you trust?
Only time will reveal if it's love or lust?
In our time of prosperity it's difficult to distinguish a friend, and
adversity exposes the truth of every man that lies within,
What is the difference between a snake and a rat?
They both will bite you and stab you in the back,
As your pockets grow your friends will multiply,
Once you're down on your knuckles they will all say good bye,
Used to cry and laugh with you . . . but all they did was pretend,
Fake love . . . Fake tears . . . And a fake grin,
One must know that with pleasure comes pain,
And a true friend will stand strong through sunshine and rain,
In a world that is cold as ice,
A faithful friend is beyond a price,
Watch your friends and keep your enemies close,
The ones that cross you are the ones you trust the most,
It's amazing all the power that a dollar possess,
Over that almighty dollar many souls lay to rest,
Be careful and watch those cut throats,
Sincerely . . . The realest thing I ever wrote . . . .

Money & The Power

CHAPTER ONE

The checkered marble dance floor of Club Sensation is semi-crowded. The multicolored fluorescent lights rotate, reflecting off the mirrored ceilings. Music by Lil Wayne blares from the concert speakers. "Let me lick you like a lollipop."

Chris stands at the bar dressed in a two piece Armani suit. A lengthy platinum iced out chain drapes down his muscular chest. He towers over the bar standing six foot eight. Chris was drafted to the NBA two years ago. He's also been label M.V.P. player of the year for the Milwaukee Bucks.

Chris' platinum pinky ring twinkles, reflecting off the multiple widescreen televisions that overlook the bar as he sips on a bottle of Louis thirteen conversating with a beautiful hazelnut skinned woman in her early twenties. From the very first moment Chris arrived at Club Sensation all eyes were on him. A majority of the women in the club has been delivering him flirtatious looks.

Being a pro basketball player, Chris always has his way with the women.

He places all his attention on Nisha, staring at her cleavage. Her hard nickel sized nipples are embossed under the lady Enyce halter top enticing him.

"So, what a beautiful lady like yo' self doing out here by herself?" Chris inquired, gazing into her ebony brown almond shaped eyes.

"I just wanted to get out of the house for a minute," Nisha answered, sipping on a shot of Hen.

"So, what you got planned for later on?" Nisha focuses on the front entrance of the club in a daze, taking her attention off of Chris. "You a'ight ma?" Chris asked, staring in the same direction.

A man enters the club violating the dress code, wearing a white Polo t-shirt, denim Red-Monkey jeans and a pair of crispy white Italian Air force Ones. He gives the security a dab as he trudges pass them without being searched or displaying any form of identification becoming the center of attention. He seats himself on the butter soft leather chair in the V.I.P section. A waitress sashays in his direction greeting him with a friendly white smile.

Nisha rises up out of her seat placing her drink on top of the bar. "It was nice meeting you Chris, but I have some business to handle. I'm sorry . . . maybe you can catch me on a rebound," Nisha apologized. She prances over to the V.I.P section with her Lady Enyce skirt hugging her curvaceous 34-26-40 frame. She seats herself beside the man she has known for 6 months. "Hey stranger, where you been hidin' for the last two weeks?"

"I had to handle some important business affairs. You know me baby. So, what you been up to sexy?"

"Now why would you ask me a crazy question like that?" Nisha leans over resting her head on his shoulder caressing his muscular arm and says, "You know I been lookin' for you. It's been two weeks since we did the nasty." Nisha proclaimed, giving him a hint.

A waitress approaches them interrupting their conversation holding a bottle of Moet. "Sir, I'm sorry to interrupt you two, but the man over there asked me to deliver this in courtesy of him to you and your companion." She pointed to Chris who is staring in their direction. They make eye contact with Chris and he nods his head. Chris cannot remember the last time he was rejected by a woman. *I can't believe she just rejected me for a nobody ass nigga.* Chris takes another sip of the Louis Thirteen.

"Excuse me for a minute baby girl," Motion said, in a smooth rich voice.

"Where you going?" Nisha inquired.

"I need to have a few words wit' somebody."

He walks over to the man he knows from watching him play basketball on television. He slowly struts to the bar to accompany Chris, clutching the bottle of Moet. Chris looks down at him as he sits the bottle of Moet atop the bar.

"Check this out playboy. I know who you is and who you play fo'. So, allow me to introduce myself." A burly built security guard steps up to the two men.

"Mr. Hopson, is everything okay over here."

"Yeah, it's okay. I'm just havin' a few words wit' my man."

"A'ight. Holla if you need me," the security guard respectfully stated.

"Like I was sayin' before we was interrupted. They call me Motion. I appreciate yo' courtesy, but that would be unprofessional of me to accept yo' offer being that I'm the owner of this establishment. Besides, I don't drink nothin' that cheap my man. So since you're a guest, It's on me for the rest of the night. And that woman over there, you can have her once I'm finish with her. Yo Ricky." Motion shouts over the music to the bartender.

"What's up boss?"

"Make sure you give my man Chris here anything he wants for the rest of the night," Motion said with authority.

"A'ight boss man."

Motion extends his hand to Chris. "It was nice meetin' you my man." Chris rejects his handshake feeling disrespected.

"I'm straight lil dawg. I just signed a contract for two point three million," he arrogantly said, staring down at Motion with a smirk on his face.

"Congratulations my man, I'm glad to hear that," Motion replied, sensing Chris' pent anger. "I guess I'll see you around. Have a nice night." Motion politely said, before walking away.

Motion returns to the V.I.P section seating himself next to a smiling Nisha. "Sorry about that baby girl. Now let's get back to where we started." Motion suggested, reaching his hand underneath the table gently fondling Nisha's thick thighs.

"Mmmm," Nisha purred with her eyes partially closed.

As the couple enjoys each other's companionship an unknown man sits in a secluded area of the club wearing a pair of sunglasses sippin' on a shot of Remy. He observes them closely bobbin his head to Pliers "I Am The Club."

Hours pass by quickly bringing the night to an end. Motion glimpses at his Jacob And Co. twelve time zone Tourbillion watch. "I'm ready to go lounge baby. What about you?"

"I'm ready when you ready bay," Nisha responded, grabbing her signature Gucci purse off the table. They embrace each other's hand and squeezes through the massive crowd of people heading for the exit.

The unknown man that has been watching them the whole night rises from his seat following behind them.

A snaky procession of automobiles flood the streets of downtown Milwaukee. Chris moves through the heavy traffic in his platinum Range Rover. The chrome 24 inch symbolic rims flickers reflecting off the street lights and blaring headlights from the ongoing traffic. A caravan of classic cars prowls Waterstreet equipped with 24 inch flat faced rims and numerous television screens glowing on the interior of the cars. A 76 Cutty with watermelon paint leading the entourage pulls up on the passenger's side of Chris' Range Rover blasting Jim Jones "Ballin."

Chris makes eye contact with the driver of the Cutty who appears to be no older that 19 years of age wearing a white t-shirt, rose gold necklace, and a New York Yankee's fitted hat. They greet each other with a nod. The glass packs on the old school automobiles growls, commingling with blaring car horns, numerous car systems, and the cacophony sound of downtown. The volcanic sound escaping the 76 Cutty shakes the surface. The driver of the Cutty bobs his head reciting the lyrics from the song. "So we lean wit' it, rock wit' it, convertible Jones mean wit' the top missin, I'm sittin' clean wit' the bottom kitted, I hopped out, my saggy jeans and my rocks glisten, bailliinn."

A black Lamborghini Murcielago Roaster swoops onto the scene pulling up parallel to the driver's side of Chris' truck. Multiple car horns blow acknowledging the driver of the Lamborghini. He waves his hand to the onlookers, as if he is the president. Chris stares into the extravagant topless sports car locking eyes on a smiling Nisha and Motion.

"Yo rookie!" Motion yelled, leaning forward in the driver's seat, with a pair of Cartier sunglasses resting on his forehead. The five karat diamond earrings in his earlobes twinkle with the movement of his head. "This what real ballers do," Motion proclaimed, reaching into his pocket. He retrieves a thick wad of crispy big face hundred dollar bills popping the rubber band off of it. He balls up five thousand dollars and tosses it at Chris. Hundred dollar bills float in the air dropping like leaves. "Get yo' weight up rookie," Motion said with a devious grin on his face. He presses the push button gear shift as the light turns green. Smoke billows from the spinning tires causing the rear end of the Lamborghini to swerve uncontrollably as he shifts gears. A piercing screech penetrates the atmosphere as he vanishes into the traffic no longer visible.

Motion arrives to his one bedroom bachelor's pad located in the town of West Allis. Motion met Nisha prancing out of Mayfair shopping mall with her best friend Denita. Nisha played hard to get for the first two weeks, which turned Motion on even more. After their first sexual encounter Motion became addicted to Nisha's sexual techniques. Motion knows that he is only sexually attracted to Nisha. The only woman he has ever loved is Ayesha, the mother of his three year old daughter. They've been living together for the last seven years.

Motion and Nisha steps into the luxurious condominium sinking into the snow white plush carpet. Nisha slips into a trance taking in the stunning beauty of the condominium.

"You want somethin' to drink ma?" Motion inquired walking over to the mini bar that is situated with several different beverages.

"Naw, I had enough to drink for the night baby," Nisha declined. Motion pours himself a drink and rolls up a blunt of purple haze. He takes a toke of the blunt. The potency of the marijuana causes him to choke. Large clouds of smoke escapes his mouth. "Damn baby are you okay?" Nisha inquired, standing behind him massaging his strong muscular shoulders kissing him on the nape of his neck.

"I've been waitin' two weeks for this baby," she admitted, fondling his magic stick causing him an erection. He grabs her by the arm pulling her closer to him locking lips. They simultaneously moan in a moment of passion. "W-Wait baby. I need to use the rest room first. W-Where is the restroom baby?"

"Just go up those steps and turn to yo' right, you can't miss it. I'll be up there in a second," Motion said, watching her apple bottom booty shift from side to side.

Motion makes his way up the steps after turning off the lights in the living room. Nisha presses end on her cellular phone. She turns around unaware of Motion standing behind her. He startles her causing her to cringe.

"My fault baby, I didn't mean to scare you like that. So, who was you talkin' to this late at night?"

"I-I was just letting my friend Denita know that I'm okay and that I probably want make it home 'til this afternoon," Nisha lied, placing her phone back inside her purse. "So, are you ready to finish where we left off?" Nisha asked, changing the subject.

"You know when it comes to you I stay ready ma." Motion grabs her by the hand leading her into the bedroom. They kiss each other wildly peeling off their clothes. They fall backwards landing on top of the bed. She unzips his pants exploring his large mandingo with her warm tongue, as he lay on his back with his eyes partially closed. He cups the back of her head, his groans commingles with the slurping sound as she bobs her head. She twirls her tongue around the head of his dick humming. She coats his dick with warm saliva. She engulfs him whole making his toes ball in a knot.

"Damn ma. You s-suckin' the shit out of this dick." Nisha uses her skillful ability, manipulating him into ejaculating. "Uuuuh shit baby," Motion groans loudly as she swallows his sexual juices. He squirms around in the king size bed as she sucks his now soft dick back to life.

He flips her on her back pinning her legs back. She grips his mandingo guiding it inside of her wetness. He slowly sinks deep inside of her moving his hips in a circular motion. She plants her french manicured fingernails in his back biting down on her bottom lip. He reshapes the contours of her fist tight pussy as he gorilla fucks her.

The 42 inch plasma screen television illuminates the room. Their shadows shift on the ceiling. He drills her from behind spreading her ass cheeks a part staring at the tattoo on her ass cheek that reads 'Bubble Ass'.

Their bodies clap in rhythmicity, as he deep strokes the pussy. She moans loudly gripping the satin sheets. He brings her to an orgasm. Her creamy white sex juice lubricates his manhood. He approaches his climax, his pace quickens and his thrust becomes more powerful.

He holds her by her small waistline hitting all pussy. Motion's stomach muscles tighten involuntarily as he squirts his sex juice allover her round bubble shaped ass.

"Uuuh shit this pussy good as a muthafucka!" Motion proclaimed, making all sorts of sex faces. He squeezes the last of the cum out of his dick. Nisha cracks a flirtatious smile looking over her shoulder. He smacks her on the ass making her round firm ass jiggle.

"Damn you got some mean pussy on you. That pussy so good it make me wanna slap yo' mama." They burst out in laughter.

"Boy you so crazy," Nisha said.

Motion climbs out of the bed. "Let me get us a towel," Motion suggested, picking up his pants heading to the bathroom.

He turns on the polish brass faucet allowing the water to run. He removes his cellular phone out of his pants pocket dialing a number. He chats on the phone in a low tone.

Nisha remains on her knees and elbows contemplating. *Finally my life is about to change. I wish I was able to have Motion all to myself. I tried my best to win him over. It's time for me to move on without him and stop wishing on a star.*

Motion struts back into the room in a pair of boxers holding a wet soapy towel in his hand. "Sorry it took me so long ma," he apologizes snapping Nisha out of her trance.

"That's okay baby." Motion cleanses her with the towel.

They cuddle under the satin sheets feeling exhausted.

Six o'clock in the morning the sun rises, leaping through the crack of the vertical blinds, shining in Motion's face. He squirms in the bed tossing and turning with his eyes partially closed. He winces from the brightness of the sun shining in his face obscuring his vision. He feels the empty space beside him and realizes that Nisha's no longer lying beside him. He glimpses at the closed bathroom door. *Maybe she's in the bathroom?* Motion climbs out of the bed. He hears the water running as he steps closer to the door. Knock! Knock! Knock! "Nisha is you in there?" Receiving no response Motion slowly opens the door scanning the bathroom, seeing no trace of Nisha. He notices a message written on the bathroom mirror.

> *Dear Motion,*
>
> *As you can see I'm long gone. I never meant for it to be like this baby, but a bitch gotta get paid. I didn't want to do you like this, so I hope there's no hard feelings*
>
> *Love Always,*
> *Nisha*

She kissed the mirror at the end of the message leaving her lip print on the mirror. "Dirty bitch, I knew you was up to somethin'," Motion mumbled under his breath in frustration.

He turns off the hot water staring into the mirror at his reflection. He is astounded by the man that is standing behind him wearing a pair of sunglasses aiming a stainless steel Sigsauer P226 9 millimeter at the back of his head.

"Put yo' hands where I can see 'em muthafucka!" The intruder rants, watching Motion's every move. "Now walk backwards real slow. You move the wrong way I'ma blow noodles out yo' ass."

Motion follows his instructions, slowly backing out of the bathroom.

A second intruder comes into Motion's view wearing a pair of black leather hitters clutching a 50 caliber. "I seen you stuntin' outside the club tossin' hundred dollar bills like it ain't shit. Now it's time for you to toss dat shit this way and make it easy. I know you got a safe in here Charlie." The intruder assumes, glimpsing around the master suite.

"Ain't shit in here man," Motion lied. The intruder strikes him across the head with the 50 caliber. Motion crashes to the floor on one knee cupping his head. He can feel the warm blood leaking from his head. "Shit!" Motion grimaces in pain.

The intruder mounts the high powered handgun against Motion's temple. "I'ma ask you one more time muthafucka. Where . . . the . . . fuck . . . is . . . t-" Click! Click!

Motion stares behind the two intruders in relief. "Drop those guns before I wet you niggas," A raspy voice demanded from their rear.

Motion's right hand man Scotty stands behind them clutching a Heckler & Koch Mp5K submachine gun wearing a poncho. Motion glares at the two intruders seeing the fear that rests in the depths of their eyes.

Motion grabs the two handguns off of the floor gripping one in each hand. "Take them hoe ass niggas in the living room. I'll be down there in a minute," Motion ordered. Scotty escorts the two men to the living room at gun point.

Motion climbs down the stairs holding a damp towel on his head with the 50 caliber tucked in the lining of his pants, clutching the P226 9 millimeter in the other hand. He stares at the intruders in silence with a questioning look on his face. His lips curves, forming an evil smile.

He seats himself on the white, leather, butter soft sofa with the gun in his lap.

"So tell me, who put y'all up to this shit?" The men disregard his inquisition.

With an emotionless facial expression, Motion aims the gun directly at one of the intruders squeezing the trigger. His hand jerks involuntarily from the powerful impact. The intruder staggers backwards collapsing on the white carpet. He grimaces in pain holding his bullet riddled stomach.

"Shit! Come on Joe please don't kill me."

"I'ma asks you again. Who sent you my way?"

"My little sister Nisha put me up to this. She just told me to rob you. We whatn't gon' kill you Joe, please let us go," he pleaded, holding his bloody stomach.

"Yo Scotty, did y'all intercept that special package for me?" Scotty chirps someone on his Nextel.

"Yeah, what up?" Chirp!

"Bring that package up in here."

"A'ight." Chirp!

Within two minutes a medium built, high yellow complexioned man standing 6'2 steps into the condo with a woman draped across his shoulders duct taped. She squirms on his shoulder with a futile gesture of resistance.

He drops her onto the floor. Motion listens to her muffled cries, having no empathy as he watches her writhe on the carpet in restraints.

He sits on the sofa staring sharply at a fear stricken woman. He rises from the sofa with a look of vengeance burning in his eyes.

Towered over the woman, he snatches the duct tape away from her mouth making her cries audible.

"Good mornin' Nisha. I'm glad you're able to join us. You probably figured it all out by now. Yeah, I heard the conversation on the phone you lying bitch. You fail to realize that you playing wit' a real street nigga." Motion explained, gently tracing her cheek bone with the handgun, brushing her hair to the side.

Nisha gazes into Motion's ignited eyes sniffling. "I-I never w-wanted it to be like this. I a-always dreamt of havin' a man like you in m-my life to take care of me. E-Every man I ever had in my life n-never treated me like you did. P-Please don't hurt us baby, I'm sorry."

"Bitch shut the fuck up! I ain't tryna hear that shit!" Motion rants, slapping her with a back hand, disheveling her hair. She lets out a ear-splitting scream. "Remember the message you wrote on my bathroom mirror? A hustla gotta do what a hustla gotta do. Ain't no hard feelings. Maybe I'll meet you at the cross road baby," he said in a raspy voice, leveling the gun to her head.

"Noooo! Please don't hurt my sister. Come on man I'll do any thi-" Blocka! Blocka! Before he could finish pleading, Motion pulled the trigger at point blank range, silencing her cries.

"Uuh, nooo Nisha!" Her brother cried deliriously like a new born baby having to witness his sister murdered in cold blood.

Motion points the gun at the other intruder with a menacing look plastered on his face. The man inches backwards towards the door trembling allover as if he is freezing. With beads of perspiration on his forehead, he says his last prayer. The intruder bumps into a burly built man standing in the door way clenching a switch blade.

He grasps the intruder sturdily, tilting his head back, skillfully twirling the switch blade like a professional butcher. A glint of light reflects off the sharp blade as he slashes his jugular. Warm blood oozes out of his neck. He topples to the floor convulsing, gripping his neck with his eyeballs rolling in back of his head, as his soul leaks out of his body staining the white carpet.

Motion's colleague Toon stands over the intruders' lifeless body. He flips the switch blade closed. Motion stands over Nisha's brother who feels that he has nothing else to live for after losing his sister. Motion's eyeballs shifts around the living room at the bloody scenery. He aims the gun directly at Nisha's brother.

"Kill me you bitch ass nigga!" he shouted. He hog spits, missing Motion.

Motion pulls back on the trigger. The gun throws up as he empties the clip leaving his body riddled with multiple bullet holes. He squirms on the floor cursing as the terror of imminent death rips his soul.

Motion calmly hands the two handguns to Scotty. "Get rid of these. Make sure y'all take care of these bodies," Motion ordered.

He strolls out of the door continuing on with his day. His three colleagues rolled the three bodies in the carpet and disposed their corpses. Scotty took care of the murder weapons.

Motion pulls into his horseshoe driveway that is lined with manicured bushes in front of his 6,553 square feet one leveled mansion.

He hops out of the Lamborghini leaving the driver's door propped in the air. He deeply inhales as he steps into his one level baby mansion that he purchased last year for a ticket. With the help of his crooked accountant he was able to buy it.

He hears the clinking sound of dishes coming from the kitchen area.

"Girl, I know exactly what you mean." Ayesha chats on the cordless house phone, placing dishes in the cabinets. She's unaware of Motion's presence. She stands in front of the cocaine white marble counter in a royal blue silk chemise with a matching thong. The diamond bracelet around her ankle glistens as she stands on her tippy toes placing dishes into the cabinets. The muscles in her calves flexes along with her movement. Motion directs his focus on her slightly exposed voluminous ass cheeks that bounces firmly as she falls back onto her heels.

Ayesha's heritage is African-American and Arabian. Her long wavy jet black hair accentuates her peanut butter complexion.

He met Ayesha in 1996 standing at the bus stop on Sherman Boulevard waiting on the bus. He pulled up along the curb in a 94 Cadillac Fleetwood he had rented from a dope fiend. When he gazed into her light gray eyes, he knew right then he had to have her. He picked her up and dropped her off at U.W.M, where she attended college. They have been together ever since that day. Motion fell in love with her personality and physical appearance.

Ayesha grew up as the only child in the family. Her father was a local drug dealer who spoiled her as a child. Although he was barely around due to his occupation, Ayesha always accepted him and loved him unconditionally.

He is currently incarcerated in federal prison for drug conspiracy charges. Ayesha is very familiar with the dope game. She respects it for what it is, and that's another thing Motion likes about her. She never put pressure on him about being out hustling for days and coming in the house late. She knows that is all a part of the game. She has hands on experience with drug dealing.

There were times that Motion would not be available. He would have her make small transactions. Once his operation became very lucrative he established a team. No longer did he involve Ayesha in his illegal activities. He keeps the game away from his family. His philosophy is, "Never shit where you lay your head."

He halts behind the love of his life, smiling impishly gripping her small waistline, collecting her attention. He grazes her ear with his warm tongue whispering in her ear.

"I'm gon' call you back girl. Somebody finally decided to come back home," Ayesha proclaimed, smiling from ear to ear.

"Uh huh, I know what y'all about to get into," Ayesha's friend Veronica stated.

"Girl bye. I'll talk to you later," Ayesha replied, hanging up the phone.

Motion slips his hand in Ayesha's thong caressing her clit. She closes her eyes in enjoyment becoming horny. He presses up against her ass with a throbbing erection. He twirls her around. They lock lips kissing and panting in a moment of ecstasy.

He lifts her up, sitting her on the counter. He slides her thong to the side grazing her pussy with his hand. He feels the warm moisture on her neatly, trimmed pussy hairs. He plants his head between her thighs. He teases her by gently kissing her luscious thighs, resting her legs on his shoulders. She cups his head in anticipation guiding his face against her pussy. She tingles all over feeling the warm passionate kisses. He teasingly licks the outer rim of her pussy. Her face contorts as he tucks his lips around his teeth locking his lips around her clit, slowly twirling his tongue.

She encircles his head with her legs humping his face with great enthusiasm. She squirms wildly arching her back breathing heavily. He inhales a cool breath of air, gently massaging her clit with his tongue. She moans loudly as she explodes into an unraveling of passions.

"Gimme that big dick baby," she said seductively.

Motion unbuttons his pants unzipping his flier. He rubs his hard throbbing dick against her wet pussy teasing her. He kisses her cleavage, slowly sliding inside of her juicy pussy. He holds her by the waist giving her only the head of his dick.

She plants her fingernails in his back. They kiss wildly in heat. He lifts her off the kitchen counter and carries her to the living room with her legs encircling his waist. They execute multiple sex positions making love on the living room couch.

She sits on his lap riding him as he grips her breasts, pinching her swollen nipples. Her wetness trickles down his balls. He holds her still pumping vigorously punishing the pussy.

In the middle of his ejaculation he hears movement coming from the hallway adjacent to the luxurious living room. Motion climbs off the couch dashing to the guest bathroom with his boxers in his hand. Ayesha adjusts her nightgown hearing the sound of their three year old daughter Joy calling for her.

"Mommy! Mommy!"

"Mommy in here baby," Ayesha answered.

Ayesha can feel Motion's juices leaking down her thighs.

"Mummy I'm hungry," Joy complained, walking to Ayesha with her one karat diamond earrings sparkling in her earlobes.

"Mommy have to use the bathroom, than I'll make you something to eat. Okay Pooh Pooh?"

"Kay," Joy replied in her youthful voice.

Motion steps out of the bathroom in his t-shirt and boxers.

"Daddddyyy!" Joy shouts excitedly, trotting over to her father with her hands extended in front of her.

"Heyyy, Pooh Pooh!" Motion said, welcoming his daughter with open arms feeling mutual. The pink barrettes clipped to the end of her long braids dangles as he holds her to the sky spinning in a circle. She laughs hysterically enjoying the playful moment.

Ayesha prances to the guest bathroom smiling at the two most important people in her life.

"Daddy me hungry," Joy reiterated to her father.

"Come on Pooh Pooh, daddy'll get you somethin' to eat. What my Pooh Pooh want?"

"Cereal daddy," Joy requested, tightly embracing Motion as he carries his bundle of joy in his arms.

* * *

TWO WEEKS LATER

Dirty Red removes 5 kilograms of cocaine out of the refrigerator sitting them on top of the kitchen table beside the 1000 gram digital scale. He cuts one of the kilos open, peeling off multiple wrappers. A strong odor lingers in the air resembling the smell of fingernail polish remover. He places the two white solid bricky layers of crystal white powder on the scale. Each one has a Road Runner cartoon character stamp on the top layer. The scale calculates the weight reading all E's, meaning that it's more than a thousand grams.

Dirty Red breaks the two bricks of soft white powder into various chunks, weighing up all 4 and a splits (4 and a half ounces) for his large clientele base.

A majority of the 4 and a split customers are teenagers trying to come up and conquer the American dream of almost every child in the ghetto, to get that first bird (Kilo of cocaine) and make a mill ticket.

Dirty Red moves close to 25 kilos a week in Westlawn Housing Projects in weight.

Dirty Red's cellular phone chimes captivating his attention, vibrating on his waist. He looks at the caller's identification seeing an unknown caller. Having an idea of who it is, he presses send answering the phone.

"Holla."

"I'm out front baby," the caller informed.

"A'ight. I'm on my way out." Dirty Red hangs up the phone and finishes packaging the first brick.

He struts out of the low income residence freshly braided with a platinum necklace dangling around his neck. Motion leans back in his cranberry colored Bentley coup GT conversing on his cellular phone. Dirty Red opens the door being slapped in the face by a cool breeze of air and the fresh smell of brand new leather. He climbs into the car joining him. They bump fist greeting each other.

"What up?" Dirty Red greeted, glancing a t the nickel plated Glock 19. "I see you got that burner with you. Make sure you be careful. Those boys been ridin' around here all day."

"I ain't worried, this one registered. Besides, I rather be judged by twelve than to be carried by six."

"I feel you baby."

Motion gazes out of the front windshield, watching all of the oncoming traffic. The streets are full of activity. A box Chevy Caprice passes by them blasting Coo Coo Cal's "In My Projects" with its license plates rattling. The driver of the car scrutinizes the Bentley in admiration driving slowly. He tosses up the pitch forks to the young thugs that are standing on the block paper chasing with their hats banged deep to the right.

"So, what's on yo' mind?" Dirty Red inquired in curiousity."

"I just wanted to let you know how much I appreciate yo' loyalty. You know I been knowing you since you had snot in yo' nose, runnin' around on the block stealin' cars, and snatchin' old lady purses. I watched you grow into a man on these streets. I got a lot of love for you. We came a long way. I'm talkin' about from the bottom of the barrel. I still remember all of those sleepless nights sittin' in the spot baggin' up dimes." Motion chuckles as he reflects on the past. "Now look at how far we came on these streets. We got the whole city on lock."

Dirty Red sits in silence listening to him closely. "The reason why I wanted to talk to you face to face is because my man called me the other day wit' a deal that I couldn't refuse. He gon' hit me wit' five hundred of those thangs for sixteen thousand a piece." The words that escaped Motion's mouth causes Dirty Red to get goose bumps.

"I can work with that. Now that's what I call a playa price. I'm ready when you ready dawg. Lets do this baby," Dirty Red said with enthusiasm.

"I got one thing that I need to, handle in order to make it happen," Motion stated.

"What's that?" Dirty Red asked with his eyebrows raised.

"I gotta find a way to get the load from Texas to here."

"Mannn, I 'ont know. That sound like it's a little too risky. If a nigga get caught drivin' that shit back, they gon' plant his ass under the penitentiary. Not only that, somebody gon' be out a lot of paper."

"That's why we gotta plan this shit out carefully. If we make about two trips like that . . . game over. A nigga want ever have to touch that shit again."

Dirty Red peers out of the car window in silence.

"What's wrong?" Motion asked, seeing Dirty Red focused on something.

"Man that's the third time I seen that green Tahoe in this area."

The truck passes by slowly. Motion and Dirty Red gazes inside the truck locking eyes with a middle aged white man, wearing a pair of shades.

"Man that look like them people," Dirty Red assumed, becoming very nervous.

"You lyin'. You seen the way he was lookin' all up in the car?" Motion asked, watching the truck turn the corner vanishing out of their sight.

"Yeah, I seen 'em. I'ma close down shop and ride out to Racine and mess wit' this shorty I knocked last week. She been tryna get a nigga to come up there."

"Well, check this out. I'ma put everything together wit' my people in Texas and I'll get back with you."

"A'ight. Cool."

They bump fist and Dirty Red climbs out of the car.

*   *   *

The high pitched cheerful sound of children's laughter interacting with the symphonic harmony of the brown Mallard ducks quacks in unison, as squirrels scurry across the manicured lawn, searching for nuts that were left behind by the earlier pedestrians.

Elliott and Bridget are at the park seated on a wooden bench facing the pond, watching the continuous activities of wild life as they lean against each other holding hands.

Elliott is Motion's only and younger brother. Elliott is 17 years old, a senior at Madison High School. Motion has managed to keep Elliott out of the streets. Elliott maintains a 4.0 grade average. Their mother is over protective when it comes to Elliott. She tries to keep him away from Motion. She feels that Motion is a negative influence on Elliott. All she wants to see is her baby boy walk across that stage and attend college.

Elliott lives with his mother in a three bedroom house on the North side of the city. She purchased the house with her hard earned money. Motion offered to buy her a bigger house in the city of Glendale, but she refuses to accept his dirty money, being that she is a God fearing Christian woman.

Motion takes Elliott on shopping sprees every weekend. Motion is like a father figure to his younger brother. They never had a father in the house. Their father was murdered when their mother was pregnant with Elliott. Their father was a well known gambler out in the streets. A man named Slick Rick put up the title to his Cadillac and loss. He couldn't accept the lost and came back and murdered their father. Their father was known as Big Fifty. He was one of the most skillful crap shooters in his times.

Bridget and Elliott has been dating ever since they attended middle school. Bridget is seventeen years old, also a senior at Madison High School. She maintains a 3.2 grade average.

Elliott tosses bread on the ground feeding the ducks. They swarm around eating the bread. Bridget smiles at the sight of Elliott feeding the ducks.

"Bridget, sometimes I wonder what it would feel like to be an animal. They seem to be at peace, without a worry in the world." Elliott stated, tossing more bread in the grass.

"I wonder the same thing sometimes." Bridget added, gently rubbing on his arm.

"Bridge?"

"Huh."

"Sometimes I wish we could fly somewhere faraway and be all alone."

"That would be so nice."

Elliott reaches into his pocket pulling out a piece of neatly folded paper. "Baby I wrote somethin' special for you. This is from the bottom of my heart," Elliott proclaimed, gazing intently in the windows of Bridget's soul.

"So beautiful, so sweet,"
A love so special and so unique.
A love so strong and very rare,
Even God had to stop and stare. staring in amazement impressed by his own work,
A creation so beautiful that he molded from dirt.
I love you so much and that's the truth,
The evidence rest in my heart with all the proof.
When my time come and I'm no longer alive,

I'll be waiting in heaven for you to arrive.
As long as I'm here on the face of this earth,
Our love will continue to prosper and give birth.
I'll never hurt you baby and I'll always be honest,
It's until death do us a part baby I promise,"

Elliott sincerely confessed with heartfelt words. Bridget holds Elliott's hand silently gazing into his eyes. Silence grows between them. Her pulse leaps crazily, her heart thudding in response. They study each other's eyes. Elliott's mouth insistently moves against her lips. Bridget curves her arm around his neck desiring more of what he has to offer.

He slowly traces down her spine with his soft touch.

*   *   *

A yellow cab arrives to the tranquil suburban neighborhood, pulling into the driveway of a single family residence. A woman peeks through the curtains aware of the visitors.

Scotty reads the meter in the cab. He reaches inside his pocket and hands the cab driver a fifty dollar bill. "Thanks fo' the ride."

"No. Thank you my friend. Me hope you use our services again," the Mexican cab driver replied, handing Scotty his change.

"No problem." Scotty climbs out the cab along with his friend of many years.

Marco is what they consider a pretty boy. He has short curly hair and resembles Chris Brown with light impeccable complexion. Motion met Marco on the block five years ago. Marco was a young hustler in the projects who use to hustle day and night, through rain and snow. Motion acknowledged his determination to rise to the top and took him under his wing. Marco reminded Motion of himself when he was a block baller. Motion introduced Marco to Scotty and it was on and popping ever since.

When Scotty served a two year prison term for possession with intent to deliver an ounce of crack cocaine, Marco supported him faithfully for the entire two years. Marco's loyalty earned him a superior position on the streets. They developed a brotherly love for each other. Scotty has a lot of respect for Marco for holding him down when he was on his knuckles. When it seemed like the whole world was turning against Scotty, Marco had his back like a true soldier.

Marco and Scotty unloaded the trunk of the cab removing two large luggage bags, dragging them to the front door of Scotty's girlfriend Candice's house. Candice's house is a low key spot they meet at once a week.

Candice is a certified nursing assistant. Usually she is at work, but today she got a day off.

She ushers them into the house greeting Scotty with a Kodak smile.

"Hey baby," she said, holding the door open for them as they struggle into the house with the luggage.

"What's up baby?"

Scotty drops the heavy luggage and falls back on the couch. He expels a loud breath in exhaustion; Candice prances over to him and falls into his lap. She fondles his solid bulky chest. Candice's soft gentle touch eases his mind. As she gazes at him with her eyes broadcasting genuine concern.

"You need to get some rest baby," Candice advised.

"I can't do that right now. I gotta get this paper," Scotty replied, staring at the two large luggages knowing that he has a long day ahead of him.

Scotty's cellular phone play's a musical tune. He glances at the caller I.D seeing his baby mother's number.

Candice already knows about Scotty and his baby mother Kanisha lives together. But, Kanisha doesn't have any knowledge of Candice.

Scotty reluctantly answers the phone. "Yeah, what's up?"

"What tha fuck you mean what's up! Why the fuck you ain't been home all night?" Kanisha scolded.

"You know why I ain' t been at home. Don't start this dumb shit wit' me today. I 'ont got time fo' this shit."

"What you mean you don't got time for this shit. Me and Junior been at home all night waitin fo' yo punk ass to come home. I know you some where fuckin' wit a bitch."

"Kanisha I' ma talk to you later."

"Fuck y-" Click!

"That crazy ass broad got issues." Scotty mumbled in agitation, tossing the phone on the couch.

"Baby mama drama huh?" Marco chuckled unzipping one of the luggage.

"Want me to get y'all somethin' to drink baby?" Candice asked, climbing off of Scotty's lap.

"Yeah, that'll be cool baby." Candice prances to the kitchen in her Lot29 jogging suit that accentuates her curvaceous frame.

"Let me grab the money machine. Motion should be here any minute now." Scotty said, walking into the living room closet.

Scotty's cell phone chimes repeatedly. He ignores the call knowing that it's only Kanisha.

Motion pulls into Candice's drive way in his Honda Accord. He places a call to Scotty letting him know that he is outside, so he can open the door. Scotty's voice mail comes on after five rings. "All y'all bitches that keep calling my man you can lose this number. This is a warning. If I catch one of y'all hood rats 'wit' my man, I'ma fuck you bitches up. No need to leave a message. Have a wonderful, hoeful day, by bitches!" Motion chuckles, finding it amusing. He hangs up the phone.

"Damn that's one crazy bitch. I feel sorry for Scotty." Motion calls Marco's cell phone.

"Holla at me," Marco answered.

"I'm outside baby boy, and tell Scotty his crazy ass baby mama on his voicemail."

"Word. That's fucked up. I'll tell 'em." Marco chuckled, hanging up the phone.

Motion steps into the house seeing bundles of money scattered all over the living room floor. Scotty stands over the ironing board, ironing hundred dollar bills, preparing them for the money machine.

They iron the money to keep it from getting jammed in the money machines. Marco sorts out all of the denominations in separate piles. Anything less than a twenty dollar bill gets tossed to the side. They call it their fuck off money.

Motion feeds the money counting machine. The money spits out of the other side moving rapidly, making a fluttery sound. It looks as if someone is fanning a deck of cards. Each of their phones rings off the hook. They ignore them and continue to do their mathematics. They used to take one day out of the week to count the money by hand. Tired of their fingers cramping and taking the entire day to count money, they decided to purchase money machines. Motion never hired a crew to count the money because he couldn't trust no one.

After six long hours of arranging money, they hear a loud deafening bang shaking the front door. The door looks as if it's about to fly off its hinges.

"Shit. Who the fuck is that?" Motion blurted.

Scotty makes a run for the window. He attempts to jump out of the window, but before he could make it out the window, he hears Kanisha shouting at the top of her lunges. He looks out the window staring at an angry Kanisha with a baseball bat dangling in her hand.

"Scotty, I know you in there. Bring yo' punk ass outside." Kanisha rants, standing on the front porch.

Candice lives in a predominantly white neighborhood. Neighbors peer through their windows witnessing the confrontation. Scotty notices her friend Sonja sitting in the passenger's seat of Kanisha's Cadillac CTS. Sonja has always been an instigator. Scotty and Sonya has never gotten along with each other.

"How the fuck this board find out where I was at?"

"Scotty you need to put yo' baby mama in her place. She gettin' the spot hot. We got over two million dollars in here. I'm not about to take no loss behind some dumb shit. If you don't handle it, I will." Motion proclaimed, as he begin to fume.

Kanisha shouts in rage, rocking her head with the rhythm of her speech. "I'ma say this one last time. If you don't come out here I'm gon' bust all this bitch windows out!" Scotty opens the front door.

"Fuck out of here with that bullshit before the neighbors call the police! Move around wit' that!" Scotty rants, fanning his hand.

"I 'ont give a fuck about no damn police! I'm tired of you neglecting me and yo' son for these triflin' ass bitches! None of them hoes supported you like I did when yo' stankin' ass was in prison doing them two years! I was that bitch driving four and a half hours every weekend to come visit yo' ass!" Kanisha speaks truthfully. Tears flows clown her cheeks as she expresses herself. Hearing her speak the truth leaves Scotty speechless.

Scotty regulates the situation by succumbing to her. He struts over to Kanisha feeling guilty for his deception. He clasps her in the warmth of his arms giving her great comfort.

"Baby you right. I'm sorry for the way I been treatin' you. I'm just tryna get this money so we can live life and have the finer things life has to offer. You know I love you baby, no matter what I do or say to you," Scotty uttered.

"A Scotty!" Marco called.

"What's up?"

"Just go home and be wit' the family, we got this."

"A'ight. Good lookin' out, I appreciate it," Scotty thanked, walking to Kanisha's car. They pull off headed home.

CHAPTER TWO

The golden glow of the early morning sunrise accents the sky, contrasting on the steel grey single level mansion. The shuttle sound of mother nature whispers it's early morning melody.

A large number of DEA agents congregate near the one level mansion, whispering in conspiratorial tones, orchestrating a plot to apprehend a suspected drug trafficker.

Special agent Rex Dillard communicates with the other agents through a concealed earpiece. One of the agents signals his colleagues with a hand gesture. They file pass the illuminated olympic sized swimming pool, adjacent to the cement veranda dressed in black fatigue gorilla suits. They clutch their M-4 assault rifles with a firm grip. The rustle of their clothing is the only audible sound, as they scurry to their assigned positions. Two agents move quickly towards the oak wood handcrafted french doors of the mansion carrying a 60 pound, solid steel battering ram with handles for a two man operation.

Motion and Ayesha are sound asleep. The 42 inch plasma screen television illuminates the master suite, making their bodies a silhouette. Motion's body jerk to the attention at the cracking sound of his front door being knocked off its hinges, crashing to the floor.

The security alarm chimes with the high pitched sound, activating his security monitors. The disturbance engrosses him, awakening him from his sleep. He glimpses at the monitors that overlook his king size bed, seeing a large group of DEA agents pouring into his lavish living room. They spread out all over the mansion.

The first thing he thinks about is his precious little daughter who is spending the night at her grandmother's house. The thought of him spending decades behind bars separated from his daughter and the love of his life races through his head.

He can hear a cacophony of loud voices vehemently shouting. They scuffle across the marble floors, positioning themselves all over the mansion. Ayesha screams deliriously in fright.

"Fuck this! I'm 'bout to hold this shit on the streets," Motion muttered, bustling across the master suite, stepping inside the walk-in-closet. He snatches a AK47 assault rifle with his heart drumming against his chest.

"Nooo, baby please don't do it," Ayesha begged, terrified, watching him position himself in front of the glass windows to the balcony. He observes an agent hiding behind the manicured bushes stretched out on the ground.

Hearing the distant sound of their footsteps moving closer, he lets the AK47 burp, shattering the windows to the balcony. Fragments of the glass rains on the floor. The blatant sound of gunfire claps as they return fire.

Motion takes cover stepping on the broken glass in his Louis Vuitton house shoes. He scrambles across the carpeted floor making his way to the master suite.

He enters the long hallway, analyzing his surroundings. He spots two agents taking cover behind the leather sectional. Obstructed by wall, he fires at the agents, riddling the leather furniture with bullet holes. A shower of bullets penetrates the 500 gallon in wall salt water aquarium. The aquarium bursts open. Water and exotic fish cascades onto the cream colored marble floor.

The agents fires from all directions piercing the walls with bullet holes. A bullet rips through the drywall striking Motion in the shoulder. He grimaces in pain feeling weak.

"You muthafuckas!" he shouts in rage. He knows that he is no competition for the mob of drug enforcement agents. Feeling defeated and outnumbered, he staggers in to the doorway as if he is emulating Al Pacino in the movie 'Scarface'.

He waves the AK47 haphazardly from side to side, aiming at everything in his sight. The once lavish living room now resembles a scene in New Orleans, after being sabotaged by Hurricane Katrina.

The M-4's sing a song promising death. Motion's body jerks uncontrollably, as bullets disperses from the muzzles of the M-4's peppering his chest. He does a death dance staggering backwards.

Motion bolts up-right in the bed, drench in perspiration, with a look of terror on his face, breathing heavily.

"Baby are you okay?" Ayesha inquired in a sleepy soft voice with her eyes partially closed.

"Yeah . . . Yeah, I'm okay bay. I just had a fucked up nightmare," Motion replied, wiping beads of sweat off his forehead. He leans over and plants a soft passionate kiss on Ayesha's forehead. "Go back to sleep baby, I'm a'ight."

He climbs out of the bed in his boxers. The Prowd Family cartoon drones on the television, reflecting a kaleidoscope of colors in his eyes. He pads to the sophisticated European style kitchen, stepping on the cold Italian marble floor with his bare feet. He opens the door to the stainless steel refrigerator. A gleam of light from the interior of the refrigerator glows, making every object in the kitchen visible. Motion removes a carton. He tilts his head as he gulps the juice greedily. He closes the refrigerator moving meticulously through the darkness, making his way to check on his pride and joy.

He gingerly walks into Joy's bedroom. He towers over her as she sleeps peacefully in her full sized canopy bed. Motion leans forward kissing her on the cheek, smelling the fresh scent of baby powder. He stares intently at his innocuous little girl who the world will one day rob of her adolescence. He falls into deep thoughts as he watches her squirm in her sleep.

A couple more moves to go and I'm out of the game. I can finally be a full time father and the best husband I can ever be. I know my luck is runnin' out. After that nightmare I just had. I know I gotta be extra careful. It's written in the bible that warning comes before destruction.

*   *   *

Lil Wanye's 'Stuntin' Like My Daddy' rips through the speakers of a mint green Lexus GS430, shaking the concrete, stealing every ones attention on the block. A young hustler is posted up in front of Ali's corner store on 27th and Burliegh. A slender built man wearing a eroded Rocawear t-shirt, faded denim jeans, and a dingy baseball cap sashays over to young hustler with his hand clenched.

"You got that work lil' dawg?"

"Yeah, I got dat. What you need?"

"Let me get one for the eight." The man opens his hand and unfolds a crumbled up five dollar bill. He scrapes close to three dollars worth of change out of his pocket. The malodorous smell of man's attire contaminates the fresh air.

The young hustler wrinkles his nose in disgust, as he backpedals keeping his distance.

"I got you on the next round young playa, don't trip. I'ma bring a lot of paper yo' way, I just need a wake up." He tucks his hand inside his pants removing a small sack of ten dollar rocks from his crotch area. He drops a ten dollar bag in the man's extended hand. "Right on little dawg. I promise I'ma bring you some action," the man stashes the rock under his tongue vanishing through the alley.

The young hustler locks eyes on the man stepping out of the mint green Lexus, planting his chocolate colored Steve Maddens on the ground. The huge mirrored Lexani rims gleams, obscuring his vision. A platinum chain sways on his neck with the rhythm of his stride.

A group of teenagers stampedes toward a Honda Accord in a disorderly fashion, chasing a potential customer. He moves closer to the young hustler with his hands tucked in his pants pocket.

"Yo' shortie, you got that work?" the man asked. The young hustler's face creases in confusion.

"Do I got some work? Man you on some bullshit. I know you ain't smokin' dat shit." He assumes, giving the man a suspicious look.

"You gon' sell me some work or what? I ain't got all day." The young hustler's face gets serious and falls into silence as he makes up his mind.

"What you tryna get?"

"I want everything you got."

"Man, you sure you ain't the police?" he inquired, glimpsing around observing his surroundings.

The man pulls out a sloppy wad of money. "I'm not on no police shit." The young hustler's eyes beams, as he stares at the thick roll of money. Sensing that the man is not the police, he removes the bag of rocks out of his crotch area.

"I got twenty seven stones left." The man hands him two hundred and seventy dollars in exchange for the bag of rocks. He watches as the man kneels down, emptying the bag of rocks, pouring them into sewer. He stares at the stranger in confusion.

"Man what you do that for?"

"'Cause I respect the hustle young dawg. The reason why I did that is because I want a little bit of yo' time."

"Man what the fuck you on dawg?"

"I just want you to roll with me for a second. I ain't on no bullshit."

"I ain't worried about that playa," he said, lifting his t-shirt up, revealing the handle of a chrome 9 millimeter Berretta. "I keep my burner on me at all times."

"Whoa killa, slow down. I 'ont want no trouble. I just wanna show you the other side of the game. I dig yo' style lil' dawg. Every morning I roll down the block I always see you out here faithfully. You remind me of myself when I was on the block tryna come up. That's why I bought the work from you. I been where you are . . . trust me. All I want you to do is roll wit' me for a minute."

"Where you tryna take me?"

"To a place called reality," he answered with a solemn facial expression.

"Reality."

"Yeah, that's what I said. So, what's yo' name little dawg?"

"Lil Wink."

"I'm Marco."

They bump fist getting acquainted. They labor across the street. Marco presses a button on his keychain, unlocking the doors. The strong smell of marijuana smoke emits from the inside of the car, as Lil Wink climbs inside sinking in the cream butter soft leather. Marco inserts the laser cut key into the ignition. The steering wheel moves automatically adjusting itself. Busta Ryhmes "Ghetto Love" erupts from the powerful sound system gripping the attention of all the teenagers traversing the block.

Marco turns down the volume. The music drones in the background. Lately Marco has been contemplating on leaving the dope game. He has been doing a lot of research, trying to formulate his game plan. His uncle Kenny that's incarcerated in the feds been putting him up on game and giving him ideas.

Marco navigates the car through the dilapidated neighborhood. Lil Wink gazes through the windows in silence.

"Let me drop somethin' on you from playa to playa. I admire yo' ambition and determination to make it to the top, but I wanna expose you to some real shit." Lil wink looks at him wide eyed, digesting every word he speaks as they move through the heavy traffic on Wisconsin Avenue.

"Man, don't you tell me you on some Martin Luther King Jr type shit," Li1 Wink stated.

"Naw, I'm not on that type of shit at all. For some reason I like you little homie. Don't think for a minute that I'm tryna knock yo' hustle. It ain't like that at all. I know how it is struggling on these wicked streets. I been where you been," Marco proclaimed, parallel parking on the side of the federal building. Marco faces Lil Wink. "Can you please do me a favor."

"What's that?"

"Put yo' heater under the seat." Reluctantly, Lil Wink slides the gun under the seat. They hope out of the car. Marco drops two quarters in the parking meter. Lil Wink follows behind him in curiosity. They stride to the front entrance or the building that reads, 'United States Federal Courthouse' in gold letters.

"Man what the fuck you bring me here fo'?"

"Keep yo' cool shortie. I'ma 'bout to show you somethin'. Everybody always see the side of the game that glitter, but I'ma show you the side of the game that's bitter."

*   *   *

A throng of teenagers pour out of Madison High School ending a half day of school, after finishing their exams. Elliott and Bridget walks slide by side carrying their book bags conversating. They stop in front of Bridget's Honda Civic. Elliott leans forward kissing Bridget. Their lips intertwines as they kiss passionately. Elliott opens the door for Bridget as she climbs into her car.

"I'ma call you later on," Elliott promised. She pulls off waving him bye. He crosses the street making his way to his Chevy Lumina that his mother bought for him. It was her way of rewarding him for doing good in school.

He approaches the trunk of the car dressed in his black and red Jordan velour suit and a pair of number four retro Jordans. He tosses the book bag inside the trunk. He places his key in the door. He is startled by the sight of someone leaning back comfortably in the passenger's seat of his car. Seeing the man's face he begins to relax, regaining his composure. He jumps into the driver's seat surprised to see his brother.

"Man you scared the hell out of me for a minute. How you get in my car without the key?" Elliott inquired in curiosity.

"You know yo' big brother got connections." Elliott cracks a smile rocking his head side to side. "I need to talk to you lil' brah. I been doing a lot of thinkin' lately. You been on my mind for the last couple of days. You got anything on yo' agenda right now?"

"Naw, I was just gon' stop and get me somethin' to eat."

"Won't you take me to the Mercedes Benz dealership on East Sliverspring. You can help me pick out a everyday car."

"That's cool, let's roll." Elliott pulls off mixing in with the afternoon traffic.

"You know I need you to go to college. I need you to help me put the finishing touches on my empire. I do the dirty work and you do the clean. I don't ever want you engage in the street life. It's a dangerous game out on these streets. See, I built the ladder for you to climb. One hand washes the other and both hands washes the face."

Elliott glimpses at Motion as he listens to his every word. Elliott admire his brother and have a lot of respect for him. "Remember our minds are the controllin' and building force in all that we create in our physical beings and in our worlds. Our minds are truly the architect, the planner, and caretaker as well as the builder of our lives. Spirit is the cause, mind is an effect, or active force that partakes of spiritual as well as material import. All manifestations of life are crystallization of spirit. Spirit is the first step in manifestation of anything in the universe. All is conceive in spirit. Spirit is our source of wisdom. Spirit is the life force energy within us. It's about what will you do wit' the spirit. What I'm tryna say lil' brah is that you can do anything you set yo' mind to. I want you to help me take this empire to the next level of the game. You know I got much love fo' you." Motion pauses briefly staring through the window.

"I mean what I said. I know moms be trippin' on me when it comes to you. She don't understand the love I have for you. The only reality I know is survival. It's a jungle out here and only the lions survive in this world."

Elliott pulls into the Mercedes Benz dealership looking at the variety of late model Mercedes Benzes. They wander around the lot looking through the windows of the luxurious automobiles.

"Let's see what they got on the showroom floor," Motion suggested. They enter through the glass doors, stepping into the lobby. A pearl white CLS550 with cream leather interior catches Elliott's eyes.

A Brazilian woman with honey blond hair, golden skin tone, wearing a two piece Versace skirt set prances in their direction. She displays a friendly smile, exposing her flawless teeth. She stands six feet with long muscular legs. Her Jimmy Choo high heel pumps clacks against the floor. She is like the coming of dawn. She looks like she just stepped off the cover of a Glamour magazine. Motion plasters his eyes on the woman mesmerized by her beauty. Her long wavy blond hair bounces with the rhythmn of her walk. The smell of Miss Dior Cherie perfume greets their nostrils as she stand face to face with them extending her hand. Motion locks his eyes on her cleavage. Her nipples bulges underneath her blouse.

"How are you gentlemen doing today?"

"A'ight," they chorused.

"Doing a little window shopping today?"

Who the fuck this board think she talkin' to? She got me fucked up. Motion is insulted by her statement. "Naw, we don't believe in window shoppin' ma," Motion replied. She appraises the two of them and the Chevy Lumina that they arrived in, finding it hard to believe his remark.

"Well, if you guys need any assistance or have any questions please feel free to ask. My name is Maria Cortez and I'll be glad to help you today," she said in a strong professional voice.

Motion stares at the beautiful woman admiring her classy appearance. She sashays to her desk leaving the smell of her perfume circulating in the air. Her booty bounces vibrantly stealing Motion's attention. He stares at her bubble shaped ass in disbelief. She has a booty so big that the average man would run out of dick before he hit the pussy, trying to fuck her from the back.

Damn she thick as hell. It looks like she got booty implants. She gotta have some black in her blood.

"You like it Motion," Elliott asked, rubbing his fingers along the hood of the CLS550.

"Hell yeah I like it. She thick as a mule," Motion said, staring at her as if he is hypnotized.

"Not her Motion, the car," Elliott corrected with a smile on his face.

"Oh my fault brah. She had me gone for a minute. Yeah that's tight. I think I can roll wit' that." Motion gazes through the windows of the Mercedes inspecting the interior and the cherry oak wood trimming.

*   *   *

"04-cr-116, United 0tates of America vs. Donald Moore. This matter is before the court for imposition of sentence. May I have the appearances please?" the judge asked.

"Assistant United States Attorney Mark Gonzales appears on behalf of the government. Good afternoon your honor."

"Denise Smith from probation."

"Good afternoon your honor. Mr. Moore is present in court with his attorney Cleo Dutch."

"Good morning Mr.Gonzales. And good afternoon to you, Ms. Smith. Good afternoon to you Mr. Dutch. And good afternoon to you, Mr. Moore. And good afternoon to you detective Logan. The matter before the court this afternoon involves the sentence to be imposed in the case of U.S. vs. Donald Moore, who, on December 10th, was found guilty following a jury trial for the offense charged in one of the indictment, namely, possession with intent to deliver fifty grams of crack cocaine nor more than a hundred grams in violation of title 21 of the U.S code section 841(B). We have now reached the stage of these proceedings where it is the duty of the court to address several questions to you Mr. Moore, as well as to the counsel. First of all, have you had an opportunity to review the presentence report prepared in your case under date of March third of this year?"

"Yes," Moore answered.

He knows that his life is about to make a dramatic change, but he respect the game for what it is. He had an opportunity to cooperate with the federal government and walk away with five years. He refused their offer.

"Similarly have you had an opportunity to review the short addendum to that report that was prepared under date of March eighteenth, of this year?"

"Can you repeat that? I didn't hear that."

"Have you read that?" Mr. Dutch cut in.

"Yes."

"Thank you. Similarly Mr. Dutch, have you had an opportunity to review both of these documents?"

"I have your honor," Mr. Dutch answered.

"Do you or your client have any objection as to any of the factual information that has been provided to the court in the presentence report and addendum?"

"We filed two objections your honor. And based on the addendum, have nothing further."

Marco and Lil Wink sit amongst all the spectators in the courtroom. Marco notices a young lady in the front row cradling a new born baby. Marco and Lil Wink witnessed the judge hand out, over two hundred years between seven defendants in a couple of hours for crack cocaine. The courtroom remains silent as the judge sits on the bench dressed in his black robe with his gray hair and receding hair lining.

"Uhmm," the judge clears his throat preparing himself to announce the sentence.

Moore's palms becomes sweaty as he tremble allover.

"Now, as to the sentencing guidelines, which the court is obliged to consult with the probation department has the following recommendations as to applicable guidelines. They include a total offense level 37, criminal history category six, which the offense level carries a guideline term of imprisonment of 360 months to life. Mr. Dutch, in light of the factual underpinnings of this case, does your client have any further objection to the court considering these guidelines that I have just spread on the record?"

"No, your honor. Understanding the Booker parameters as they are advisory for the relevant conduct portion," Mr. Dutch answered.

"All right. Thank you Mr. Gonzales, does the government accept those guidelines?"

"Yes, we do your honor."

"Very well. That being the case, and the court having no dependent basis to disagree or otherwise suggest a different guideline construct, I do here with adopted before me Donald Moore to life imprisonment without the possibility of supervised release."

The words the judge spoke resonated in his head. He drops his head in disbelief feeling numb. He can no longer hear the litany of voices chanting in the courtroom. Mr. Dutch massages Donald's shoulder as he sits in shock. The U.S Marshals rises from their seat ready to escort the defendant to the holding cell. An older woman in the audience dabs her eyes clenching a piece of cloth within' her long artistic fingers. A toddler whines in the courtroom. The young lady in the audience cries hysterically unable to restrain her emotions. Her stomach muscles tightens uncontrollably. She begin to feel weak in the knees.

Donald is the father of her new born child. He is the only man that she has ever known. He's the only person in the world that seems to love her.

"Nooo. Please don't take him away from me. Pleaseee let him come home wit' meee." She drops to her knees holding the only thing that she have in the world. The federal government took all of their worldly possessions. A new disturbing sensation courses electrically through her body. Lil Wink feels sorry for the woman. Instead of a courtroom he feels like he is at a funeral service.

"See this the side you never see until it's too late. This game comes wit' a big price that most people can't pay. He was a stand up nigga no doubt." Marco proclaimed, feeling the couple's grief and sorrow. "A lot of brothas had a dream of becomin' the next Michael Jordan, some had a dream of becomin' a millionaire drug dealer and wake up an inmate strugglin' to make commissary. Once you get locked up all those Benzes, Bentleys, Lexus', and Range Rovers loses its value, they depreciate. You can have all the millions you want, but when you in the belly of the beast all you can do is spend two hundred and ninty dollars a month like everybody else in prison. All you get is three hundred minutes a month. My uncle used to put me up on game all the time.

I'm tellin' you lil' homie, the federal government is playin' for keeps. When the lights go out and it's time to do that time, all those niggas you was crackin' bottles with gon' turn against you to save their own asses. You got two choices when it comes to the feds. You either do yo' time like a man or live yo' life as a rat havin' to watch over yo' shoulders. This is the place I call reality and this shit ain't no game . . . trust me."

*   *   *

A rumbling sound vibrants the windows of the Mercedes Benz dealership, seizing the attention of the employees that are conversing on the phones, shuffling through paper work. Maria peers through the glass windows. A black Aston Martin Vanquish with tinted windows pulls up on chrome 22 inch Astanti rims. The car system over powers everybodies conversation. It sounds as if King Kong is stomping on the concrete, having a temper tantrum. Employees and customers stare at the extravagant vehicle in awe. The huge chrome rims gleams being kissed by the sun. The music drops in silence making everyones conversation audible.

A man climbs out or the car with a tapered fade spinning 360 like a bag of Ramen noodles, wearing a pair of Gucci sunglasses, black casual Gucci blazer, and a matching pair of leather Gucci loafers. A soft breeze passes by blowing his blazer open exposing his cell phone that is clipped to his waistline. Carrying a leather Gucci briefcase in his hand with his Blacplain rose gold faced watch slightly exposed underneath his sleeve. He connects eyes with Maria. He removes his sunglasses tucking them in the inside pocket of his blazer.

He strides in her direction with strong confidence. She looks at him surprisingly, recognizing his face from the encounter they had earlier today. Maria studies the meticulously groomed man. The smell of his Sean John cologne wafts the air. Maria smiles at him and says, "I see you came back." Her elegance intrigues him greatly as he stares into her hypnotic eyes.

"Yeah, so I can finish my window shoppin' as you referred to it earlier. I want you to know I'ma man of business baby and playin' around is not the way I get down."

"I'm sorry if I offend-." He cut her off in midsentence, before she could finish apologizing.

"There is no need for an apology. Just make it a valuable lesson and never judge a book by its cover. Well, since we cleared the air I would love to rewind everything and introduce myself. My name is

Mr. Hopson and I take it that your name is Maria according to yo' name tag."

"Yes, that is my name Mr. Hopson. Is there anything specific that I can help you with today Mr. Hopson?" She smiled seductively. He stands gallantly in front of her desk.

"Since you asked politely, it is somethin' that you can help me wit'. Earlier my lil brother picked out that Mercedes Benz CLS 550 over there," he points to the car, "I would like to purchase that."

Maria flicks her hair away from her shoulder shuffling through the file cabinet. She slides an application in front of him.

"I need you to fill out this application with your current information. I just need to run a credit check on you before we begin the process."

"I 'ont think that is necessary sweetheart," Motion glimpses around and sits the black Gucci briefcase on top of the desk. "Today I'm payin' cash." He pops the briefcase open, exposing large stacks of big face hundred dollar bills neatly stacked. Maria stares at the money wide eyed in disbelief. She never had a customer walk into the dealership and pay cash for a car.

"You know by federal policy I have to report any transaction that exceeds ten thousand dollars."

"No problem. I'm puttin' it under my corporation name." She looks at Motion with a different perspective. Motion stares at her glossy full lips. His mind drifts off as she exchanges the credit application. *She know she's fine as hell. I wouldn't mind dickin' her down.*

"Sir . . . sir."

"My fault baby. What's up?"

"I need you to fill out these forms."

"By the way, I want it imported from Europe."

"I can make that possible. The only thing about that is you'll have to wait two to three weeks."

"That's no problem."

She hands Motion an ink pen to fill out the paperwork.

CHAPTER THREE

T he shiny rims flicker as Marco turns the corner, detouring through the tattered neighborhood. The air conditioner hums in accompaniment to the hip hop music escaping the sound system.

"You see that boarded up duplex right there?" Marco points to a house in the middle of the block.

"Yeah, I see it. What about it?" Lil Wink replied, inspecting the house carefully.

"You can buy that house for one dolla."

"One dolla. Yeah right. Get the fuck out of here."

"Fa real, no bullshit. I been doin' a lot of research on the real estate game. I didn't believe it myself until I did my home work. I never knew that it was so much money out here. I'm talkin' about that legal money. I been studying up on C-corporations, chattel mortgages, foreclosures, and equity loans." Marco proclaimed. Lil Wink stares at Marco as if he is speaking another language.

"Man I never heard of none of that shit before."

"Ignorance is the primary weapon of containment. A great man once said, 'the best way to hide somethin' from black people is to put it in a book.' We now live in the information age. We have gained the opportunity to read any book on any subject through the efforts of our struggle for freedom. We still refuse to read. We rather buy a pair of Nike shoes instead of investing our money in a business. A lot of people think that having a Mercedes Benz, and having a big house gives them status, or that they have accomplished their ultimate dream. Materiality ain't about shit," Marco stressed with a serious look on his face.

"You just seen what happened in that courtroom. This world is controlled by the United Snakes of America. Life is not a fuckin' game. We became a target market for any business, especially the penitentiary.

We are the minority in this country, but in prison we are the majority. When scientist created crack cocaine they created a modernized slave master. The dope man addicted to sellin' that shit and the pipe head is addicted to smokin' that shit. Check this out homie." Marco pulls up on the block scanning the scenery.

"The reason why I took you on this short ride is because I see somethin' in you. I know you're a smart young man. I got a proposition fa' you. How much do you make a week hustlin' on that block?"

"About a stack a week."

"Dig this. I'll pay you fifteen hundred dollas a week to get off the block and go to school. If you maintain a good grade point average I'll throw you a bonus. How that sound?" Marco stares at Lil wink as he contemplates.

"Bet."

"But, if I catch you on the block, deal off, cool?"

"Cool." Lil Wink agreed.

They give each other dab sealing the deal.

* * *

Coupe rattles the dice in his clenched fist with strong confidence, huddled up in a circular formation. The foul stench smell of urine lingers in the alley. A group of young hustlers place their bets.

"I say he hit fo' ten." Coupe rolls the dice and snaps his fingers. The dice spins side by side like two tops. All of their eyes are plastered to the dice as they anticipate victory. The dice stop spinning on six ace and he craps out. The mix throng of hustlers falls into an uproar as money exchanges from hand to hand.

The dice rotates around the circle clockwise. Coupe drops a twenty dollar bill in the center of the circle in frustration.

"Back man got 'em," Coupe proclaimed.

A slender young man shakes the dice making them clack together, poetically chanting.

"Six ace in yo' mutha fuckin' face."

The dice lands on six ace setting Coupe back another twenty. Kev has a reputation for breaking up the gamble.

"Stop lockin' the dice and let me get some shake," Coupe stated, glaring at Kev with a sinister look on his face.

"Catch what you don't like," Kev replied unaware of Coupe's quick temper. Coupe peels off two twenty dollar bills off his now thin wad of money dropping them on the ground.

"Shoot fourty." Kev matches Coupe's forty dollars, rattling the dice in his hand. He throws the dice followed with a snap. The dice lands on four deuce. "Anotha twenty say you don't hit," Coupe said nonchalantly. Kev matches his twenty feeling confident. Kev roll a five and an ace on his fourth roll. Kev makes an attempt to grab his money. "Yo point, was eight not six," Coupe lied. Kev's comrade Tyson intervenes on their conversation.

"His point was six," Tyson advocated.

Anger gleams in Coupe's eyes as he lock eyes with Tyson.

"Ma fucka this ain't got shit to do with you!" he snapped, reaching under his shirt pulling out a .44 Mag. The chrome handgun glimmers in his hand. He flexes his jaw muscles causing his temple to move. Intoxicated with fear, Tyson backpedals with his hands in the air.

"My bad man. You right, 'ont got . . ." Coupe bites down on his lower lip squeezing the trigger. Boc! Boc! Boc! Coupe's hand jerks involuntarily with every squeeze of the trigger. Tyson staggers backwards crashing into two aluminum trash cans. The thunderous sound of the baby cannon leaves their ears ringing. Gunsmoke lingers in the air.

Tyson lies on the ground against the garage with three bullet holes in his chest. He convulses, his Vision blurs, his body grows cold, and his world becomes complete darkness. The three shots he took to the chest introduced him to his death.

Coupe tucks the cannon back into his waistband, glaring at a fidgeting Tyson.

"Anybody else disagree wit' me?" Coupe asked, scanning the sea of fear stricken faces.

"Naw'll," they chorused.

"Roll these ma fuckas," Coupe demanded, having no remorse for the coldblooded murder he just committed.

Kev shakes harder than the dice clutched in his hand.—He releases the dice rolling a seven. Coupe rakes up the money in the center of the circle.

"Next!" Coupe said breaking the silence.

"I'm striaght dawg," the next shooter said.

"Me too. I'm cool."

The next man says, "I gotta go check on my moms, I'll holla."

The huddle disperses one by one feeling a great deal of relief. Coupe stands up and struts over to Tyson. He lies on the ground bleeding profusely. Coupe kneels down beside him, fumbling through his pockets.

Ever since Coupe been wanted for a double homicide he became even more vicious and stonyhearted. He knows once his luck run out as a fugitive, the game is over. Coupe is known as a stick up kid and a coldblooded killer.

He removes a large wad of money out of Tyson's pocket. *It's time fa' me to holla at those niggas in the projects now. I need me a big come up so I can get little.* Coupe disappears leaving the murder scene.

*   *   *

Scotty pulls in front of the Greyhound bus station downtown in a convertible JK8 Jaguar with the top down exposing the rust colored leather interior. He scans the streets watching the excited bustle of activity downtown. Automobiles whir by rapidly moving up and down the street. The mundane sound of car horns blare and the suffocating odor of burning sulfur pollutes the air.

Scotty's European girl Becky climbs out of the passenger's seat prepared to take a long trip to Minneapolis, Minnesota.

Her long red hair flutters as a breeze of fresh air passes by. The slender young woman wears a Gap skirt, prescription glasses, a Gap halter top, and a pair of sketchers. Becky is a college student in Minneapolis. Scotty met her 6 months ago at a college party. Scotty never dated a white woman, but for Becky he made a special exception. He knew that he could use her in the future to his advantage considering it to be a white man's world and all of the racial discrimination.

Scotty strides smoothly to the trunk of the car in a pair of designer sunglasses. He opens the trunk removing Becky's luggage that contains two zip loc bags of X. The luggage has a false bottom. He sits the luggage on the ground. He gently grabs her chin with his thumb and index finger brushing her hair away from her cheek and gives her a peck on the lips.

"You make sure you call me as soon as you make it there. My man gon' pick you up from the bus station. Be careful baby. I would like to spend sometime wit' you, but I gotta handle this business," Scotty lied. Becky listens to him intently, staring into his ebony brown eyes. "Don't stop and talk to nobody. You hear me?" Becky nods her head in agreement. She picks up the luggage willing to do anything for Scotty.

"Love you honey," Becky said, making her way to the four glass doors.

Scotty climbs into the car pondering, watching her until she was out of his sight. ***Dumb bitch. She really thinks I give a fuck about her.*** The X-pills will be worth fifty thousand once they are transported to Minneapolis. He pulls off mixing in with the heavy traffic.

Scotty struts into Styles beauty salon and barbershop. His heavy platinum necklace sprinkled with diamonds, as they bounce against his chiseled chest. He glimpses around the luxurious 20 booth beauty salon and barbershop. The strong smell of fingernail polish remover slaps Scotty in the nose as he struts pass the beautiful nail technician, who greets him with a friendly white smile. The buzzing sound of hair clippers accompanies the hip hop music dispersing from the surround system. A group of awaiting customers are seated on a leather sectional watching BET on the 60inch plasma screen television.

A young woman under the hair dryer whispers to the woman seated beside her. "That's ol' boy that be at club Sensation. I heard him and his boys doin' it big. He knows he's fine as hell girl." She looks at the candy that drapes down his chest twinkling.

Scotty approaches his barber Ismail. They slap palms greeting each other with a handshake. Scotty discreetly slipped Ismail a hundred dollar bill when they shook hands.

"Sup baby?" Ismail greeted.

"Tryna keep my head above water in this white man's world."

"I feel you on that. I got you as soon as I finish my man."

"Cool baby." Scotty browses around the shop killing time.

Ismail finishes with his customer and removes the apron from around his neck shaking the hair off of it. Ismail makes a hand gesture signaling for Scotty. He climbs into the chair. Many of the awaiting customers complain, mumbling under their breath.

"You must be going to the concert they havin' at the Bradley Center?" Ismail asked, preparing to give Scotty one of his famous haircuts.

"Naw. I'm tryna get money. Right now I 'ont got time fo' that. I know its gon be plenty hoes up there though."

Scotty holds his head still staring at one of the many beautiful beauticians' doing hair. He watches as she arches her back with her ribcage pressing against her skin, exposing her pierced navel. She unwraps the towel on her customer's head and her long, silky black hair spills on her shoulders.

He shifts his focus on a Porsche Cayenne truck pulling to the curb in front of the shop in a reserved parking space. A beautiful woman with a butter scotch complexion steps out of the truck in a two piece Ralph Lauren pants suit. She appears in the doorway prancing in her high heel pumps like a black stallion, garnering everyone's attention. The beauticians and the barbers acknowledge their employer with a wave of the hand. She returns a wave followed with a smile.

Scotty's eyeballs dances as he studies her perfectly shaped sculptured hour glass body in admiration, mentally undressing what he considers to be a fine piece of art. She labors across the black and white checkered floor, making her way to her office. The sound of her heels clacks against the pavement, becoming distant with every step. She closes the door behind her. The soft smell of her perfume drifts about.

"Damn she strapped like a ma fucka," Scotty softly blurted.

"Ain't she?" Ismail added. "I haven't seen her with a man since I've known her. Ever since her man caught that fed case, she hasn't been the same I heard. That woman looks young, but believe me she's a certified vet." Ismail told, finishing Scotty's haircut.

"I know she's about due now."

"You just be careful Scotty. I hear her man is still heavy out here in these streets. They say he's still pullin' strings from behind the walls."

"I ain't worried 'bout that," Scotty replied with confidence.

Elane steps out of the office and stands in the doorway motioning for one of her employees.

"Tiera!"

"Huh."

"Can you do me a favor and keep a eye on things until I get back? I have a very important meeting to attend to."

"Okay, I'll handle this Elane, gon' and handle your business."

"I appreciate it. I owe you one girl," Elane thanked, walking back into her office to retrieve her belongings.

Scotty sees an opportunity to approach her. He stares at her round, onion booty that will make any man's eyes tear up. Her classy style and pure beauty turns Scotty on. He doesn't realize that he is not in her league. With perfect timing, he climbs out of the barber chair.

"A'ight Ismail, you stay up baby." They bump fist saying their goodbyes.

Scotty struts behind Elane. As she reaches for the door Scotty kidnaps her attention. He had his eyes on her quite sometime. He never had the courage to approach her out of the many times they crossed each other's path. Today he feels different for some reason. He unloads his game on the veteran.

"Let me get that fo' you sweetheart. Don't know woman as fine as yo' self got any business opening doors. Allow me to get that for you." Scotty puts on his gentlemen performance, by holding the door open for her. They exit the establishment standing in front of the building. "Can you spare me a moment of your time?"

"Go ahead."

"I was wondering if you can give me the opportunity to take you out fo' dinner one day, whenever you got some free time on yo' hands."

"I'm sorry baby. It looks like you're a little bit to young for me."

"Age ain't nothin' but a number ma. Maybe you can teach a young man like myself, a thing or two. So, how old are you if I may ask?"

"Lets just say, I'm probably old enough to be your mama. Besides, my man been gone for seven years and I'm well taking care of. It isn't nothin' you can do for me."

"It ain't about me being able to take care of you. It's the fact that I can make you happy. Now, let me ask you a question, are you happy?" She pauses with a lost of words.

"I couldn't be happier," she lied. Seeing the hesitation Scotty knew he had hit the right spot.

It has been seven years since she was last sexually active. She haven't been on a date or had any romance in her life since her lover been absent from the world.

"That's what yo' mouth say, but yo' eyes tellin' me somethin' different."

Knowing his statement is full of truth, she cracks an artificial smile and prances to her truck, disregarding his statement. He jumps into his Jaguar and watches her taillights as she vanishes.

*   *   *

TWO WEEKS LATER

Ayesha sits in the back of a stretched Cadillac Escalade being escorted to Giovanni's Italian restaurant. The chauffeur pulls up to the front entrance. The valet parking attendant opens the door for Ayesha, ushering her into the restaurant. She glimpses around, prancing in her high heel pumps. She steps into the restaurant.

"How are you doing today ma'am?" An Italian waiter greets her in his heavy accent, smiling cordially.

"I'm doing fine." She can't wait to enjoy the surprise that Motion has for her.

"Follow me," the waiter instructed, leading her through the luxurious restaurant. Her eyes bounce around the restaurant. She doesn't see any customers in sight. Curiosity invades her, causing her to wonder. She hears someone playing Luther Vandross' "Here and Now" on the piano, her and Motion's favorite love song. The soft, rhythmical harmony seems to be playing under her skin promising romance and exquisite heartache.

The waiter leads her to the table that's situated for two. Motion reserved the entire restaurant for their romantic evening.

He slides the chairs from under the table, allowing her to be seated. Pink rose pedals are sprinkled all over the table. The burning candles flickers, reflecting in her almond shaped eyes. Motion's fingers dances on the piano keys as he gazes at the beautiful Goddess. A smile pulls at the corners of her mouth as she stares at the man she knows to be very romantic, but known as a cold blooded hustler in the streets.

He rises up from the grand piano dressed in a white Prada button up shirt, black slacks, and a pair of black Prada loafers. She can see his chiseled chest bulging against the silky fabric. He slowly strides in her direction. He seats himself across from her. He gently embraces her soft hands, silence engulfs them like a gentle storm. He breaks the silence speaking in his rich deep voice, expressing himself to the love of his life. In his eyes she is his angelic enchantress. He leans forward looking through the windows to her soul.

"I'm so glad to have you as apart of my life. When I'm wit' you, I know I'm in the presences of someone who truly love me. You always give me inspiration. You know how to lift my spirits up and take my thoughts to another place, where my troubles seem so far away. I compare you wit' things like the sunshine in the morning, the most beautiful flowers in the fields, and the happiness I feel on the best days of my life. You bring me feelings that know no limits, and smiles that will never go away. You filled the empty pages of my life." The words he spoke sinks into the deepest part of her heart. Her eyes sparkle, becoming misty. They look into each other's eyes as if they are searching for each other's soul. Over the years Ayesha's love gave a new meaning to Motion's life.

The waiter interrupts them by sitting a bottle of red wine on the table, grilled shrimps, fresh seasoned bread, and lobster tails.

"You two enjoy your meals. If you need anything else please feel free to call me."

"Thank you," Ayesha replied. He pops the cork on the bottle of wine, filling their glasses.

"Enjoy," he said politely, walking away.

The movement of the waiter's body creates a slight breeze, causing the flame on the candles to sway. They entwine their arms, taking a sip of the wine.

"Motion, this means so much to me. You always manage to bring me happiness. I want you to know that there is no man on the face of this earth that can take your place. You're the most important thing in my life, my heart, and everything I could ever want in life. It seems like each day that you leave the house a part of me leaves with you. I know you're taking care of business. Lately I've had a lot on my mind. There is something I want to ask you."

"What's that baby?" Motion asked with a serious facial expression.

"When are you going to quit? I'm just curious. We have everything we could ever want. We have a beautiful daughter, a big house, cars, money, jewels, a business, when do we call it quits? Don't take what I'm saying in the wrong way. I just want to spend more time with the man I love and do family things. I know you love me with all of your heart, but lately I've been feeling lonely," she sincerely admitted.

Motion always knew deep down inside that she would one day ask him that question.

"I knew the time would come and you would ask me that question. I know you just didn't wanna ask me. But to answer yo' question, I been thinkin' about givin' the game up and going fully legit. After I bust these last couple moves I'm finish," Motion said, his eyes gleaming with nothing but sincerity.

"So, how long is these last couple of moves suppose to take?"

"No longer than six months, I promise."

"If you don't you know its drama right?" Ayesha said in a playful mannerism.

Motion smiles at her remark grabbing a shrimp. He takes a bite of the shrimp and feeds her the other half.

After two hours of romance and finishing their candle light dinner, Ayesha glazes at Motion displaying a tiresome look. He lifts his gaze from the drink with his eyes revealing genuine concern.

"What's wrong baby?"

"My feet is getting sore in these heels."

"I think I gotta cure for that." He reaches under the table grabbing her feet. He slowly removes her heels. She rests her french pedicured feet in his lap as he massages them with expertise. She murmurs in pleasure as he watches her eyes close.

"Mmmm. Come on baby I think it's time to go," She suggested.

"I agree." Motion grabs her high heel pumps, looping his arms under her legs picking her up. He carries her to the front entrance.

"How was your evening?" The waiter asked.

"It was perfect," Ayesha answered.

"Let me have your vehicle brought around the front." The waiter picks up the phone.

No longer than two minutes the valet attendant pulls up to the front entrance in Motion's Bentley coupe.

"Damn ma I should've brought my umbrella," Motion said watching the heavy rain pour down.

The parking attendant leaves both of the car doors open for their convenience. Holding Ayesha in his arms, he exits the glass doors. The fierce wind flutters their clothes as it blows the rain violently. He moves hurriedly sitting her in the passenger seat. Her damp dress sticks to her flesh. Motion jumps into the car blowing out a short breath of air.

"It's pouring down like a mutha fucka out here," he blurted. The rich bass from the car system knocks softly at a low volume. The heavy rain taps on the windshtild singing like soft music.

"I really enjoyed myself baby. Every minute with you mean so much to me." Ayesha said, her voice soft sounding like she should be singing a solo in heaven. He leans over and their lips meet, just a nibble, just a tease that threatened to grow into a hungry bite. He gazes into her eyes in silence.

"It's just the beginning of true love," he whispered. A car horn blast, but the sound is muffled by the closed windows.

They weave through the heavey traffic. Motion's profile is in shadows, being struck intermittently by the streetlights.

*　　*　　*

Motion and Ayesha stand face to face in their bedroom. He brushes a strand of her hair back off of her forehead. His fingers gently drops slowly down her cheekbone, along the warmth of her throat, tracing her collar bone making his way to her firm right breast. He grazes her nipple with the palm of his hand. He grips her chin guiding her lips to his. Their mouths lightly touch. She tilts her head back and their tongues explore each other's mouth. She loops her arm around his neck thristy for more of his compassion. He lifts her off her feet, off the carpeted floor laying her on the bed.

Moonlight leaps through the window shining on her flesh. His eyes goes on a journey as he studies her body. He devours her body like lovemaking is an art to be crafted and praticed solely on her. He can hear the sound of her heart softly drumming against her chest playing a soft harmony. She tingles allover feeling the warm passionate moist kisses on her body. He removes an ice cube from the icetray and puts it in his mouth. She tenses up, as the coolness of his tongue introduces itself to her clit. A short moan pierces her lips as her body adjusts to the cool temperture of his tongue. He nibbles on her luscious thigh teasingly.

She claws the back of his head with her french manicured nails clenching his head, as if she is holding on for dear life, biting down on her bottom lip in attempt to restrain her moans. He uses his lips to grasp her pearl tongue swirling his tongue like a magic wand, bringing her to ecstasy.

She squirms around arching her back gripping the bed spread. He slides his tongue up and down her wetness to console her, as he savors her love juices. He traces down her thighs with his love wand, shifting his focus on her soft pedicured feet. As he plants passionate kisses, he darts his tongue around her ankles, to the top of her feet. He veers to the base of her foot licking it torridly, easing his way to her perfectly structured toes, sucking each one with the same amount of attention, as if they were molded for his mouth.

Finishing her other foot, she leans forward cupping the back of his head, giving him a seductive stare, letting him know that her feet is satisfied. They lock lips and he feels the quivering touch of her mouth. His heart skips a beat as they shift positions. She holds his throbbing erection, nibbling on his balls. The warmth of her breath sends a compassionate sensation traveling down his spine.

She grazes his hardness with her tongue, enveloping half of his 9 inch mandingo in her mouth. She coats his man hood with her warm juices. She fixes her gaze on him, licking her lips in a circular motion, stroking his pipe. She tucks her lips around her teeth and engulfs him whole. Her head bobs, as she slowly works her way up and down his shaft. Her diamond earrings sparkle in the darkness, being struck by the moonlight that is leaping through the picture window.

He wraps her long silky hair in his fist, trying to fight back his urge to explode. Unable to control his hormones, he succumbs, ejaculating in her mouth jerking in voluntarily. She swallows his sex juices, his toes curl up, and his rod slowly softens. It feels as if she has drained the life out of his body. She uses her skillful ability and sucks his manhood back to life. Her heart rate soars with adrenaline as she anticipates his loving. She climbs on top of him, lowering her body, clenching her teeth, taking every inch he has to offer her. It feels as if she has melted through his flesh, and their bodies has joined. She makes all sorts of sex faces as she grinds against his pelvis. Motion watches her with a steady gaze, studying her flawless features, pulling the upper half of her body against his solid muscular chest. Her lengthy hair curtains their faces. He kisses her lightly on the lips, tasting her peppermint breath. Motion manipulates their position by shifting his body weight, now on top of her.

He twirls his hips slowly, holding her soft hairless leg in the air, planting gentle warm kisses on her firm muscular calf. A luster of sweat coats his strong back, as he continues to stroke her in a slow rhythmical pace. The low tone of her moan is like music to his ears. The melody of their love making mingles with the sound of soft rumbling thunder. The lightening pulsates, seeping through the window displaying the contrast of dark and light, outlining their naked bodies. The signature Gucci spreads is rumpled and tangled beneath them.

Three hours and six powerful orgasms later, Motion climbs out of the bed tireless, staring at her tear drop shaped booty feeling like the luckiest man in the world.

Motion leans back on the chaise, smoking a blunt of Acapulco Gold marijuana. He blows out a billow of smoke gazing at the stars that glimmers like dew against the velvet expanse of the sky pondering and having flashbacks.

I can't believe I made it this far in the game. Here I am a young black man who grew up in the projects that manifested and conquered the American dream. I remember when I kept takin' losses and was about to give up on what turned out to be a multi-million dolla enterprise.

Motion's thoughts goes back down memory lane. Motion walked into his one bedroom apartment with nine ounces of powder cocaine concealed under his maroon Averix coat with its cream stitching, coordinating with his maroon colored timberlands with it's cream soles. He kissed Ayesha on her lips as she sat on the living room couch Indian-style, watching the Cosby Show on the 27 inch screen television.

"Heyy boo?" she said, as she held the remote in her hand. "Somebody seems like they're in a good mood." Ayesha stated, watching him walk into the kitchen, placing his coat on the back of the kitchen chair.

"That's right, I'm back in baby," he announced excitedly. He tossed the quarter bird on the kitchen table, along with his 9 millimeter Ruger P94, with one up top, off safety.

It was almost two weeks since Motion finally re-upped, usually he would cop a half of bird, but he had to pay his daily extravaganzas over the last two weeks.

He opened the zip loc bag, inspecting the solid chunk of powder he bought with his last sixty five hundred dollars. He retrieved his cooking utensils out of the cabinet, preparing himself to cook the powder. He tries to break the powder into pieces, but it is to solid.

"Damn this shit hard as a mafucka," Motion mumbled under his breath. He grabbed a hammer out of the kitchen drawer and tapped the solid chunk with just enough pressure to break it into various pieces. He weighed a hundred grams at a time on his hundred gram capacity digital scale. The package weighed 252 grams on the dot, causing a smile to stretch across his face. He poured the powder into a pyrex pot and weighed up 63 grams of Arm & Hammer baking soda. He poured a quarter cup of water into the pot, mixing it together with a fork. He sat the pot atop the the fire, bringing it to a boil. The dope foamed up, forming into a brownish oil base. Motion shrinks back, wrinkling his nose from the loud odor resting in the air. He carried the pot to the sink, running the cold water. He held the rim of the pyrex pot slightly under the water, allowing a small amount of cold water to get inside. He became frustrated, seeing that the dope would not harden up.

I'ma kill that nigga if this some bullshit. This look like that re-rock shit. He tried to make it form.

"This shit short as hell," he said aloud, his face flushing with anger. He drained the water out of the pot and stirred the gummy substance with a fork. He swirled it around until it locked on the fork, looking like a upside down carmel apple without the nuts. He sat the small boulder on a ceramic plate, letting it air dry. Looking at the short dope, his stomach dropped, ice and malice coursed through his bloodstream. He dropped the dope on the digital scale half wet. The scale read 89.6 grams. He reaches to his hip and flips his cellular phone open. His blood boiled as he dialed Shake's number.

The phone rang four times and went straight to the voice-mail.

"You reached Shake holla back." Motion hung and dialed the number four more times getting the same results.

I'ma kill that mafucka. That was the last of my money. I'ma catch that nigga in traffic and air his bitch ass out.

Motion's cellular phone chimed bringing him back to reality. He answered the phone thinking it was Shake.

"Man I need to holla at you. That was some bullshit you gave me," he said in an angry tone.

"Hold up, you got the wrong man, this Scotty."

"Aww, my bad. I thought you was that bitch ass nigga Shake. He fucked me over," Motion explained. He realized that he was on the phone and regained his composure. "I'll just holla at you about it later. I need to sit back and do some thinkin'."

"A'ight fam, holla."

"One." Motion flipped the phone closed, walking into the livingroom.

"What's wrong baby?" Ayesha asked. She noticed that something was bothering him.

"Nothin' ma. I just got a whole lot of things on my mind. It seem like every time things start going good some bullshit happen. It seem like I'm hustlin' backwards." He fell back to the couch, blowing out a deep breath of frustration.

Ayesha moved closer to him, massaging his shoulders feeling his pain. "Don't worry baby. I know you'll figure out something. You just have to be patient. If I have to work extra hours to make us some extra money that's what I will have to do. You know this is both of our struggle. I'm here baby nomatter what it comes down to. I love you with all of my heart and I will stand by my man," Ayesha expressed with heartfelt words easing Motion's mind.

"I know you got my back ma. That's one of the reasons why I love you so much." Motion paused briefly before finishing. "One day I'ma take you of out the ghetto . . . I promise."

Two days past by and Motion's cell phone rang early in the morning. He leaned over answering the phone.

"Yeah."

"That ain't the way to answer yo' phone."

"Man who is this? It's too early in the damn morning to be playin' fuckin' games," Motion said irritatingly.

"Man this yo' cuz nigga, wake up. All you get out of sleep is a dream."

"Shit it's better than what I been gettin'," he retorted.

"I feel you. What you doing later on tonight? I'll be up there this evening. The military gave me a two week leave."

"Yeah. Come on through we can get out fo' a minute. I ain't got shit else to do. Everything has been slow motion lately. A nigga doing bad as hell. This nigga played me the other day. It ain't shit out here right now.

"I'll holla at you when I get there."

"A'ight. I'll holla at you then."

"A'ight baby." The phone went dead.

Motion rose up out of the bed and took a long hot shower.

Eddie lives in Chicago, but he is stationed in Africa. It has been a year since Eddie and Motion last seen each other. He moved to Chicago when he finished high school. Within a year later he joined the military.

Later on that night Motion heard a knock at the door.

"Who is it?" Motion shouted from the livingroom as he approached the door.

"It's Eddie," he answered.

The closed door muffled his voice, making it sound like he is far away. Motion unlocked the door, ushering Eddie inside.

"What up cuz?" Motion said enthusiastically.

They gave each other a manly hug with one arm in between them, bumping their fist against each other's back.

"You ready to kick it or what?" Eddie asked with a grin gleaming across his face.

"No doubt. Let's do this."

Eddie and Motion have a lot of resemblence. Eddie is darker than Motion and a little taller than him.

They stepped out of the apartment building, jumping into Motion's Cadillac STS.

"So tell me cuz, what's been going on wit' you?" Eddie asked.

"Nothin 'man, just strugglin' out here. I been takin' a lot of losses lately. It's a lot of bullshit dope floatin' around out here. I can't catch for shit." Motion complained.

Eddie pondered for a brief second, looking out the window massaging his chin. The heater in the car hummed in the background blending in with the radio.

"You know what? I might be able to solve yo' problem. I gotta close friend that might be able to help you. He used to smuggle dope through the military M.A.C flights. He's a Dominican guy out of Chicago. The last time I spoke to him was about six montha ago. I'ma give him a call and see what's up wit' him. You just lay back fo' a minute, but I'm tellin' you if I make this happen you gotta come correct. This dude is about business strictly, real heavy in the game. I always knew him to be a straight up dude. I'ma ask him to do a favor for me. So I'm puttin' my name on the line," Eddie stressed with a serious look on his face.

"You know 'ont play no games cuz. All I'm tryna do is get money or die tryin'. I always believe this. If you plant good seeds . . . you'll receive good deeds."

ONE WEEK LATER

Motion stood in front of Chicago's Amtrak station on 95th snuggled in his leather Pelle Pelle coat, shivering with his hands tucked in his pockets. His teeth chattered as he paced back and forth with his hoodie on, sheilding him from the cold stinging breeze that swept the street. Vapors escaped his mouth and his nostrils, dancing in the atmosphere, slowly fading away as he glimsped around. Ice crunched under his Timberland boots as he paced around impatiently. The volcanic sound of the trains traveling underground sounded like a hurricane moving under the earth. Every vehicle that pulled up collected Motion's attention. After what seemed to be a long fifteen minutes, a pearl white Lincoln Navigator turned the corner with it's headlights blaring, obscuring Motion's vision. The truck pulled up to the curb. The passenger's window slowly descended.

"Get in," the driver instructed.

Motion made a brief observation of the man's features. His description was just as Eddie described him. **This gotta be Julio**. He climbed into the passenger's seat escaping the cold weather of the Windy City. It felt as if his body was melting from the heat. Motion glanced over his shoulder seeing an unknown man seated behind him in the darkness. The only thing that Motion could identify is the huge outline of his frame and the man's diabolical eyes that gave him the creeps.

"What up?" Motion greeted respectfully as the man pulled off.

The diamond Rolex watch on his wrist sparkled as he twirled the steeringwheel. He disregarded Motion's words and spoke without turning his gaze to him.

"Let me get straight down to business. I'm Julio. I know Eddie probably told you a lot about me, but let me put it to you like this. The only reason why I chose to meet you is because Eddie told me a lot of good things about you. He told me that you good people. He also told me that you tryna get a big eigth, but I 'ont do nuttin' that small."

Motion looked at Julio with a look of disappointment. Julio pulled back in front of the Amtrak station. ***Don't tell me I came down here for nothin' in this fuckin' cold.*** Julio reached to the door panel as if he was unlocking the doors to let him out. He pressed a button and reached under the dashboard, pulling a brick shaped package out of a secret compartment. He tossed the package into Motion's lap.

"Check this out homes. All I want is seventeen fo' that. If you run off on me, it's nothin' major. I won't come lookin' for you. If you come back that mean you got a chance to make more money. It's a lot more where that came from."

Motion reached into his pocket grabbing his last $2,800.00 dollars.

"Keep it." Julio refuse to take the money and unlocked the door. Motion wanted to jump high in the air and shout yes, as he tucked the brick in his waistband, covering it up with his shirt.

"Before you go I want you to remember this Motion. Without loyalty a man will never reach prosperity. If you be true to the game . . . The game will be true to you." Motion hopped out of the truck being attacked by a cold gust of wind.

Motion made it back home after a long three and a half hours on the Greyhound. He unlocked the door to his apartment being stopped by the security chain.

"Hold on baby," Ayesha said. He could hear the sound of the chain rattling as she unhooked it. "Hey boo," Ayesha said excitedly, kissing him with enthusiasm.

"Man we been waitin' for you all day," Scotty proclaimed, hanging up his cell phone. "How everything go?" Scotty questioned.

"How did everything go. I'ma show you how everything went."

Motion unzipped his coat and removed his shirt. He had the brick duct taped to his chest, wearing it like a bulletproof vest. Scotty's eyes enlarged at the sight of the kilo taped to Motion's chest.

"Help me take this off baby." Ayesha assisted him.

He sat the kilo on the glass kitchen table and tore a hole in it, taking a piece out of it. He stashed the rest of it in the kitchen cabinet. "Come on Scotty, lets go holla at Pops."

Pops is a veteran drug addict that test all of their product.

Motion gave Ayesha a kiss on the lips. "I'll be right back baby. I need to make a quick run."

"Okay baby."

Motion and Scotty hurried out the door. They pulled up in front of a tattered apartment building. As they approached the door to the lobby, a group of teenagers exited the door with their pants sagging, with their baseball caps tilted deep to the left. Motion entered the building with Scotty trailing behind him. Knock! Knock! Knock!

"Yo, who is it?"

"Motion!"

The door opened quickly at the sound of Motion's voice. A tall slender man with lengthy dreadlocks, a dark complexion, and dingy clothes answered the door. The sides of his face looked like the bottom of a Nestle Crunch bar. He ushered them into the apartment.

"What up my man? What y'all got fo' me?" Pops inquired, already having an idea of why they were there.

"I need you to test somethin' fo' me." Motion reached in his crotch area, removing a small package of crystallized powder. He dropped the package into Pops extended hand. Pops dropped the powder in a pyrex tube and sprinkled a small amount of baking soda on top of it. He poured a teaspoon of water into the tube and pulled his cigarette lighter from his pocket. He struck the lighter allowing the fire to heat the bottom of the tube. His eyes were glued to the pyrex as if he was a scientist in the labatory studying a project. He placed the tube under the cold water, chilling the bottom of the tube. The cocaine base hardened instantly, forming into a pearl white boulder with a pinkish tint. That was the first time Motion and Scotty ever seen crack that color.

Pops chopped a ten dollar piece off of it. He grabbed his glass pipe out of his pocket, adjusting the Choreboy. Being a true connoisseur, he placed the rock on the glass dick. Motion and Scotty watched him closely as he took a blast of the dope. A billow of smoke flowed from his nostrils, whirling in the atmosphere, slowly evaporating. He sway his head in silence as if he was disappointed.

Pops lifted his head looking like the living dead. His lips started twitching, making him look like a retard. That was the first time that they ever seen Pops react like that.

"Pops! Pops! You alight?" Motion asked, watching a drooling Pops. Scotty started getting spooked as he stared at him. He snapped out of his convulsions regainning his composure. Pops fixed his eyes on Motion.

"I ain't had no dope like this since Ronald Reagan was in office. This shit right here gon' make you a millionaire. Whoever you got this shit from, you need to go kiss that mafucka and thank 'em. This shit you got right here gon' take everybody out of business." Pops stated.

Motion used his vicious whip game, turning the kilo of cocaine into 45 ounces. He sold $50.00 sixteenths and $100.00 dollar eightballs at 3 grams each, making $42,000.00, taking no shorts. Motion gave Julio his $17,000.00 and bought him his own brick for $17,000.00. Ever since than he never looked back. He stayed loyal to the game like a true hustler.

Motion flicks the burning blunt into his olypmpic sized swimming pool with a large smile on his face. He hops off the chaise and goes back inside the mastersuite to accompany his love. He cuddles against her warm flesh and falls into a deep sleep.

*   *   *

Homicide detective Jeffrey McCormick pulls in front of a single family residence in the Crown Victoria. Before stepping out of the car he looks at his notepad, double checking the address. He climbs out of the car strutting to the front door in his charcoal gray, two piece suit.

His black polished shoes clack against the sidewalk. He rings rings the doorbell and waits patiently for someone to answer. He hear the muffled sound of a woman's voice.

"Who is it?"

"Detective McCormick!" He stares at the darkness in the peephole as someone peeps through it. An older woman opens the door with a look of concern plastered on her face.

"Can I help you detective?"

"Yes ma'am. My name is Jeffrey McCormick of the homicide unit and I'm conducting an ongoing investigation. I need to talk to Kevin Wilkins."

"He's not in any trouble is he?"

"No ma'am. I just need him for questioning."

"Please come in. Kevin!" she shouts. "A detective is here to talk to you."

Kevin steps out of his bedroom fidgeting. He knows why the detective is there to see him.

"Kevin, I'm detective Jeffrey McCormick with the homicide unit. Results from the forensic lab shows that you were at a homicide scene. I'm sorry, I'm going to have to take you in for questioning."

"I'm not being arrested am I?"

"No, your not Mr. Wilkins. This is just procedure. I spoke to a few other people that was at the scene, but they're not willing to cooperate. So first of all I want to ask you, are you willing to cooperate and answer my questions truthfully?"

"Yeah, if you promise to let me go when you finished."

"That's no problem Mr. Wilkins, like I said you are not being arrested. All I need you to do is give me your assistance."

"Officer, this will not place my son in any danger will it?"

"No ma'am. The debriefing will remain confidential, so you have nothing to worry about," Mr. McCormick explained, convincing Kevin's mother that he will be safe.

Ms. Wilkins embraces her son with a motherly hug and a kiss on the cheek.

"I'll be up and waitin' on you to come home," Ms. Wilkins said, watching the detective escort Kevin out the door.

A boxed Chevy Caprice turns the corner, rolling down the block headed to Love's Liquor store across the street from Kevin's. house. The driver of the car recognizes Kevin's face. He eases on the brakes, observing Kevin as he climbs into the Crown Victoria. Coupe glares at Kevin and makes an imaginary gun with his thumb and indexfinger, pointing in Kevin's direction.

"Bang! Bang!" he whispered, nodding his head with a devilish smirk on his face.

Kevin never noticed him driving pass. Coupe deviates from his course of direction, leaning back in the seat, easing off without being seen.

*　　*　　*

Marco and Scotty pulls up at Gloss & Floss detail shop. Scotty spots a familiar woman sheilding her eyes, peering through the window of a pearl light blue Ferrari 360 Modena equipped with 22 inch mirrored flat faced rims that shines with a wave of light, along with the ultra thin tires, coated with Black Magic.

"Damn ol' girl strapped," Marco stated, locking his focus on the woman. A smile spreads across Scotty's face.

"You must know her?" Marco asked.

"Somethin' like that." Scotty answered, giving Marco a dab. "I'ma holla at you later on about that."

"A'ight."

Scotty hops out of the Lexus and close the door. "I wish you would give me the same attention as you givin' that car," Scotty blurted, stealing Elane's attention as he approaches her from the rear.

She lifts her gaze from the window of the car staring at a smiling Scotty. "I wish I was the lucky man drivin' that car. If I was I'll probably be able to spend a little time with you."

"Maybe, but I think this is a little too extravagant for a man of your caliber," she replied in a soft strong sophisticated voice.

A breeze of wind flutters her wrap. She brushes a strand of hair away from her face, tucking it behind her ear. The firm fitting Rocawear velour jogging suit she has on accentuates her shapely 34-23-43 frame. Scotty discreetly glimspes at the camel toe imprint between her thick thighs. It looks like God molded her from liquid.

He struts away shaking his head side to side with a grin growing on his face. He steps into the small detail shop. He converses with one of the uniformed employees. Scotty drops a twenty dollar bill into the man's hand. He exits the building with a set of keys jingling in his hand. He presses a button on the keychain. The driver's door to the Ferrari pops open making a swishing sound from the air pressure as the door rises skyward, exposing the oatmeal colored interrior. Elane's mouth drops open in disbelief, as Scotty climbs into the sports car closing the door. The driver's window slowly descends. Scotty leans back in the driver's seat with his eyes glued on Elane, as she stares at him looking dumbfounded.

"Lesson number one baby. Never underestimate a man." Scotty winks his eye at her and smashes down on the gas burning rubber, shifting the stick. A loud screech pierces the air sounding like an angry tiger. The rearend of the Ferrari swerves uncontrollably with a billow of smoke fogging her vision, as he zips out of the lot.

CHAPTER FOUR

M otion struts across the parking lot carrying his daughter in his arms, as Ayesha sashays beside him dressed in her House of Dereon halter top, and sweat pants. Her pierced navel is exposed, accentuating her flat chiseled stomach.

Elliott and Bridget trails behind them holding hands. An aurora of lights dances in the air, illuminating the lot, looking like a scenery in Las Vegas.

"Da da 'ook." Joy pointed at the moving rides.

The wide spectrum of eclectic sounds that are heard at every carnival reverberates throughout the lot. The clacking sound of the rollercoaster ascending pierces the air as it reaches towards its peek before making a dramatic drop.

Loud, joyful, ear piercing screams rips through the atmosphere, along with hysterical laughter. Calliope music erupts from the windpipe organs. A carnival hawker stands next to the basketball game, soliciting the large crowd of customers.

"Step right up and try your luck! Five tries for one buck."

Motion hands Elliott a thick wad of money. "Go snatch us some tickets brah. We'll be over there by the basketball game."

"How many tickets you want me to get?" Elliott inquired.

"Get a thousand of 'em. Rides on me tonight."

"A'ight." Elliott and Bridget walk off to the ticket booth. Motion approaches the basketball game holding his bundle of joy.

"Here take Joy fa' me so I can win y'all some prizes." Motion sits Joy down and Ayesha holds her soft tiny hand.

"Step right up sir and take your best shot." Motion hands the man a five dollar bill. "How many tries would you like today sir?" the man asked politely, exposing his rotten teeth.

"Twenty five shots." He passes Motion the miniature sized basketball.

Motion shoots the ball and misses three times in a row. "Damn," he muttered.

"Come on baby you can do it," Ayesha cheers him on.

Motion makes the next five shots.

"That's what I'm talking about bae," Ayesha said excitedly. Motion makes 14 out of 25 five shots, leaving him with 14 tickets.

"Daddy me want teddy bear," Joy proclaimed.

"Which one boo?"

"Dat one," Joy answered, pointing at the biggest bear hanging on the wall.

"How many tickets I need to get that bear?" Motion asked.

"That one right there is a hundred tickets."

"Well, that mean it's time to get the party started."

Motion reaches into his pants pocket pulling out a hundred dollar bill. "That should give me five hundred shots. I need to win one for my wifey and one for my little princess. So that mean I gotta make two hundred shots out of five hundred."

"Da da, me wanna shot the ball." Joy said, staring up at her father with her innocent baby brown eyes.

"Okay boo. I tell you what. We gon' win this together okay?"

"Kay."

Motion lifts her up off the ground and hands her the ball. She grabs it with her tiny hands as he positions her in front of the basketball hoop.

"You ready boo?"

"Uh huh," Joy responded, moving her head up and down. She uses all of her strength and throws the ball. It bounces off the rim having the bomerang effect. Motion retrieves the ball and hands it back to her.

"You can do it boo come on," Motion encouraged.

She throws the ball making a perfect shot, hitting all net. "Yahhh," Joy shouted excitedly, clapping her hands along with Ayesha.

"That's my boo. I knew daddy's little girl could do it," Motion applauded. "Now its daddy turn."

"Kay."

Motion hands her to Ayesha so she can have a clear visual. Motion throws the ball skillfully making a perfect shot. Ayesha and Joy cheer him on as he shots the ball repeatedly. Elliot and Bridget makes it back from the ticket booth. Motion makes ten successful shots attracting a large crowd of spectators.

A long line of awaiting customers accumulates behind him as he finishes his shot.

*　　*　　*

ATLANTA FEDERAL PRISON U.S.P

Vegas stands in the shower. The hot water drizzles down his four foot nine chiseled frame, as he rinses the soap off of his body. He cups his hands under the cascading water, filling them with water. He splashes the water on his face, tracing his facial features with his eyes closed. Water glistens on his cleanly shaved head.

Vegas is a 47 year old veteran, who has been incarcerated for the last seven years on his thirty year sentence. Vegas ran a large scale drug ring in the city of Milwaukee. He has a lot of street credibility and clout. Physically, he is small, but financially he is a gaint with money and the power.

With one of the most powerful attorneys in the country on his team, he managed to give back a life sentence.

He turns the knob affixed to the tiled wall, turning off the shower. He reaches for his drying towel that is draped across the bar inside the shower stall.

A tall muscular built inmate with french braids, and multiple tattoos on his arms, struts toward the shower room. He is carrying his drying towel and a bag of hyigene products. As he attempts to enter the shower room, a short burly inmate blocks the doorway.

"Hold on playa. No disrespect, but this area is off limits 'til Vegas get finished," he proclaimed with authority. He has his arms crossed in front of him revealing his large biceps.

"I 'ont give a fuck about a nigga name Vegas! He don't own this mafucka!" the muscular inmate barked, disregarding the man's statement. He tries to muscle his way through the doorway.

Another inmate approaches him from behind; locking his arm around his neck, holding a razor sharp sank against his throat. The muscles in his forearms bulge as he tighten his lock.

"Mafucka didn't you hear what the fuck he said? Vegas in the shower. Next time you be disrespectful I'ma cut yo' muthafuckin' throat open. You hear me mafucka?" He apply more pressure to the man's neck. "Mafucka answer me!" the inmate said in a raspy voice, jerking the man's body.

The sharp blade causes him to get his mind right. He nods his head. "Y-Yeah," he grimaces in pain with his face contorted, grasping for air.

Vegas steps out of the shower room wearing a heavy white robe with his drying towel draped across his shoulders, his lips pluckered, whistling the harmony of Curtis Mayfields' "Freddy's Dead" as he strolls down the tier pretending like he never noticed the confrontation.

Vegas steps inside his small cell, removing his robe. He sits on the edge of the twin sized bed. He slips into his tan khakis and crispy white Airforce Ones with its gummy bottoms. He gazes into the 8x11 mirror that overlooks the stainless steel sink, inspecting his meticulously groomed shadowed beard.

"Still lookin' like a million bucks," he said aloud, smiling in the mirror, nodding his head. He glimpses around sneakily and unscrews the mirror, detaching it from the wall. He reaches into the hole behind the mirror, removing a small white envelope, thumbing through ten hundred dollar bills. He hears the distant sound of footsteps and jingling keys approaching in the direction of the cell. He moves hurriedly stashing the envelope underneath his pillow. He grabs one of his urban novels entitled "Dream" and feigns as if he is reading. The audible sound of the keys jingling in front of his cellblock causes him to lift his gaze from the soft covered book, locking his focus on correctional officer Korbic.

The inmates named him Shakedown because of the random searches he conduct daily. He did a cell search last year that lead to a seizure of 8 sanks, two pounds of marijuana, and two ounces of powder cocaine that placed the institution on lockdown for two weeks.

Shakedown stands in front of Vegas' cell with a military style haircut, glaring through a pair of shades.

"Inmate Hawkins, room search," Shakedown informed. "Please step out of your cell," Shakedown instructed.

Vegas exits the room already familiar with the routine.

Vegas' cellblock get searched more than any other inmate in the facility.

He plants his palms on the wall above his head as Shakedown pats him down thoroughly, from shoulders to ankles. He orders for Vegas to remove his socks.

"Step to the side inmate Hawkins, while I conduct my room search. Something is tellin' me that today may be my lucky day and your worst day," he proclaimed, entering the cell wearing a pair of latex gloves.

He moves directly for Vegas' bed and lifts up the mattress, searching under it. He drops the mattress and lifts up the pillow. He locks his eyes on the envelope that lays on in plain view. He opens the envelope feeling like a lucky man. The corners of his mouth curves, forming a crooked grin. He tucks the envelope into his pocket, replacing it with a cell phone and a quarter pound of hydro. He sits on the edge of Vegas' bed shuffling through one of his Don Diva magazines killing time.

Ten minutes past by and Shakedown steps out of the cell. "Your good to go inmate Hawkins. You got lucky this time," Shakedown stated, putting on his best theatrical performance, strutting down the hall in his tight fitting uniform.

Vegas slides back inside his cell closing the door. He reaches under his pillow grabbing the package of marijuana and the cell phone. He sits at the stainless steel desk rolling up a blunt. He strikes a match and blazes up the pencil thick blunt. He takes a toke of the blunt to the head and blows out a thick cloud of smoke with his eyes partially closed, as he contemplates.

It won't be long before I'm back on the streets. My plan is finally coming together. Milwaukee . . . Milwaukee . . . here I come. Vegas press the power button on the cell phone feeling good as ever under his circumstances. He punches a number in the phone calling his woman, who has been riding with him like a true soldier for many years. She answers the phone on the third ring.

*   *   *

Elliott and Bridget rises from their seats after thirty minutes of sitting motionless for the artist, as he sketched an animated cartoon version of them.

"Whew, I think it's time for something to drink." Bridget suggested, stretching her stiff bones.

"I hear that baby. I'm dying of thirst," Elliott added, holding the finished piece of artwork in his hands. "He did a good job on this. Look at you baby. If you were a cartoon character you'll be the finest," Elliott complimented.

"You have to tell a sista that." She flicks her long hair behind her shoulders as if she is posing for America's Top Model, doing a sexy pose. "I know baby, I get it from my mama," she playfully said with her flawless white dentures on display.

"Oh yeah. Well, I guess that mean I get it from my daddy huh?" Elliott chuckled.

Motion holds Joy in his arms moving through the thick disorderly crowd of children racing to the many rides. Cotton candy is allover Joy's hands and clothes. She licks the cotton candy off of her sticky fingers.

"Boo you making a big mess," Ayesha said, wiping Joy's hands with a damp papertowel.

"Ooow dada 'ook." Joy points to the colorful illiminated carousel.

"You wanna get on the carousel boo?" Motion asked, talking over the loud deafening sound of children yelling in excitement.

On their way to the carousel Motion spots three children wearing sad faces, staring at their mother with glassy eyes, as she scolds them.

"I told y'all mama I ain't got no more money, now come on, it's time to go. Don't make me have to repeat myself."

Motion looks at the children feeling sorry for them. It made him think about when he was a kid. His mother struggled raising him and Elliott. He remembered the hard times they had growing up in the projects, sharing the same clothes, drinking Kool Aid out of pickel jars, and standing in front of gas stations pumping people's gas for chump change.

He walks up to the woman with a look of sympathy written across his face. He taps her on the shoulder. "Excuse me Ms.Lady." The woman looks over her shoulder with a puzzled facial expression.

"Do I know you from somewhere?" she quizzed, studying Motion's face as he holds Joy in his arms.

"Nah, you don't know me, but' I know the struggle that you goin' through raising them three children."

The woman is trying to figure out where he is going with the conversation. He hands her 50 tickets and five hundred dollars. The woman stares at the money in disbelief, shifting her gaze on Motion as if he is God. She cups her mouth with her open hand.

"Are you serious?"

"Than a heart attack," he smile, glad to see the woman's appreciation.

"You gon' and take yo' kids and finish havin' a good time."

"Thank you so much whoever you are."

"No problem," Motion responded, watching the woman who was almost in tears. He pats her son on the head. The little boy tilts his head back looking up at Motion. "You make sure you take care of yo' mama lil' man. You hear me?" The little boy rocks his head up and down shyly in silence. "Now gon' and enjoy yo' self." Motion turns around and struts away. He can hear the joy in their voices as the children jump in the air cheerfully.

"Yaaaah."

Motion carries a large bundle of stuffed animals that he won for Ayesha and Joy. Ayesha carries a sleeping Joy in her arms as they make their way to the car, accompanied by Elliott and Bridget.

"Bay it's kind of chilly out here," Bridget complained, rubbing her shoulders and arms. Elliott wiggles out of his throwback jersey and places it over her shoulders.

"Is that better baby?"

"Yes baby." She replied in her soft voice. "Thank you."

They climb inside the car ending a long day of laughter and happiness.

*   *   *

A large assembly of Christians are congregated in the sanctuary at Born Again Baptist church, listening to Pastor Thomas deliver his sermon.

"It's truly a blessing to be in the house of the lord today.

75

Can I get an amen?"

"Amen," the audience shouts in unison.

"I would like for you to turn to Romans, chapter twelve verse two in your bibles and I quote, do not be conformed to this world, but be transformed by the renewing of your mind, that you may prove what is good and acceptable and perfect will of God. Now see my brothers and sisters, until we begin to think right we can't please God or do his will, because see the mind never stop and that is the easiest place for Satan to do his battle. I once heard a woman say that I was brainwashing people. I laughed and then I replied, the brain needs to be washed because it's filthy."

The assembly erupts in laughter. An old woman with gray hair wearing a large white hat shouts, "Amen! Speak that holy word." She fans herself with her hand, fighting back the hot room temperature. Pastor Thomas scans the sea of happy faces.

"My brothers and sisters today I beg you to fix your thoughts and let Jesus into your hearts. At this time we'll let our choir priase the lord in song. The doors of the church are now open."

Kevin and his mother Ms. Wilkins are seated in the front row of the sanctuary. A young man sits in the fourth row dressed in a black pin striped Zoot suit, wearing a pair of sunglasses with a bible in his lap. He glimpses at Kevin and his mother as they watch the Pastor deliver his speech.

It's time fo' me to change my life. My mother was right; it ain't nothin' but death on them streets. I can't believe my homie is gone just like that over a crap game. He didn't deserve that father. Maybe it was time for him to go. God I pray that you forgive me for my sins. Kevin stares at the Pastor as he continues to speak.

"Let's bow our heads and pray. Our father in heaven we come to you in prayer to thank you for this day that you have given us to worship you. We pray that your word reflects on us for your word says let your light shine before man that others will see it, and glorify the father. We pray for world peace, we pray for the soldiers that are gone to war and for their families at this time. We also pray for families that word reside in them. Forgive us for our sins known and unknown. We thank you for guiding us each day in Jesus name Amen."

"Hallelujah, thank you Jesus," Ms. Wilkins shouted, feeling jubilant. A compassionate spirit courses through her body. She embraces Kevin's hand and closes her eyes, thanking the lord for allowing her son to get baptized and turn his life over to the lord.

Kevin has been out of the streets for the last two weeks. He never thought in a million years that he would be a member of the church. Pastor Thomas stands in front of the congregation with his hands extended in front of him. The choir sings a soft harmony, dressed identically in purple robes as the pianist strikes the piano keys, blending in with a smooth melody.

"I know it's somebody out there in this crowd that is ready to give their life to the most high. I know your out there some where. Don't be ashame to turn your life over to the giver of life. Please stand up and step forward. I'm not asking you to do this for me, I'm asking you to do this for the good lord."

Pastor Thomas studies the crowd and the young man seated in the fourth row rises from his seat, staring at the Pastor through the lenses of his sunglasses.

"Now that's what I'm talking about, please step forward young man, don't be afraid. I know it's not easy, please come my way it's going to be alright. You're in the house of the lord."

The young man eases by the people sitting on the wooden benches carefully, clutching his bible. "Hallelujah!" The crowd of church members give him a round of applause as he moves down the aisle making his way to the front row of the sanctuary. A large crucifix overlooks the sanctuary. *I can't wait 'til I take off this suit and get out of these shoes.* The young man stands in front of the Pastor and opens his bible. "Pastor can you read this for me?"

"Sure I can son," Pastor Thomas answered, accepting his bible.

He reads the highlighted words in the book of Revelations, chapter twenty two, verse thirteen. "I'am the alpha and omega, the first and the last, the beginning and the ending."

The young man opens his suit jacket, producing a nickel plated .44 Mag. Pastor Thomas cringes in shock dropping the bible on the floor. Coupe spins around aiming the gun at a startled Kevin. Coupe bites down on his bottom lip and squeezes the trigger repeatedly. The barking sound of the powerful handgun reverberates throughout the sanctuary, along with the loud ear-piercing screams. The assembly scatters around the church in a disorderly fashion, running for safety.

Kevin's body is folded up on the wooden bench. The smell of gun powder floats in the air.

Coupe steps closer to Kevin's corpse unloading two additional rounds. The impact of the handgun causes his body to jerk and topple to the floor. His head traces a trail of blood down the bench. Ms. Wilkins screams hysterically, cradling her only son in her arms rocking back and forth. "Noooo, Nooo, my babbbyyy."

Coupe tucks the gun under his suit jacket, kneeling down grabbing the bible. The church is now empty. Coupe strolls down the aisle never looking back at his victim. He exits the church hearing the distant sound of sirens. Coupe's protege Steve pulls up to the curb in a stolen Chevy. Coupe brushes imaginary dust off his suit jacket and glimpses around calmly before jumping inside the car. ErrrrK! The tires screech as they pull off hurriedly with the engine roaring.

*   *   *

Buzzz! Ghino the jeweler presses a button behind the counter of Igloo's jewelry shop, allowing Scotty inside the estabishment. The Asian jeweler greets him with a friendly smile.

"Sup Ghino?"

"What's going on Scotty?' Ghino replied. Ghino is in his late twenties. He inherited Igloo's jewelry store from his deceased father.

"I got yo' message. I would've came yesterday, but my hands was full," Scotty explained.

"No problem, I know how it is when your a baller. Let me get yo' piece for you. I'm sure your going to like it." Ghino goes to the back room behind the counter and return with a platinum chain with it's custom made medallion attached to it reading 'Money makes the world go round' in diamonds with a big faced hundred dollarbill in the middle that spins.

Scotty nods his head with a smile of satisfaction forming on his face.

"You like it?" Ghino inquired.

"Do I like it? Hell yeah I like it." Scotty grabs the piece of jewelry off of the cush velvet tray inspecting it. He loops it over his head and looks into the mirror. The 25 carat diamond sprinkled medallion sparkles like a disco light. Scotty reaches into his pocket dropping a thick wad of hundred dollar bills on the display cabinet.

"That's 20 grand. That should cover the balance." Ghino grabs the wad of money and fans it with his finger tips.

"No need to count it. That's that all there money." Scotty retorted, he spins around and heads for the door with the $70,000 piece adorning his neck.

"Thanks," Ghino said pressing the button to buzz him out.

Toon sits in the driver's seat of his artic silver Denali accommodated with chrome 26inch Havoc XL rims talking on his cellular phone. Marco is in the back seat playing the Sony Playsation 2. Marco's fingers moves rapidly as he presses the buttons on the wireless controller. Scotty climbs into the Denali with the chain dangling from his neck looking like a rapper. Scotty spins the hundred dollar bill center piece and holds it up to Toon.

"You like this shit don't you?" Toon glimpses at the platinum piece and hangs up the phone.

"I see you doin' it big baby. Ghino plugged you on that." Toon stated. Marco pauses the game and leans forward in his seat stealing a quick look at the chain.

"Yeah that's tight right there. You should've got God make the world go round with a black Jesus on a crucifix in the center." Marco said, leaning back in his seat.

"God." Scotty blurted with his face twisted up. "God ain't never did shit fo' me. This the only God I know." Scotty slams a thick wad of money on the dash board. Money falls all over his lap. "God ain't never made it happen. I made this shit happen." Scotty pounds his fist against his chest. The liquor he drunk earlier has him a little tipsy and hyperly active. "Money is power and power is money. This how I eat everyday. I watched my mama pray all my life and shit never happened fo' us. I had to get out there and get it! You feel me?" Scotty stressed. The smell of alcohol emits from his breath lingering in the atmosphere.

"Calm down baby," Toon blurted, bringing the engine to a soft roar.

He presses a button on a remote awakening the four 15inch gorillas. The deep powerful bass vibrates the rearview mirrors. Their ears tingle from the loud bass. Marco feels as if he is being punched in the back.

Marco bobs his head to the rhythm of the beat, playing Grandtheft Auto on the Playstation 2 with the Audiovox headsets on.

Heads turn as the volcanic sound rumbles in the concret as they veer through the downtown area chopping on the 26inch chrome feet.

They pull up to Big Mama's soul food carry out restaurant stealing the attention of all the bystandes. Everything seems to be moving in slow motion as the bass drops hard, shaking the truck.

Scotty notices a familiar vehicle parked in front of them. He peers through the windows searching for the occupant of the vehicle. Toon presses a button on the remote bringing the music to mute.

"What's wrong dawg?" Toon inquired, as Scotty studies the scenery.

"Ain't nothin' wrong," Scotty replied. "It just looks like I' ma bout to have a little fun." He massages his chin with his thumb and index finger, with a devious smile on his face.

"I 'ont know what you up to Scotty, but make sure you grab me a grape soda."

"Make that two of 'em," Marco added.

Scotty hops out of the truck, his platinum chain sways as he struts into the restaurant. The bell hanging above the glass door jingles as he makes his entrance, becoming the center of attention. He called their order in to avoid the long wait. Big Mama's is always packed with awaiting customers anticipating the tasteful bite of the soulfood.

Scotty's eyes shifts around the carry-out restaurant in search of the owner of the S.U.V. He plasters his eyes on who he considers to be the most beautiful women on the face of the earth. He puts on his best performance and acts as if he doesn't see he. He feels a vibration on his hip. The melody of his customized ring tone escapes his cellphone. He retrieves one of the cellular phones attached to his waistline. The woman turns around now aware of his presence. He chats on the phone watching the woman through his peripheral vision. He hangs up the phone and trudges over to the pick up window.

"Excuse me. Do you have a call in order fo' Scott?" He asked the older woman standing at the window arranging the prepared orders in the paper bags.

"I think I do, let me see." The woman replied looking at all the reciepts attached to the bags. "Here it is."

She grabs the bag and rings up the order. Scotty pays her for the food. He grabs the bags out of the window. Scotty feels someone tapping him on his shoulder. He turns around face to face with Elane.

"How you doing stranger?" She askedin her soft sophisticated voice.

"I'm doin' a'ight."

"I see that," Elane replied, appraising the platinum chain that is hanging from his neck.

"Check this out baby. I would like to sit here and elaborate wit' you, but I'm in a rush right now baby." Scotty proclaimed, demonstrating his Oscar winning performance. "Maybe you can give me yo' number and I'll get wit' you."

"That sounds like a good idea, but unfortunately I don't have access to any writing utensils."

"No problem baby," Scotty said, reaching for his waistband for one of the cellular phones clipped to his waistband. "Here, take this. Just make sure you answer when I call." Elane accepts his cellular phone, placing it into her purse.

"I'll be waiting on your call," Elane said, as Scotty exits the restaurant.

CHAPTER FIVE

EL PASO, TEXAS

Motion leans back in the butter soft leather interrior of Julio's Mercedes S600 conversing.

"After you move these five hundred thangs, I'ma hit you with five hundred more thangs. I'm talking about the best dope in the United States of America. I hate that you're about to get out of the business. I'ma miss doin' business with you. Out of all my customers you have maintain your loyalty from day one." Julio peers through the tinted windows of the Mercedes that conceals them.

"Like I told you from day one, my word is all I got as a man. If a man can't keep his word he ain't shit. I came a long way and I thank you fo' all you have done fo' me," Motion said.

"Motion you have nothin' to thank me for. Everything you have came from your own diligence and determination. You never asked me for nothin', that's why I always had a lot of respect for you. Me don't have respect for a man that keeps his hand out. You will always have my friendship for life. I appreciate your business and most of all, your loyalty."

Julio's cellular phone vibrates, seizing his attention. "Hola," Julio answered in spanish. He nods his head as he listens to the caller. "Buen, adios." Julio flips the phone closed and turns the ignition bringing the engine to life. "Everything ready."

"Cool. Let me hit my people so they can meet us there." Motion churps Scotty on the Nextel.

* * *

Mayfair shopping mall is crowded. Many civilians traverse the parking lot bustling in and out the mall, carrying shopping bags, and loading them into the trunks of their automobiles.

Coupe roams through the cluttered parking lot scanning the environment in search of his next victim, gone off that ecstasy. He spots the perfect candidate and reaches for his nickel plated .45 automatic.

Ayesha prances to her convertible BMW M3 coupe in a pair of Jean Michel pumps, with a pair of Chanel sunglasses sheilding her eyes. She is carrying multiple shopping bags. The ten karat diamond Cartier braclet sparkles on her wrist as she guides her daughter safely through the parking lot. She pops the trunk with the keyless entry.

"Mummy, can we go get ice cream?" Joy asked.

"Yeah sweetie."

"Yaah. Thank you mummy," Joy said excitedly, her eyes gleaming with joy and happiness.

I'ma break this bitch off. If she start screamin' and shit, I'ma blow her brains out. Hopefully she'll make this easy. Coupe eases out of the car. He opens the door, clutching the only friend he feels that he have in this world.

*   *   *

A midnight blue Dodge Charger Daytona arrives at the Amoco gas station resting on a set of large chrome rims with dark tinted windows, concealing the driver of the car. The hot beaming sun baths the streets making the chrome rims gleam.

Nickel sits in the driver's seat of his Ford Thunderbird thumbing through a thick wad of money. He is parked on the side of the gas station. He shifts his gaze to the Dodge Charger and stuffs the money in a purple Crown Royal bag. The Dodge Charger pulls up besides him. ***This nigga right on time.***

Nickel climbs out of the car. He jumps into,the Dodge Charger removing the money underneath his Milwaukee Brewer's baseball jersey.

"What up Toon?" Nickel greeted.

"What up man? What's good?" Toon replied, his cellular phone is ringing of the hook. Toon paints his index finger skyward. "Hold on fo' a second Nickel." Toon answers the phone. "Yeah . . . A'ight . . . Be there in a minute." Toon hangs up the phone. "My bad baby. What up though?"

"Here you go." Nickel hands him the Crown Royal bag. Toon places the bag under his seat without inspecting it. "It's all there?"

"Yeah, it's all there," Nickel answered.

Toon's cellular phone goes off again. "Reach under the seat," Toon instructed, looking at the caller's identification.

Nickel pulls a ziploc bag from under the passenger's seat containing a half of brick (half a kilo).

Nickel examines the large chunk of powder and tucks it underneath his jersey. Toon answers his cellphone.

"Yeah, holla at me."

Nickel climbs out of the car. "I'ma be gettin' back at you in a minute.

"A'ight." Nickel closes the door and jumps into his car. Toon dips out of the lot and vanishes. Nickel stashes the half of kilo in his console. His cellphone chimes, "I make it rain. I make it rain."

"Yeah what up?" Nickel answered, feeling blissful. "Yeah it's all good. Just left my man a few minutes ago. Just give me a minute and I'll holla at you . . . A'ight." Nickel hangs up the phone not realizing that he just ran a stop sign. A blue and white patrol car appears out of nowhere pulling behind him. He can hear the sound of the engine roaring as the patrol car approaches the rearend of his car. He begins to fidget knowing that he's riding dirty. ***Shit! Where the fuck they come from. I should get little on that cracker. Fuck it, he can't do nothin' but write me a ticket.*** Nickel stares at the red and blue lights dancing in his~rearview mirror.

*　*　*

Dirty Red maneuvers the big body S55 Mercedes Benz through the busy intersection, bobbing his head to the rich bass that is ripping through the 12 inch JL Audio subwoofers. He stares through the soft tinted lenses of his semi rimless aviator sunglasses by Kennth Cole. He pulls up to a red light and glimpses into the rearview inspecting his crispy zigzagging cornrows feeling like a ghetto superstar. He sits motionless at the redlight. The Mercedes appears to be moving as the chrome 22inch Sprewels windmill. The dime sized diamond stud earring shimmers as he turns down a horseshoe shaped street. He turns down his car system, as he enters the tranquil suburban neighborhood with impeccable manicured lawns.

He dips into the alley and presses a button on his keychain allowing himself access to his garage. As the garage door ascends, he pulls into it slowly. The door descends as he parks the car.

Roof! Roof! Roof! His bull master barked, jumping around hysterically rattling the thick chain he is attached to, causing Dirty Red to become suspicious. Dirty Red exits an additional door adjacent to the fenced in yard. He glances around with caution in search of anything usual. This is the first time his dog has displayed such behavior. Unaware of anything strange, he pulls the door closed behind him.

Roof! Roof! Roof! What's wrong wit' that damn dog?

A man steps from behind the garage with his hands in his pockets. Dirty Red springs back in fear, reaching for the Glock 19 tucked in his waistband. The triangle barrel of a .45 auto presses against his temple answering his question. The assailant bashes him across the back of his head brutally with the gun. Dirty Red falls to his knees loosing his balance. Slowly he regains his composure. The bullmaster growls leaping forward being yanked back by the chain attached to its collar.

An old model Cadillac Sedan Deville pulls beside the garage with it's trunk ajar, with a sheet of plastic covering the interior of the trunk. The assailant shoves him in the ribcage with the gun.

Dirty Red stands in the admidst of three tamed bulls. His face creases, as he agonizes in pain. Dity Red stares at the unfamiliar man walking in his direction. The man removes Dirty Red's gun from his waistband.

"Check dis out partner," the man speaks in a calm mannerism. "If you follow my instructions I'll let you live. I'ma let you know dis right now. I' m not into killin', but if I have to make dis a homicide, I won't hesitate to squeeze dis trigga." The man stands in front of Dirty Red nonchalantly with his hands in his pockets. *How the fuck these niggas find out where I live.*

He can tell by their style and demeanor that they are not amateurs. The man signals his colleagues with a head gesture. The men place him in handcuffs and escorts him to the trunk. He knows that he has no other alternatives so he follows their instructions.

Roof! Roof! Roof! The dog contiunes to bark attracting attention. Dirty Red's fiance peers through the window sensing something wrong. She grabs the cordless phone to call Dirty Red's cellular phone.

*　　*　　*

ATLANTA FEDERAL PRISON

"Mr. Hawkins you have a visit," Correctional Officer Pulaski announced, standing in front of Vegas' single cell.

"A visit," he said aloud. *I'm not expecting no visit today.* He leans upward in the bed, looking at his digital clock. *It's three thirty, visiting hours over wit'.* A confounded facial expression forms on his face.

He slips on his neatly creased tan khakis and his coffee colored Timberland boots. He walks pompously down the corridor, entertaining himself with numerous thoughts, as he moves closer to the visiting area. *Maybe this is the day that I been waitin' for.* A short chubby female correctional officer presses a button. Click! Click! The door pops open allowing him to make his entrance into the visiting area.

Vegas hands the correctional officer his institutional issued identification card, upon making his entry. She pats him down for contraband. He scans the empty visiting room. The female correctional officer escorts him to a room that is only used for professional visits. Being that it has been a lengthy time since he has engaged in any sexual activity, Vegas studies the woman's body for a brief second, as she stands in front of him opening the secured door. *Her ass flat as hell. I wouldn't mind tappin' that ass right now.* Vegas thought, feeling a slight erection forming underneath his tan uniform. The seven years in prison lowered his standards. If he was in the free world he wouldn't give her the time or day.

He struts into the room in the amidst of three Europeans sitting at the round table in a circular formation, dressed in double breasted designer suits. They greet Vegas with friendly smiles, as he makes his appearance.

"Good evening Mr. Hawkins, have a seat," Mr. Lindsay greeted with a hand gesture welcoming him.

Vegas sinks into the firm cushioned, high back chair already familiar with two of the men.

Mr. Lindsay is the superior federal agent on his case, seated to his right is the United States prosecutor, who prosecuted him six years ago.

Vegas fixes his eyes on a beautiful white female with ocean blue eyes, long blond hair, and a two piece cashmere skirt set. This is the first time Vegas met the woman. She appears to be no older than 28 years old. ***Damn, that white broad fine as hell.*** Vegas feels his manhood rising for the second time as he stares at her cleavage. The woman cracks a short friendly smile as if she is reading his mind.

"You're probably wondering why your attorney isn't present. To satisfy your curiousity, Mr.Davocci is on his way. He had a meeting to attend, so he will be a little late," Agent Lindsay informed.

"So how are you holding up in here?"

"I' m cool, but it could be better."

Before Mr. Lindsay could reply a well dressed Italian man struts into the room in a charcol gray Giorgio Armani suit, black Testoni shoes, and various diamond rings glistening on his fingers. He totes his black leather Prada briefcase. His jet black short curly hair bounces with the rhythm of his stride.

"Good evening ladies and gentlemen."

"I' m glad you're able to join us Mr.Angelo Davocci. I know you.'re a busy man these days," Mr.Lindsay retorted, addressing his friend of many years. The two of them attended the same college.

"You know how it goes when you're the top ten most powerful defense attorney in the country." Angelo Davocci boasted, brushing imaginary lint from his blazer before taking his seat. He bump fists with his long time client and business partner.

"Now that you finally made it to join us, let me get straight down to business," Mr. Lindsay suggested. Vegas never thought he would be sitting at the round table congregating with the federal government conspiring to take the next man away from his love ones. He became one of the things he always despised, a snitch. He finally realized what they mean when they say, pressure bust pipes. Vegas returned back to court on a Rule 35 motion, earning the title of a certified rat. The federal government issued him some false documentation to provide to the inmates to guarantee his safety. They also promised to grant him his freedom for his substantial assistance on behalf of the government.

* * *

Motion climbs out of Julio's Mercedes laced in a white Polo short set with the baby blue embriodered Polo logo and a pair of crispy white Rockports. He tosses up the peace sign, holding his two fingers in a V-shape, as Julio pulls off with a dusty cloud lingering behind his car.

Gravel crunches under Motion's feet as he struts over to accompany his two men crew. They are positioned around a 92 Ford Explorer that contains 500 kilograms of the puriest cocaine in the United States Of America. This is one of the biggest loads Motion has ever dealt with and his first time picking up his own shipment out of state.

"I got some bad news for ya," Scotty stated with a look of disappointment written across his face.

"What's that?"

"Our driver never showed up."

"Fuck! If it ain't one thing, it's another thing."

Motion's face crinkles in frustration as he paces the surface.

"How we suppose to get all this shit back home?" Scotty inquired, as Marco stands beside him quietly.

"I know I ain't driving that mafucka home. If we get caught wit' that much dope, we'll never get out the joint. It's enough dope in there to supply the whole state of Wisconsin," Scotty continued.

Marco sits on the hood of the Durango they rented, along with the Chevy Impala SE. They rented the vehicles in two different names so they can't be linked to each other.

Motion's eyes are faintly visible behind the lense of his Gucci frames, as he contemplates the next move. Coming up with a solution to their dilemma, he reaches into his pocket, producing a butterfly knife. Marco and Scotty stare at Motion with a puzzled look plastered on their faces. He kneels down beside the Ford Explorer and slashes the two front tires.

"What you do that for? Now we really fucked up," Scotty proclaimed, staring at Motion as if he has loss his mind. He pops open the hood and cuts the battery cables.

"Man you crazy," Scotty stated. Motion pays no attention to him. He flips open his prepaid cell phone, calling Triple A towing service.

"Trilpe A towing service, how may I help you?"

"I need a tow truck. My truck just broke down on me."

"Where is the truck located sir?"

"Hold on."

Motion glimpses around to find the address. He gives the address to customer's service, providing them with all the information they need. He flips the phone closed giving them giving Marco and Scotty the run down.

"Check this out. I want you and Marco to follow the tow truck once they pick up the truck. Me, I'ma be close by keeping an eye on things. Once the tow truck reach Milwaukee and drop the truck off, we gon' let it sit for three days in Candice's driveway."

Marco and Scotty listen intently as Motion explains his plan to them. Marco looks at him in amazement.

"Damn, you a genius Motion. I would've never thought of that."

Motion winks his eye at Marco and says, "I was born for this shit."

*   *   *

Coupe takes the only friend he have off safety, approaching Ayesha from behind as she leans forward, placing shopping bags inside the trunk. His eyeballs dances as he studies his surroundings, making sure that it is free of spectators.

As he levels his gun, a car turns down the aisle of parked automobiles. He takes a fleeting look over his shoulders becoming startled. Swiftly, he tucks the gun back into his waistband, changing his course of direction. A Wauwatosa patrol car roams the parking lot. The officer who appears to be racist watches Coupe closely, as he eases back into the car in a casual manner, trying not to look suspicious. His heart beat soars, as the officer eases on his brakes. He reads the license plates.

Ayesha leans into the passenger's side of the car fastening Joy's seatbelt. She hops into the car backing out of the parking slot, unaware of the blessing she just received.

The license plates on Coupe's car comes back clean. The officer continues patrolling the area. Lately they've been receiving several complaints about automobiles being broken into.

"Damn that was a close call. That cracker had to fuck up my come up," Coupe grumbled, pulling off in search of another victim.

* * *

The canine unit arrives as Nickel sits in the back seat of the silver Crown Victoria in handcuffs, in the state of turmoil. He watches as the canine becomes hyperly active, clawing at the dashboard, detecting illegal narcotics. Nickel knows what is about to transpire. He is overwhelmed by the intensity of his emotions. He bangs his forehead against the plexiglass that divides him from the occupant of the squad car in sheer frustration. His emotions go chaos as he ponders. He visualizes his girlfriend who recently informed him of her pregnancy. He buries his chin in his chest, swaying his head, blowing out a short breath of air. His heart begins to feel heavy at that point.

Fuck I'm suppose to do now. My parole officer ain't tryna hear this shit. Ain't no way I can explain being in possession of a firearm, two ounces of hard, and a half of thang soft. Nickel tries to figure out a solution to his problem. Being a second time felon, he knows his unborn child will probably be an adult by the time he makes it out of prison. *No way, it's not gon' happen like that. I'm comin' up out of this shit.* Nickel promised himself, as an idea surfaced his mind.

* * *

Dirty Red's fiancée Janette called his cellular phone for the umpteenth time only to receive his voicemail. Captivated by dismay, she dials Motion's prepaid cellular phone with no luck at all. The only thing she received is a busy signal.

Her heart pumps with trepidation as she exits the back door to conduct her own investigation. Their dog trots in her direction brushing up against her pacing back and forth.

"What's wrong boy?" Roof! Roof! The dog leads her to the ajar garage door and Dirty Red's keys that lay on the pavement. "Red baby are you in there?" Receiving no answer, she pushes the door all the way open, inspecting the inside of the garage. The only trace of Dirty Red is his Mercedes Benz parked in the garage along with his keys.

"Oh my God, something is wrong," she blurted, storming out of the garage with the dog trailing behind her. Panic sweeps through her body as she emerges inside the house to call for help.

CHAPTER SIX

Marco and Scotty rushes inside Club Sensation after receiving an emergency call from Motion. They march into Motion's office. He sits at the end of the long mahogany table seated in the leather high back executive chair with his fingers interlaced in front of him, his forehead resting on his hands. Hearing them make their entry, he lifts his head. Toon is seated beside him with a distressed look on his face.

"What's goin' on? Is everything a'ight?" Marco questioned in concern, shifting his gaze from Toon to Motion waiting for an answer.

"It's Dirty Red . . . some niggas kidnapped him," Motion uttered, running his cupped hand down the length of his face.

"Who the fuck did it? And why they do it?" Scotty cut in.

"I 'ont know, we waitin' on them to call b-" Before he could finish his sentence his cell phone chimes. He glances at the caller's ID aware of someone calling private. He answers the phone with no hesitation. Everyone in the office listens intently as he speaks. "Hello."

"This the deal. I'ma man that means business. I don't believe in killin', but if any police get involved or any funny shit, this mutha fucka's dead. Just to let you know that I mean business." Boc! Boc!

Motion flinch from the sound of gunfire in the background.

"Awww shit! You muthafucka!" Dirty Red shouted, groaning in pain, after being shot in both feet.

"I want five hundred grand by one o'clock sharp this afternoon. Drop the money off on Sherman and Millroad at the gas station across from the cemetery. Sit the money by the payphone." Click! The line goes dead. The caller doesn't give Motion a chance to negotiate.

Knowing that the man mean business. Motion prepare to put everything into progress to save his crony. He would give up everything he has to save his man's life. There is no garantee that they'll let him live, but Motion was not about to take that chance.

"What the fuck we suppose to do now? We can't let these muthafuckas get away wit' this shit. Word on the streets will travel so fast and niggas'll think we soft." Toon barked with fire in his eyes.

"Just keep yo' cool. I'ma find out who's responsible for this shit, but first things first. We have to save our man. The same thing goes if it was one of y'all. We family and family stick together. We gotta maintain our composure and play this shit smart. Right now they got the upper hand. We gotta play by their rules."

*   *   *

Elane picks up the cordless phone and dials Scotty's number. She receives no answer. In the first week of them dating, they went to the movies, park, bowling, and to a jazz club. She felt real comfortable in his presence. The moment he disappeared from her sight, she felt as if a part of her went with him. It has been a lengthy time since she's engaged in any sexual activity. Her heart skips a beat at the thought of Scotty. She had to regulate her hormones around him. The slightest touch of his hard hands caused her to quiver. She hangs up the phone. *Why he's not answering his phone. I been calling him all day. Maybe he taking care of some business? Maybe he with another woman? Let me stop thinking like that. Why I'm getting attached to him? I already have a man I love. I can't do this anymore. I have to call it off. I don't want to hurt nobody. He's a good person. I have to keep my distance.* Elane flops down on the Italian leather sofa in her flower patterned chemise staring at the ceiling.

*   *   *

"I'm glad this is my last year of school. My mother is real proud of me. There is nothing like seeing the sparkle in my mother's eyes. I always promised her and my brother that I was going to finish school and go to college," Elliot said, peering throughthe front windsheild of the car, occassionally glimpsing at Bridget.

They are on their way to a 12:15pm movie.

"How you think you did on your exams?"

"You know I aced that with no problem," Elliott bragged.

"I'ma genius, remember?" He cracks a smile revealing his flawless dentures.

"Oh yeah."

"That's right."

"Well, maybe you should've took mine for me then genius." Bridget retorted with a smile extended across her face.

He embraces her soft, firm, french manicured hand.

"All you had to do was say the word baby. You know I'll do anything for you sweetheart."

"I'll keep that in mind for the next time we have a test."

They chuckle as they pull into the parking lot of the movie theater.

* * *

Kanisha calls Scotty cell phone repeatedly, becoming agitated. She slams the phone down on its receiver. She hurls the dish in front of her that she prepared for them. The ceramic plate crashes against the wall. The dish scatters all over the cream marble floor, along with the food.

"I'm tired of this shit," she exclaimed, pulling at her hair. Scotty promised to have lunch with her.

She leans forward at the meticulously set table with her head down, feeling downhearted. Tears erupt from her eyes crawling down her wrist. She dashes the tears from her misty eyes. *Why he keep treatin' me like this? He could've at least called me. Why do love hurt so bad? What is it that I' m doing wrong?* Many questions cross her mind leaving her confounded.

* * *

Motion navigates the hard top Bentley Coupe into the gas station, analyzing the area for any suspicious activity. Before hopping out of the car, he takes his twin Glock 40's off safety, grabbing the book bag out of the back seat that contains five hundred thousand in big face hundred dollar bills.

He glimpses over his shoulders as he steps to the payphone. He sits the bag down beside the payphone as he was instructed. Just as he was about to walk off the payphone rings. He stops in his tracks gazing at the payphone in curiousity. Hesitantingly he picks up the phone.

"Yeah, what up?"

"Look inside the slot of the payphone. It should be a set of car keys in there. White Camero parked on fifty fifth and Millroad." Click!

Motion sticks his hand inside the slot finding the car keys. *I hope my man a'ight.* He says to himself, as he struts to the car. He glances over at the payphone one last time and notices that the bag is no longer there. He continues to stare at the empty spot in disbelief. He knows that whoever he is dealing with is not an amateur.

Scotty and Marco is parked a block away in a green Corsica with dark tinted windows.

"I know Kanisha mad as hell at me right now. I promised her I was gon' have lunch wit' her. She just gon' have to understand that my nigga needed me. I can't even think straight right now," Scotty stressed.

"I feel you. This seems like some shit that only happen in a movie. Once this is over wit' I'm out. I got big plans. I'ma 'bout to take that real estate to anotha level. These streets gettin' too dangerous and the feds . . . them muthafuckas splittin' niggas heads to the white meat."

"You 'ont gotta tell me, I know, believe me," Scotty stressed.

"Why you ain't gave this shit up yet?" Marco inquired.

"This might sound fucked up, but . . ." Churp! Churp! Scotty is interrupted by his Nextel. "What up?"

"Man y'all need to get over here quick." Hearing the sadness in Motion's voice Scotty questions him.

"What's wrong? Where you at?" Churp! Churp!

"I'm on fifty fifth and Millroad hurry up." Churp! Churp!

"Is Red a'ight?" Churp! Churp!

"Man it's fucked up . . . just come on."

Scotty dips off hurriedly with his heart drumming against his chest.

*   *   *

Janette emerges through the glass doors of St. Joseph's hospital, after receiving a call from Scotty. Her eyes are puffy, having been up on a four day binge worried about Dirty Red. She storms up to the receptionist station with a worrisome expression on her face, in the state of confusion. "Ma'am could you . . . please tell me where I can find Jermy Battle. I'm his fiance. I need to find him." Janette said in a quivering voice, sniffling.

The blond haired woman seated behind the desk in a baby blue scrub looks in Janette's misty red rimmed eyes.

"Calm down ma'am. Let . . ." Janette rudely interrupts her in the middle of her speech.

"What the hell you mean calm down! My fiancé some where in here fighting for his life!" She snapped, drawing attention to herself.

The security officer rushes over to the woman. "Excuse me ma'am, what seems to be the problem?"

"I'm trying to find my fiancé and this, lady, tells me to calm down," she explained.

"It's gonna be a'ight ma'am. I know who you're lookin' for. He's in room 115 on the third floor in the intensive care unit. I heard you say his name."

"Thank you sir!" Janette said, moving quickly towards the elevator.

The pulsing beep of the cardiac monitor drones in the background. Motion towers over Dirty Red along with Scotty and Marco.

They stare at their brutally beatened friend, who can't see because of his swollen eyelids. Dirty Red's head is wrapped up, making him resemble a mummy. He is suffering a mild concussion. His stomach sucks in and out as he breath, attached to the I.V.

Motion drops his head inhaling deeply, brushing his hand across his deep spiral waves, feeling downhearted.

Somebody gon' pay for this shit. Motion said to himself.

"Who did this shit to you Red?" Motion questioned, hoping that Dirty Red is able to respond.

A silver of light penetrates his eyes as he struggle to stare through his swollen eyelids.

"I 'ont know. H-He had a tattoo on his neck that said Thump." In his drowsy voice he continues. "It had to be an inside . . . job. How dem niggas know where . . . I live? I never drive straight home. They . . . was already there . . . w-when I got there. Somethin' ain't right about this. I . . . Always be on point." Dirty Red managed to explain, grimacing in pain.

"We gon' find out who did this shit to you. And when we do, that mutha fucka gon' pay in blood," Scotty proclaimed.

"You know I got yo' back Red. It's whateva," Marco sincerely stated.

"I'ma find those hoe ass niggas. I promise you that. They won't get away wit' this. It's not about the money. It's the principle. If they would've asked fo' more I would've gave up anythang fo' my nigga. I know you would do the same fo' me if it came down to it," Motion stressed.

"I-I know my nigga. Maann, I'm tired. I need some rest. Y'all . . ."

Janette bursts through the door moving rapidly with all eyes locked on her. They can see the distorted look on her face.

"Baby." She called, stepping between them with teary eyes. "Please tell me your okay." She cried holding his hand against her forehead.

"Baby . . . I'm okay. It's gon' . . . be a'ight." Hearing the sound of his voice reassured her that it is going to be okay.

Scotty comforts Janette by gently rubbing her back.

"We gon' leave y'all two lovebirds alone," Scotty said.

"You take care Janette and make sure you keep an eye on my man."

Motion whispers to Scotty and Marco, as they exit the room.

"I'ma handle this situation. I'ma call an old friend of mind. Y'all just lay low."

"A'ight."

They exchange manly hugs giving each other dap.

"One."

*   *   *

Scotty hangs up his cellular phone after chatting with Toon, making him aware of the situation that transpired with Dirty Red.

"Damn, this been a long day." Scotty mumbled under his breath.

His keys rattle as he inserts the key into the front door of his condominium. He knows that he has a lot of making up to do. He closes the door behind him, being greeted by the sound of the television.

"Kanisha!" Scotty called out, walking towards the kitchen, receiving no response. A worrisome facial expression grows on his face as he glimpses around at the disorderly kitchen. He pulls out a military issued 357 automatic from his waistband, assuming that he has an intruder.

He peeks around the doorway, easing throughout the residence in search of Kanisha. *I hope my baby is okay. Maybe somebody just broke in? Naw, her car still in the driveway.* Considering the situation that occurred with Dirty Red, Scotty refuses to take any chances.

He peeks inside the bedroom at a sleeping Kanisha, cuddled up under the sheets sleeping peacefully. "Whew, I was worried fo' a minute," Scotty said aloud, sitting his gun on top of the dresser.

He removes his attire and crawls into the bed. Feeling his body weight shifting the bed Kanisha awakes from her sleep. Seeing Scotty staring at her, she turns away from him with an attitude, giving him the silent treatment.

Scotty presses up against her warm flesh and whispers into her ear.

"Baby I'm sorry." Feeling the warmth of his breath on her ear triggers her hormones. Upset with him, she tries to restrain her sexual desire. She scoots away from him. He pulls her back in his direction massaging her shoulders. Reluctantly, she pushes his hands away.

"Get yo' hands off of me!" Kanisha snapped. "I'm tired of you lying to me. Then you come up in here acting like you ain't did shit wrong. You think . . ."

"Hold up baby. Give me a chance to explain."

"Go ahead. Gon' and feed me another one of your lies."

"Motion called me when I was on my way to the house. Somebody kidnapped Dirty Red."

"Huh!"

"Yeah, he at the hospital. He's in bad shape. If you don't believe me you can call the hospital and check for yo' self," Scotty truthfully admitted.

Even though Scotty lied to her numerous times before, she accepted his words to be the truth.

"I believe you baby. We don't have to go through all of that. Next time just call me and let me know instead of havin' me thinkin' you out there fuckin' with one of those chicken heads."

"Baby I promise next time somethin' like this happen I'll make sure I call you baby. I don't want you going crazy thinkin' I'm out there fuckin' off. Besides, I 'ont want no baby mama drama." Scotty jokingly said, trying to break the tension.

"That's right. You don't wanna go there. I'm one bitch you don't wanna play with." Scotty chuckled, pulling her close. "I'm serious," she added.

"Whoa killa, slow down." Scotty kisses her succulent lips in between him smiling, gazing into the windows of her soul. Kanisha closes her eyes, as he grazes her neck with his warm tongue. The warmth of his touch sends a chill traveling down her spine. He explores every inch of her body as they go on a journey to lover's land.

*   *   *

Dog Catcher sits on the bench at Lincoln Park smoking a cigarette, reading a Milwaukee Journal newspaper. The sun beams on his dark complexion causing him to perspire. Being a professional hitman, he surveys the area watching a beautiful Hispanic woman pushing a baby stroller, carrying a diaper bag. The JLO velour jogging suit she is wearing accentuates her shapely physique. She sits the diaper bag on the ground and kneels down. The print between her thighs form the imprint of a camel's toe.

Dog Catcher finds himself lusting, having an erection. ***She look good as hell to just had a baby. If I whatn't here on business I'll get at that broad.*** He flicks the reminder of his cigarette into the grass, blowing out a billow of smoke, waiting patiently for his associate to arrive.

He watches an older couple standing in the amidst of a flock of pigeons feeding them breadcrumbs.

The evening sun pours westward forming a corona around the shape of a man. Dog Catcher squints hard against the light as the man struts in his direction. Dog Catcher reaches underneath his shirt and clutches his 8 millimeter, discreetly aiming at the subject, who has an icy look in his eyes. A long platinum chain sprayed in diamonds, dangling from his neck, obscuring his facial features.

Dog Catcher shields his eyes with his hand to get a better visual of the man approaching his direction.

"Don't panic, it's only me," Motion proclaimed, taking a seat beside Dog Catcher.

"You know I gotta stay on point at all times. You can't afford to slip in this game." Dog Catcher preached, not knowing that Motion is already one step ahead of him. "So what's the problem? What is it you need me to do?"

"I need you to find out who kidnapped my man Dirty Red."

"Do you got any idea of who might've did it?"

"All I can tell you is that he got a tattoo on his neck that say Thump."

"Hmmm, Thump, Thump," Dog Catcher ponders, massaging his chin.

Motion glances at the beautiful woman sitting on the bench opposite of them with the baby stroller facing her, talking to what appears to be a new born baby.

"I think I might know who that is. If it's who I think it is, it might cost you a little more. The person I have in mind is a professional stick up kid. I ran across his path a few times. It's gon' be hard gettin' next to him. S-"

"What it's gon' cost me?" Motion interrupted.

"Mannn." Dog Catcher sways his head. "I need at least fifty grand."

"I tell you what. If he's dead in the next twenty four hours, it's a fifty thousand dolla bonus."

"Word."

"To start you off its seventy five thousand in that diaper bag."

Motion rises off of the bench and beckons his head at the woman seated at the bench. Dog Catcher shifts his focus on the woman walking off pushing the baby stroller.

"You on point ain't you?" Dog Catcher stated, watching the woman vanish through the grassy area.

"That's right. Remember what you said? You can't afford to get caught slippin' in this game." Motion struts away finding his way to his Bentley coupe, catching up with the woman pushing the stroller.

"You did a good job Shasha," Motion congradulated.

"You know me do anything for you papi," Shasha replied.

Shasha is a Puerto Rican mami that Motion met on the Eastside through her brother Jose, who was murdered two years ago in a home invasion. One of the intruders was Jose's right hand man. They robbed him for three kilos and $48,000.00 in cash. They never knew that Shasha was in the house. When authorities questioned her, she gave them false information. She wanted the men responsible for her brother's death to pay in blood.

She found Motion's number in Jose's cell phone and informed him of who killed her brother, knowing that her brother spoke highly of Motion. 72hours later the men who killed her brother was staring at the sky. Every since then Motion sensed the killer instincts in Shasha's eyes and took her under his wing.

Motion removes the AK47 assualt rifle out of the baby stroller and stashes it inside the trunk, along with the stroller. He closes the trunk and glimpses over his shoulder noticing a green Tahoe exiting the parking lot. *It seem like I seen that truck before. Maybe I'm just trippin'.* They climb into the car and Motion brings the engine to a soft roar. The Clarion LCD screen slowly spits out the dashboard. Motion taps the screen and 2 Pac's "Hail Mary" pours out of the speakers. He dips out of the lot with one thing on his mind, revenge.

* * *

The rustling sound of Toon counting a large sum of money from a previous transaction is suspended by his cell phone vibrating, dancing on the kitchen counter. Toon has been pumping non-stop for the last three days. He reaches over answering the phone.

"Yeah, what up?"

"Chillin'. I need to see you. I'm down to my last zone. I need anotha hal-"

"Hold up Nickel. You know you can't be talkin' reckless on my line like that." Toon cut him off becoming skeptical.

"My bad Toon," Nickel apologized.

"I'm not tryna be rude playboy, but you gotta be careful on these phones. Just meet me at Wendy's on fourty seventh and North Avenue in fifteen minutes," Toon instructed.

"A'ight."

"Holla." Click!

* * *

"Oouuch, mommy." Joy's face crinkles from pain as she sits between Ayesha's legs getting her hair braided.

"Oops, mama sorry."

"Kay."

Motion strolls into the house sinking in the plush carpet tossing his keys into the ceramic bowl on the cocktail table.

"Heyyy dadddy!" Joy burst out in glee, her slanted eyes flashing with happiness at the sight of her father.

"Heyyy, lil mama." He kneels down and kisses his pride and joy on her dimpled cheek. "What yo' mama gettin' you all pretty for?"

"Grandma comin' to get me."

Motion flops down on the couch beside Ayesha, giving her a peck on the lips.

"You miss me?"

"Nope." Ayesha replied with her lips pursed, finishing Joy's hair.

"So it's like that?" Ayesha chuckles.

"Boy, I'm just playing with you. I miss you every time you walk out that door sweety."

"Awww, ain't that sweet," Motion mischeviously said, leaning to the side to give Ayesha a second kiss with more meaning.

"Oowwl daddy. Y'all bad." Joy interrupted their moment of passion. They laugh at her remark, ending their kiss.

"Pretend like you didn't see that."

"Kay, me won't tell grandma."

"Yeah, don't you do that. Grandma'll give mama and daddy a whippen."

"I'm not gon' tell."

"You promise?" Motion curves his pinky finger to seal the deal.

"Promise." They lock fingers.

"Daddy gon' go down stairs, give me kiss." Motion leans down and she pecks him on the cheek.

"Be good for daddy, okay?"

"Kay." Motion head to the basement to relax his mind after a long stressful day.

*   *   *

Toon leans back in the leather seat of the car, maneuvering through the thick traffic. The sound of a car horns blare as he switch lanes. An uncomfortable vibe crosses through his bones, as he travels West on North Avenue, nearing his destination.

He peers through the light tinted lenses of his Dolce & Gabbana designer frames scanning the scenery. He passes by many tattered buildings stained with graffiti, deciphering gang literature. This is the place he always known as the concrete jungle. Seeing no signs of Nickel, he punches speed dial on his cell phone. Nickel answers on the first ring.

"Yeah."

"Where you at? Toon asked.

"I'm pullin' up right now," Nickel lied.

"A'ight." Click!

Officer Bodo Gajevic sits on a side street in a gold Durango, accompanied by his partner, conducting surveillance in the area. Toon's Dodge Charger pulls into the parking lot of Wendy's, its large chrome rims sparkle, obscuring the vision of the pedestrians who are traversing the parking lot.

The Dodge Charger parks at an angle, the sound of screeching tires startles the onlookers, as drug enforcement agents surrounds the Dodge Charger.

"Freeeeze, F.B.I, get out of the vehicle with your hands up!"

A party of angry faces are scattered throughout the parking lot, aiming high powered handguns from different directions, anticipating Toon's arrest. As they eagerly wait for their target to exit the car, their adrenaline flows with excitement. Unable to see through the dark tinted windows, they positioned themselves behind the doors of their vehicles.

The driver's door swings open slowly and a coffee complexioned female exits the car with her hands extended in the air, wearing a Chanel skirt set, Aldo high heel pumps, big looped earrings, and a Fantasia style haircut.

The party of angry faces forms into a look of disappointment, seeing that Toon is not in the car.

"Turn around and walk backwards," Bodo ordered, admiring the muscular legs on the woman and her viciously curved body that will make almost any married man commit adultery.

Toon rides by slowly in the rental car scanning the disorderly crowd of law enforcement agents, searching his car thoroughly for the half kilogram of cocaine.

"I knew that nigga was on some bullshit," he muttered, stashing the half of brick in the console, vacating the area. Toon made it a habit to follow his first thoughts. He learned a valuable lesson from his past experience and others. A smart man learns from his mistakes and a wise man learns from the mistake of others.

*   *   *

Motion lounges on the butter soft leather sofa, stretched out with his legs crossed, watching "God Father" on the 65 inch plasma screen television that overlooks the lavish basement. The screen illuminates the semi-dark basement along with the in-wall, saltwater aquarium that contains a baby shark.

Ayesha exits the bubbled glass elevator that descends from the upper level of the mansion to the basement, stepping in her Manalo Blahnik alligator skin boots with two inch heels, sinking into the plush carpet, her steps soundless.

Motion sips on a bottle of Courvoisier XO Imperial. The soft touch of Ayesha's hands massaging his shoulders abducts his attention. Her divine embrace is his refuge from the outside world.

The love she possess for him is the essence of his happiness. She seasons the nape of his neck with warm moist kisses. She lifts his spirits with each kiss.

"Baby you miss me?" she said in a low seductive tone, her sweet melodic voice is like music to his ears.

"You know I miss you," he said, tilting his head, gazing into her sparkling eyes, which stirs his emotions and heightens his anticipation. The radiance of her flawless smile warms his heart.

She sashays over to the stainless steel wetbar and activate the surround sound system. R-Kelly's "Whine for me" pours out of the speakers. The flourescent lights shifts around in the basement. She twirls her hips as she approaches the black marble top circular customized stage with the chrome pole in the center.

Climbing on the stage, she slowly peels off her robe, introducing the exquisiteness of her heavenly sculptured body, which inflames Motion's deepest passions.

Twirling her hips, laced in the tiger striped lingerie set, she stares at a watching Motion as she curves her indexfinger in a come here gesture. In his eyes her body is a poetic masterpiece. Her stunning beauty melts him into submission. With a smile gleaming across his face, he slowly saunters in her direction, gazing in her eyes. With his every nearing step, her heart skips a beat.

The sweet rich smell of her Chanel perfume wafts the air. Ginuine's "Difference" replaces R-Kelly. Motion pulls out a large wad of hundred dollar bills popping the rubberband. He tucks a hundred dollar bill in the elastic of her thong, going along with the program. She kneels down dancing with the rhythm of the music, as if she is a professional stripper. She cradles Motion's head in her hands, burying his face between her cleavage.

He tucks another hundred dollar bill into the pelvis area of her thong, showering the stage with hundred dollar bills. Unable to resist her perfectly curved body, he grazes the rich texture of her skin with his indexfinger creating chaos within her body.

She turns around giving a full visual of her round, juicy firm ass that would make any grown man cry. She manipulates the muscles in her right ass cheek to the rhythm of the music. Motion's eyes widen with excitement as she entertains him with her skillful performance.

No longer able to restrain his hormones that are screaming for satisfaction, he slides her thong to the side, exposing her meticulously groomed pubic hairs. She arches her back and her fleshy mound forms a hump, allowing him more access. Her soul hungers for his companionship. She gazes over her shoulder as he spreads her ass cheeks, grazing the outer rim of her asshole.

Teasingly, he works his way slowly to her clitoris, sensitizing the area around her vulva, and her inner thighs, nibbling around her clit inviting goose bumps. He strokes her pubic area and outer lips with a feather light touch. She shifts her body weight, eager for his love making. He continues to tease her, breathing hard on her flowered opening, kissing it all over, purposely missing her clit. While sucking and licking, he hums on her vulva and clit sending sound vibrations, licking her from the bottom right above her hole, he works his way up to her clit. Holding her lips open, he forms his hands in a triangle shape with the tips of his fingers meeting just above her clit. He pops her clit out flicking his tongue up and down gently with his lips locked around her swollen clit. Not allowing her to cum, he slows down the pace letting her anticipation build up, enabling her to build up pressure. He stiffens his tongue and sticks it into her wetness. She grips his ears demanding his loving.

Motion picks her up from the stage, carrying her to the stainless steel pool table, laying her on her back at the edge of it.

He licks around her opening, darting his tongue into her wetness, tongue fucking her, thrusting it as deep as he can. He goes slow then fast, teasing her with the tip. He tosses her knees behind her head, giving her a tongue fucking that she will never forget.

Loud moans escapes her parted lips. Ayesha's body begins to convulse, her legs trembles becoming weak. He gives her an ecstasy which is not of this earth. She lifts her body forward resting on her elbows. He gazes into her soft green eyes mesmerized by her beautiful features. He embraces her french manicured hands, slowly pulling her close to him, locking lips. They explore each other's mouth. Ayesha unbuttons his shirt exposing his chiseled chest. She massages his chest and nibbles on his nipples, sending a tingling sensation racing down his spine. He faintly groans, enjoying the gift of her passionate touch. Slowly working her way down to his waist, she unfastens his pants; they drop to his ankles followed by his boxers. They switch up and he sits on the edge of the pool table leaning backwards with his palms planted on the surface of the black clothed pool table. She gently strokes his large mandingo, which makes her hand look tiny, staring into his eyes.

The clear lip-gloss that coats her full lips and her hair pulled back in a bun on top of her head turns him on. She grazes the length of his shaft with her warm tongue causing him to tense up.

Simultaneously licking his balls and jerking him off, she envelopes him into her mouth using lots of mouth and hand pressure. She has half of his dick in her mouth with her saliva dripping from her hands, contracting her cheeks she takes him deeper inch by inch, rotating her head side to side. She puts on her best throat game relaxing her throat muscles. Motion's toes curl up as she bobs her head quickening the pace, like making him cum is the matter of life or death. If the world were able to see her work right now, Superhead would lose her title.

Motion cups her head with both hands releasing his juices and all his tension into her mouth. She swallows his sex juices and seductively twirls her tongue across her upper lip. She climbs atop the pool table completely naked with only her knee length gatored skin boots on. Her basketball rounded ass cheeks bounces with a firm shake, as she steps in the center of the pool table.

"Lay on your back," Ayesha ordered. She loves to take control

Motion's limp dick stretches to its full length at the sound of her demanding voice. She squats down with her back facing him, grabbing his brick hard magic stick with it's veins crisscrossing. She spreads her ass cheek. The wetness glistens around her opening. She guides him into her pussy and grips his ankles. Biting down on her lower lip, she bounces up and down crashing against his pelvis area taking all dick. Motion smacks her ass causing her flesh to ripple.

"Yes!" Smack!

"Yes!" Smack!

"Mmmm, shit!" Smack!

"Ride this big dick!" Smack!

"Ooooh yeah baby." Smack! Ayesha's pussy becomes juicer with every smack. Her sex juice trickles down his balls as she rides him hard. Their bodies clap in the rhythm of their freak session. Motion's eyes are plastered on her ass. He wishes that their love making would never end.

*   *   *

The Staple's lounge is semi-crowded after long hours of socializing. Thump purchased drinks for the entire bar becoming the center of attention. Thumps sits at the bar, his eyes are blood shot red from the hydro that he smoked earlier that night. The flourescent lights twirls, shifting illuminated patterns allover the interior of the bar. Lil Jon and the Eastside Boyz erupts from the concert speakers vibrating the bar, as if it is being shaken by an earthquake. Bobbing his head feeling mellow, he sips on the shot of Remy V.S.O.P blended with cranberry juice.

Two men seated on the other end of the bar steals a look at Thump's diamond faced rolex he bought from Ghino the jeweler.

"Man them niggas must've hit a good lick. They been doin' a lot of splurging."

"I see," the other man replied. It wasn't long before word traveled all across the city. The streets always talk.

Thump's partner steps out of the restroom and walks up behind him, leaning down shielding his mouth with one hand saying something in Thump's ear. Thump nods his head in agreement hopping off the stool. He pulls out a thick wad of money peeling off a hundred dollar bills, dropping it atop the bar. They exit the bar being greeted by a fresh breeze.

The trees that line the street rustles, swaying from the soft midnight breeze. As they walk along the sidewalk, Thump stumbles over a Corona bottle, it clings as it slides across the pavement into the grass. Thump regains his balance.

"Damn nigga, you fucked up ain't you," Ball stated.

"I'm straight," he replied, pulling out the key to his brand new Acrua, fitted with large mirrored 22incn rims.

The keys jingle as he presses the button to the keyless entry unlocking the doors. Churp! Churp! The dimly lit streetlights reflect off the rims as they climb into the car.

"I know my bitch mad at me for being out all night."

"You know how that shit go, she'll get over that shit." Ball added, checking his cell phone for any missed calls.

Thump pulls a pack of Newport cigarettes out of the console before pulling off. Music by DMX spills out the Bose sound system as he sparks up the fresh cigarette. Pulling up at the redlight, Ball notices a woman along the side of them in a green Neon giving him a flirtatious look.

"A Thump, look I think this broad choosin' me." Thump looks into the car beside them.

"Man you trippin', that ain't no broad, that's a nigga." Ball takes another look knowing what he just seen.

"Man I told you. That's a broad nigga, you blind as fuck." This time the woman twirls her tongue seductively, rolling down the window. Ball glances at Thump and back into the car.

"Man that X got you fucked up. You need to stop using that shit fo' real."

The dark complexion man in the Neon looks at them with a devious smile pulling at the corners of his mouth, revealing a gold trimmed tooth.

"Man I know I ain't trippin! I seen a bitch in that car." Ball sees a glint of light in his peripheral vision. Before he could figure out what was transpiring, the barrel of two nickel plated .45 Desert Eagles are pointed at his face.

Boc! Boc! Boc! Boc! Boc! Boc! The man hands jerk repetitiously from the powerful impact of the guns.

Shards of glass rains on top of their heads as they fold up shielding their heads with their hands. The engine roars as Thump smashes on the gas slamming into a light pole. The clapping sound of gunfire reverbrates, contrasting with the ear piercing sound of whining tires. The car horn blares from the weight of Thumps face buried in the steering wheel. Ball feels an excruciating pain slicing through the base of his skull as he fumbles under the seat in search of his gun, with his heart drumming against his chest.

The man slowly nears the wrecked vehicle that has smoke billowing from its hood. The smell of antifreeze, burned rubber, and gas lingers in the air.

Ball sees the man shadow shifting along the pavement. What Ball considered to be the lifestyle was nothing, but the death style.

Ball stares into the man's devilish eyes as the man aims his gun. Boc! Boc! His body jerks, and his life slowly leaks out of him. He aims the gun at the back of Thump's head. Boc! Boc!

"The Dogcatcher always catch his dog," he said to the dead corpses. He blows the barrel of the guns and struts to the stolen Neon vanishing into the darkness.

*   *   *

Motion's cellular phone rings playing its customized ring tone. "This is the life of a, this is the life of a, go getta, go getta." The sound of the phone vibrating inbetween rings on the gleaming cherry oak wood nightstand awakes him from his sleep. He rubs the corner of his eyes, yawning stretching his body. The phone glows in the darkened master suite giving Motion a clear visual. He answers the phone in a sleepy monotone.

"Yeah, what's up?"

"Channel six," Click! The caller hangs up the phone. Motion feels around fumbling under the satin sheets in search of the remote from under her thigh.

"What you doing baby?" Ayesha inquired.

"Nothin' baby. Go back to sleep and get yo' rest."

Motion presses a button and the 42inch plasma screen television descends from the ceiling, filling the mastersuite with a soft blue glow of light. He flicks the channel to Fox six news.

-News flash-

"This is Raphael O'donnel reporting to you live with breaking news. Earlier this morning at approxiately two thirty seven two men were gunned down on the city's North side. Authorities estimate that at least twelve rounds was fired from a semi-automatic weapon. Both men were shot numerous times. At this time there are no suspects in custody and no motive to why this tragedy transpired".

They zoom in on the bullet riddled Acura, smashed up against the light pole looking like a crushed soda can, blocked off with yellow tape. An array of detectives roam the crime scene conducting a thorough investigation.

"The men have not yet been identified. If anyone have any information that can lead to an arrest and conviction please call one eight hundred, seven, seven, seven, five, five, four, four. As we receive the news, we'll try and keep you updated on today's events. This is Raphael O'donnel reporting live for Fox six news."

CHAPTER SEVEN

A Chinese man is seated on the red and black carpeted floor playing a mouth organ made with seven bamboo pipes, delivering a high pitched melody, similar to the opening of the David Carradine Kung fu show.

A carved, jade disk hangs on the wall. Multi-colored ceramics are situated all over the restaurant. A soft spring breeze pours through the windows, fluttering the calligraphy patterned curtains. The smell of roasted sweet potatoes, deep fried pastries, sliced crisp roast duck, thin rolled pancakes, and sweet sauce made from soybean paste floats in the atmosphere.

Scotty and Elane sits on the floor indian style across from each other on a rug. Elane tries eating her food with the chopsticks. Each time she comes close to taking a bite, the dumpling stuffed with shrimp falls back onto her plate. Scotty chuckles at her lack of experience with the chopsticks.

"How do they use these things?" Elane questioned.

"Here let me show you how to use them," Scotty suggested with a warm smile plastered on his face.

Skillfully he picks up the dumpling with the chopsticks. She leans forward with her eyes partially closed taking a bite of the food.

"Mmmmm, now this is what I call tasty." Scotty gazes at her mesmerized by her sex appeal. The way she bit the dumpling turned him on. He imagined her taking him into her mouth. He has been dating Elane for a little over two months and they have not yet engaged in any sexual activity.

Elane always managed to keep her distance, even though she wants to satisfy that desire that has been burning in her body over the years. She is tired of the toys and playing with herself. Elane has always maintained her fidelity, although her man is incarcerated. There is not a moment that she doesn't feel guilty about dating Scotty. But for some reason he is starting to grow on her heart.

After minutes of Scotty feeding her, she attacks him with a question.

"So what made you bring me to a place like this when you have a baby mama at home? What makes me so special?"

She studies his eyes waiting for a response.

"You want the truth or you want me to lie?"

"I want the truth."

Scotty returns a gaze with a look of sincerity. "It's somethin' very special about you. I never had a woman of yo' class before. You have a good personality, self sufficent, and most of all your the most beautiful woman I have ever laid my eyes on. Whatever it is, I can sense the presence. I guess you can call it chemistry or better yet, the possibility that we on the same page. Truthfully, I want our friendship to blossom and elevate to somethin' much bigger than life itself. I believe that our friendship is the union of two spirits destined for everlasting happiness."

"I got to give it to you. If I was ten years younger I would probably fall for that."

"I mean what I said sweetheart. I had my share of women, but it's somethin' different about you. Your a very intelligent woman and down to earth."

Scotty leans closer to Elane, staring into her eyes with his facial expression registering a serious look. Elane eyes him back with lifted eyebrows.

"When I look into yo' eyes I see sincerity, loyalty, devotion, and a woman that's in need of a real man. Right now, you just afriad because you know that I'm too much of a man for you."

"Too much for me. Yeah right. I think you better put that the other way around." Elane chuckles in between her statement.

"You know what else I think?" Scotty pauses as if he is waiting for an answer. "I think you're afraid of true love. I'ma tell you somethin' about me for the record. I don't bite my tongue for nobody. Excuse my language, but pussy comes a dime a dozen baby and true love comes once in a life time."

With a loss of words, Elane says the first thing that comes to to her mind. "Answer this, why do men cheat when they have a good woman at home? I never understood that." Scotty studies her beautiful facial features, the curly hair at her temples, and her full lips. Her forty years on this earth barely marked her face in a negative way. She kind of reminds him of Angela Bassett.

"Let me put it to you like this. I can't answer that question for all men, but I can give you my perception."

"And what's that?" she asked with a look of curiousity in her eyes.

"I cheat because I haven't found that woman that can satisfy all my desires. A woman that can answer my every need mentally and physically. I never found that woman that I can call my soulmate. I wanna woman that's sad when I'm sad. When I'm hurt, she hurt. When I'm happy, she's happy. When one fall, we both fall. When one rises, we both rise. I want a woman that's willing to sacrifice her life for me if it came down to it. I want that woman that's gon' stand strong like a soldier when I lose my balance. A woman that's gon' be my crutch when times get tough. When it rain she gon' still walk with me. When it storm she gon' walk with me. I think you might be that woman to meet those qualifications. So far the only woman that I've been runnin' into lately don't love a nigga. They love what that nigga can do for them, and I'm only keepin' it one hundred wit' you baby."

"So what about the men? All they want to do is get in between our legs and get a quickie."

"Check this out ma. I'm not worried about what everybody else want. I'm worried about me and you. I just want you to know that I wanna be more than just yo' friend. I want you to be that other half of me. I would even like to say I wanna be wit' you fo'ever, but unfortunately we don't live fo'ever."

Elane looks into his eyes as if she is hypnotized by his words.

It seems like he knows just what to say. I like a man that speaks his mind and knows how to take control. I can't believe that I'm thinkin' like this. What's wrong with me? I can't turn on my man, I love him.

Scotty embraces her soft hands, massaging them by moving his thumbs in a circular motion. His touch communicates more than words as he watches her silently. Her heart hammers at the base of her throat as she reads the intent of his gaze. His winning touch warms her heart, as their lips come closer inch by inch.

A woman locks her focus on the couple from a distance, making her way over to them quickly with an angry facial expression as they enjoy their romantic moment.

*　　*　　*

Motion dips into the gas station in his Lamborghini, its chrome rims flicker as he pulls up to the gas pump. Joy is sitting in the passenger's seat laced in a gold and brown Gucci signature short set, her thick curly hair twisted in four ponytails. Joy plays with the remote to the car system turning the volume up and down. Dora the Explorer plays on the in dash LCD screen.

Motion peers through his Gucci designer lenses with a signature Gucci visor, shielding his skull. Joy loves to ride around with her father and spending quality time with him. Motion glimpses through the review mirrors making himself aware of his surroundings at all times. He refuses to get caught up slipping.

A man leans up against the wall on the side of the gas station chewing on a toothpick, twirling it around in his mouth, eyeing the lamborghini. He eases over to the car sneakily, reaching his hand under his nylon jacket.

Motion's cellular phone chimes stealing his attention.

"Can me answer the phone daddy?" Joy inquired, reaching for the phone.

"Go ahead boo."

"Hello . . . Yeah . . . You wanna speak to my daddy? . . . Kay?" Joy hands the phone to Motion. "Huh daddy."

"Yeah what's up?"

"Mr. Hopson." A soft sophisticated feminine voice comes from the other end.

"Speakin'."

"How are you doing Mr. Hopson? This Maria Cortez at the Mercedes Benz dealership. Your car just arrived an hour ago. You can pick it up any time before five o'clock. The owner would also like to thank you personally for your business. If that's an inconvience I can arrange to have the car delivered to your residence."

"I tell you what. If you promise me dinner, I'll be there at five o'clock." Silence falls between them.

"Uhmmm, that might be possible. I think I'm going to take you up on that offer."

"A'ight then, five o'clock."

"A'ight." Click!

Motion hears the rustling sound of the man's clothes as he makes his approach, he leans back greeting the man with the barrel of his blue steel .45 automatic Smith and Wesson, pressing it against the man's ribs. He startles the man, making him drop the two packs of white tube socks on the ground, raising his hands above his head backpedalling.

Motion bites down on his bottom lip, gripping the trigger with a firm embrace. Recognizing the man's face, he lowers the gun.

"Man Poochie, what you tryna do, get yo' self killed. You 'ont suppose to walk up to nobody car like that," Motion stressed.

"My bad my man," Poochie said, picking up the two packs of socks. The smell of alcohol rips through his pores wafting the air along with the malodorous smell of his underarms and the scent of cigarettes.

Poochie is one of the neighborhood dopefiends who hangs out at the gas station hustling for petty change. He poeticlly chants as usual.

"Check this out young smoove, won't you help a black man out so I can bust this move. I know you young cats jugglin' those big knots, so gon' and show me a lil love and buy some of these socks."

Poochie flashes his dentures exposing his decaying teeth. Motion sways his head with a silent chuckle.

"Hey lil cutie pie."

"Hi. Daddy who is that?" Joy asked, staring at the aging man.

"That's Poochie sweet heart."

"That's your friend?"

"Yeah boo, that's my friend," Motion lied.

Motion arches his back as he reaches into his pocket producing a large wad of money. Poochie eyes the money as Motion shuffles through it. He lets out a short whistle rubbing his hands together as if he is putting on lotion. Motion peels off a twenty dollar bill dropping it into Poochie's extended hand.

"Keep the socks, just pump the gas fo' me." Motion hands him thirty more dollars.

"My man. I knew you was a good dude. No matter what nobody say about you. I'll be right back." Poochie struts inside the gas station with his smooth signatured pimp walk.

*   *   *

The lemon lime drop top 72 caprice equipped with a 572 big block and 26inch chrome rims, rounds the corner on Sherman and Burliegh. The chrome grill on the old school glimmers, delivering a blinding flash of light.

The distant sound of the car system garners the attention of the students who are milling the semi-crowded streets, as the car makes its approach traveling south on Sherman boulevard. The warm summer breeze slaps Marco in the face.

"Dizaaam." A teenager shouted excitedly. "Look at that ma fucka right there." He told the other teenager walking besides him.

"Yeah, I like that ma fucka. He got that ma fucka wet. For a minute you had me thinkin' you seen a big booty bitch."

Marco moves through the now heavy 3:00 o'clock traffic in front of Washington High School. Lil Wanye's Carter three escapes the sound system. The deafening sound of the car system greets the ears of the students pouring out the school building.

The four 12inch gorillas in the trunk vibrates the surface. Hard rich bass punches against Marco's chest. A group of teenage girls proportioned in all the right places, dances in the middle of the street staring at Marco seductively. They wave at him and he returns their wave with a smile, wishing they were a little older.

It has been a month since Marco retired from the dope game. He has purchased two duplexes located on the cities Westside. Usually he drives his Ford pick up truck, but today he decided to take the day off and enjoy himself. He made a promise to himself that he will never get back into the dope game. Over the last year he accumulated enough money to go legit. For many of years he watched a large amount of dope boys get lost behind the walls.

Lil Wink tosses his bookbag in the back of the car and climbs into the car sinking into the white leather interrior. They slap palms curling the tips of their fingers in unison. Marco turns down the music.

"What up my man?"

"Same 'ole thang as usual, tryna focus on finishing this year of school," Lil Wink replied, blowing out a short breath of air, swaying his head. "Man it's hectic."

"Just be patient and hang in there youngin'. Trust me, in the long run, this gon' all payoff."

"I'm tryin' Marco, I'm tryin'."

Lil Wink looks up to Marco, he's the big brother that he never had. Marco takes him shopping every weekend and hits his hand on a weekly basis. Lil Wink grew to love Marco like family and he'll kill for him in a heart beat.

"I wish I would've stayed in school, but I was to busy tryna run the streets and survive in this concret jungle. I never had a father figure in my life or a mother around. The streets taught me how to be a man. My only motive was gettin' money. If it didn't make dollas, it didn't make no sense. Know what I mean?"

"I feel you. That's the same way I felt, but now I see the bigger picture. I loss two of my mans last month, that could've been me out there." Lil Wink stated, peering through the front windshield in silence with a serious look plastered on his face.

"Thank God it ain't you lil homie. I couldn't imagine somethin' like that happenin'. All I wanna do is see you walk across that stage next years 'cause I got big plans for us. You just keep doin' what you doin' and I promise you it's gon' get better, trust me on this."

* * *

Scotty and Elane shifts their focus on the angry woman towering over him, being interrupted.

"You not kiss in me restaurant. You get room," she snapped. Scotty mocks the Chinese woman's accent.

"Me sorry. Me not mean to disrespect you. Meet room." They chuckle at the comical moment as she storms off

"Boy you crazy. I think it's time that we leave before your friend comes back and whip your butt."

"Me not worried, me know hung fu baby." Scotty joked, making emphasis with his hands, like he is about to chop the table in half. Elane laughs, tucking her hair behind her ear. She clutches her Hermes Birkin bag and climbs to her feet.

"Well, me not want to see you fight. So me say lets go." Scotty looks at a beautiful Elane admiring her sexy features.

"A'ight boss lady." Scotty pays the bill leaving a twenty dollar tip. He loops her arm with his, guiding her out the front entrance of the restaurant.

*　*　*

Motion pulls beside Maria's Mercedes in his Aston Martin, dropping her off after going out for dinner.

"I really enjoyed myself Maria. This is the first time I felt close to anotha woman since being with girl. It's somethin' real special about you." Maria listens intently as Motion speaks wholeheartedly. "If I was a single man, I would love to wake up every morning in the presence of a beautiful Goddess like you. I have a lot of respect for you and I don't want to be responsible for a broken heart. The only reason why I chose to keep it authentic with you is 'cause you're a sweet person. A woman like you is hard to find. But, I'ma tell you like this ma," Motion pauses, licking his lips. "If things ever go bad between me and my woman . . . . you'll be the first person I call . . . believe that." Maria gazes into the depths of Motion's eyes seeing only one thing, sincerity.

"I'm going to keep that in mind papi. I appreciate you being honest with me. I know it took a lot for you to do that." *Sho' did. Damn Motion, have you loss yo' fuckin' mind?* His little head talks to him. *Don't piss up that fine piece of pussy.*

"I really enjoyed myself this evening and I'll always cherish that memory as long as I live. Who knows what the future hold?" Maria stated. He embraces her soft warm hand, gazing in her eyes in silence. He leans into her seat and kisses her on the cheek.

"You take care of yourself ma. And remember what I said."

"I will." She opens the door exiting the car, leaving the scent of her rich sweet perfume lingering in the air. Motion watches her as she jumps into her Benz waving bye.

*　*　*

Elane falls back into the brown suede sofa blowing out a short breath of air. "It's been so long since I've had any time to myself,"

Elane proclaimed, kicking off her Chanel alligator and lambskin high heel pumps.

Scotty seats himself beside her. This is the first time Elane has invited a man into the home that her and her boyfriend shared many years ago.

"This is a nice place you got baby. I know this pad had to cost you a fortune. I knew you had it going on, but I didn't think you was layin' like this." Scotty scans the interior of the 4700 square feet estate in awe, that looks similar to the houses you see on MTV Cribs. The house is meticulously decorated to perfection. The sweet smell of potpourri floats in the air. A 84 inch projection screen overlooks the living room.

"When you're a hard working black queen like myself you deserve nothing but the best." Elane displays her kodak smile, gazing into Scotty's eyes.

"Since a black queen deserves the best, allow a black king to give you the best," he replied, looking at her facial expression anticipating her reaction.

"You sure you're ready for a real woman?"

"You sure you ready for a real man?" Elane stares at him in silence. Scotty leans forward reaching for her leg taking control. He plants her soft french pedicured foot in his lap. He grips her bare foot with his hands, rotating his thumb in a twirling motion on the upper fleshy part of her foot. A soft moan escapes her parted lips.

"Mmmmm, that feel so gooood," she whispered, her eyes partially closed.

Scotty studies her flawless facial features as he massages her feet. Every bone in her body craves as he licks and whisper in her ear. She feels the hunger for physical contact explode violently within her, leaving her legs weak. *Its been so long since I felt this good. I can't believe I haven't felt this way for a long time. I just have to keep myself from falling in love.* She lies back burning with passion. Her pulse leaps crazily as his fingers traces along the sides of her feet. He leans to the side inching towards her. He moves her hair to the side, gazing into her eyes moving closer. He brushes his lips softly over her, inhaling the sweet scent of her fragrance. She parts her lips in a breathy, speechless invitation, allowing his tongue to wonder in between her lips. As their mutual passion grows he probes a little deeper. Slowly and gradually they explore each other's tongue. Their tongues dance in each other's mouth at a slow, compassionate pace. He savors the flavor of her like it's his favorite dessert. Their kissing lingers notes of sultry jazz as they exchange a series of kisses.

He snaps the button on her tight fitting Roberto Cavali jeans, unzipping her pants. He traces down her neck working his way to her cleavage area, unbuttoning her blouse. She holds his neck as he peppers her exposed golden brown nipples with warm kisses. He peels off the rest of her attire introducing her perfectly shaped body, kissing around her pierced navel. He traces her thighs with his finger tips, feeling the silkiness of her unblemished butterscotch complexion.

Scotty eases his way to her ears and whispers into to them making a request.

"Huh." A look of perplexion travels across her face, as she becomes intrigued by his request. She rises to her feet; her hypnotic body captures his eyes, as she makes her way to the kitchen area. Scotty removes his clothes stripping down to his boxers, anticipating a moment of love making. Elane returns with a towel and a glass of warm water fulfilling Scotty's request. Her luscious, thick thighs rock from side to side, as she strides in his direction gazing into his eyes. He grabs the towel and lays it on the sofa, removing the warm glass of water from her other hand and guides her to the sofa. He takes control making her seat on the neatly spread towel.

Scotty sits on the floor between her legs, greeted by her wet, glistening womanhood and the fresh smell of fragrances. He grazes her inner thighs with the warmth of his tongue. He slips an Altiod breath mint into his mouth and begins to demonstrate his platinum tongue game.

As he grips her clit with his firm lips, he twirls his tongue slowly making passionate love to her clit. The strength of the mint gives her pussy a cool, tingly sensation, causing her reflexes to tense up.

After minutes of minty cunnilingus, he takes a sip of the warm water and holds it in his mouth. He continues to perform his tongue game on her, allowing the warm water to flow from his mouth onto her pussy.

"Mminm, baby it feel so . . . good. Please don't . . . stop." A series of moans escape her parted lips, as she arches her back, clawing the sofa. The sensation of the warm water causes her reflexes to involuntarily relax, initating a climatic moment for her. A silence scream shakes her body, as she releases a powerful orgasm. Occupied with sexual gratification, her act of infidelity is far from her mind. She explodes into an unraveling of passions.

"Uuuuh baby, uuuh, ooh, what you doing . . . to . . . me?" Elane moaned, squirming on the sofa, swaying her head in ecstasy.

Scotty grabs her hands and they entwine fingers, staring into each other's eyes. His love muscle throbs, standing at attention. He rubs the length of his shaft against her puffy pussy lips feeling her wetness. He uses the head of his dick to message her swollen clit. He slides the tip of his dick in her opening, barely going inside of her. He swirls the head of his dick around in her pussy, then pulls out. He uses the sexual juices on the head of his dick and rubs her clit in a swirling, teasingly motion. She arches her back moving her pelvis towards him, craving his love making.

"Give it to me baby please, I want you," Elane begged.

"You want it baby?"

"Yesss, pleaseee," she relied in a sexy voice. Scotty slides half way into her tight fist pussy. Ooooh baby." Elane embraces his muscular arms tightly, puncturing his skin with her long fingernails. He holds her ankles sinking deeper inside of her. He struggles, her cumming makes it easier for him to dig deeper. Their pubic hairs connect and he feels her pelvis bone. He watches the creamy juices that streak his mandingo as he penetrates her.

After two hours of sex, they fall asleep on the sofa in the warmth of each other's arms.

CHAPTER EIGHT

Toon parks his Dodge Charger in front of Chocolate City strip club. He steps out of the car being slapped by the cool midnight breeze, which flutters his burnt orange Gucci button up shirt. He presses the button to his alarm system. Churp! Churp! The lights on his car flash. He strides to the front entrance of the strip club in his dark blue denim Gucci jeans, and his burnt orange alligator skin Timberlands that is the same tone as his button up.

As he enters the club he is greeted by a buffet of half naked women. A bouncer stands 6'2, wearing a firm fitting shirt with security printed across it. He stops Toon upon his entry. Very familiar with the procedure, Toon hands the bouncer his identification card and a crispy twenty dollar bill. After a routine pat search, he lets him into the club.

Toon scans the club with a searching gaze. He spots his man Franis seated at a table for two adjacent to the stage. He has a stack of hundred dollar bills in front of him focused on the performing stripper.

Franis is Toon's jamacian connect he met six 2 months ago through his female cousin Nakesha. This is his first time dealing with Franis directly. Nakesha conducted their transaction receiving $2,000.00, in courteous of Toon, for her services. Toon plans on leaving the cocaine business. He knows that the cocaine business is to risky, especially since the close call he had with Nickel. Seeing how lucrative the marijuana business is, he decides to diversify to marijuana because it carries less time.

As Toon makes his way towards Franis, someone grips him by the wrist, stopping him in his tracks. He turns around to see a beautiful goddess standing right before his eyes. The woman resembles Kimora Lee Simmons in the face with a body like Serena Williams.

"Did you enjoy my show?" the woman asked, standing there in a red thong aud a pair of laced knee length high heels by Chinese Laundry.

"I'm sorry baby I just stepped through the door, but maybe later on we can hook up and you can entertain me with a private show," Toon replied. He pulls out a thick wad of money and tucks a twenty dollar bill in her thong.

"Maybe," she said, twirling her tongue across her lips in a flirtatious mannerism. She sashays away rolling her hips hard teasingly, gazing over her shoulder at a watching Toon.

T-Pain's "I'm in love with a stripper" crones in the back ground. Toon glances to his right at the stripper giving a lap dance as he takes a seat beside Franis. Paying no attention to Toon, Franis make paper airplanes out of hundred dollar bills. He tosses them at the stripper on the stage bouncing up and down, making her voluptuous ass clap.

"Damn." Toon blurted, infatuated by the woman's baketball bottom and her skillful ability. A slim figure stripper standing 6'1 in her highheel pumps approaches Toon from behind. She massages his muscular shoulders and his chest feeling allover him.

"Mmmmm, baby that's what I'm talkin' 'bout," Toon said, enjoying the soft touch of her hands. She eases her hands down to his crotch area and massages his manhood, causing him to grow hard. She whispers into his ear. "Mmmm, daddy you packin'."

She prances over to Franis and massages his shoulders as he continues to toss hundred dollar bills. She leans forward brushing his lengthy dreadlocks to the side, whispering in his ear. Franis hands her a hundred dollar bill and she struts away smiling.

Franis lights up a blunt stuffed with strawberry hydro. He faces Toon and blows out a billow of smoke. He peers through the haze of smoke with his blood shot red eyes.

"What's up wit' ya mon?" Franis asked, breaking the silence.

"The same ol' thang, tryna get that money," Toon replied, glimpsing around at all the beautiful strippers.

"I hear ya rudeboy. So what ya tryna do mon?" he asked.

Franis never discuss any business until he is sure everything is safe. The stripper that gave Toon a massage was searching him to make sure he isn't wearing a wire. After whispering in Franis ear letting him know that he is clean, he pays her off with the hundred dollar bill.

"I'm tryna get three hundred pigs. I hope you can make it happen." Franis lets out a short chuckle.

"Me got whateva ya wont man." Franis speaks in his heavy accent.

Franis slides him a black device that looks like a pager.

"What this fo'?"

"That's da garage door opener ta get ya bud man. It's a piece of paper in ya console wit' address. Me people got ya money already." Toon looks at him in shock, wondering how did he manage to get in his car without triggering his car alarm. Franis reads the expression on Toon's face as he frames his lips.

"Don't bother ta ask man, jus' go get ya ganja rudeboy." Toon raises up out of the seat and heads for the door.

*   *   *

Elliott pulls up in front of his house, parking behind his mother's Chrysler PT Cruiser. He is exhausted from his long day at school. It's hard for him believe that he only has two more weeks of high school remaining. Due to his credits, he only has to attend school for an half of day.

As he exits the car, he spots a slender built man cutting through his neighbor's yard.

"What's poppin' young Fifty?" Poochie greets Elliott by his father's nickname. Poochie and Elliott's father Big Fifty was close friends before he was killed. Poochie watched Motion and Elliott grow up. He used to hit their hands and show them love because of the respect that he had for their father. Poochie was once the man back in the early eighties. One day he came home after dropping off two kilos of cocaine and found his fiancé and 6 year old son tied up in the bedroom shot in the head execution style. Poochie couldn't bear the pain that embraced him daily, so he started getting high off his own supply, trying to escape the reality. E even contemplated on committing suicide by putting a .44 Magnum to his head, but realized he didn't have enough heart to pull the trigger.

"Everything a'ight? I'm just glad that I'm almost done with school. I'm ready to get this over with so I can get myself together for college,"

Elliott replied, grabbing his backpack and his school clothes out of the back seat.

"You need some help wit' that youngsta?" Poochie asked, reaching for some of the things in Elliott's hand.

"Naw, I'm straight. It ain't much."

"Well, you think you can lend ol' school a little bread?"

"Lend? That means you plan on payin' me back right?" Elliot asked, walking up the steps to the front door.

"Well, you know what I mean you technical lil' nigga," Poochie said jokingly.

"Man Pooch what happened?" Elliott questioned, placing his belongings on the porch fuddling with his keys. "I mean, I heard you was the man back in the days. I heard you had long money." Elliott hit a nerve on Poochie. He stares at Elliott reminiscing on the days when him and Big Fifty was getting laid and paid. His addiction kicks back in.

"Well, young Fifty, I don't have time to talk about that right now, but if you let me get that five spot I promise the next time I see you, I'll let you know a little bit about me and yo pops," Poochie said, meaning every word of it.

"Bet, but next time I see you, be ready to talk." Elliott fishes through his pocket pulling out a small wad of money. "Here, and don't go do nothin' I wouldn't do."

"I'm cool young Fifty, I'm cool," Poochie replied, clearing two steps at a time making his way to the alley. He stops in mid stride.

"Aye, by the way," Poochie said gaining Elliott's attention before he could step into the house.

"What's up now?" Elliott said in an irritated manner.

"Congratulations young Fifty." Poochie cracks a smile, revealing his brown stained teeth. Elliott stands there in shock surprised at Poochie's words.

"Thanks Pooch."

"I'll make sure I have a graduation present for you the next time I see you."

"A'ight." Elliott watches as Poochie dashes across the yard, making his way into the alley.

* * *

Shasha relaxes in the beautican's chair at Styles barber and beauty salon with her eyes closed, as Tiera flat irons her long thick hair. Elane sashays through the glass doors entering the shop, greeting the nail techniean with a warm smile.

"Hey Elane."

"Hey girl."

Tiera notices something different about Elane as she strides in her direction, making her way to her office. She seems to be in a good mood. Tiera can see a glow in her eyes that she haven't seen in a very long time. Elane flashes her flawless set of teeth.

"Hey Tiera," Elane greeted.

"Hey to you too. What got you feelin' so good today?" Tiera questioned, locking eyes on a smiling Elane.

"Oh, let me take a guess. It must be that new man you been talkin' about."

"I plead the fifth," Elane said, heading into her office.

"I never seen that woman in such a good mood before. She been seeing this one dude name Scotty. I hear him and his boys doin' it big. I wonder what she gon' do when Vegas get out. She been tryna get him out for a couple of years. I know how she feel, my man is in the same situation. So I know what she's going through. I don't blame her for gettin' a little . . . You know what I mean."

"Yeah, I know what you mean mami," Shasha replied, learning about Scotty's new mistress. It isn't a surprise to her. Whenever she goes out with Motion to handle business, she witnesses Scotty's work first hand.

Shasha gazes through the large glass windows locking her focus on a titanium silver Cadillac Escalade EXT pulling in front of the building. The Vredestin tires wraps the shiny 28inch rims like fine fitting boots, delivering a smooth nimble roll. A woman seated under the hair dryer popping gum in her mouth, stares directly at the luxurious vehicle as if she is hypnotized. Two men climbs out of the truck entering the shop.

Shasha looks at the two unknown men strutting pass the nail tech and the women seated at the dryers with their mouths hanging open. Shasha never seen them around before.

One of the men has a hersey brown complexion with a Steve Harvey lining, accentuating his perfectly trimmed beard. A Datlantis watch hugs his wrist with its floating diamonds dancing in the bezel.

The other man resembles Laurence Fishburne, appearing to be in his early forties. A pair of Cartier frames conceal his eyes, and the three carat VVS1s twinkles in his earlobes. They walk directly into Elane's office, closing the door behind them.

"They must be new around here. I never seen them before," Tiera proclaimed, finishing up with Sasha's hair.

"I never seen them around here before either. Maybe they from out of town," Shasha added.

"Maybe. Because if they was from around here I would know. You know how them hoochies be runnin' their mouths around here."

"You ain't never lied mami."

Ten minutes later the two unknown men struts out of Elane's office. The dark complexion man glimpses over his shoulder making eye contact with Shasha. He nods his head with a slight smile pulling at the corners of his mouth, exposing his gold grill. Shasha returns an innocent smile, watching them closely as they exit the building.

Scotty betta be careful. Mami seem like she's bad news. Shasha's instincts kicks in, as she watches the truck pull off into traffic.

*   *   *

Motion leans back on the couch, staring at the 36 inch HDTV that plays an old series of the "Jeffersons." Dishes are clinking together as Ms.Hopson organizes the dishes, placing them into the cabinets.

"Motion, come and help me put these dishes away." Ms.Hopson called from the kitchen, standing on her tippy toes trying to place dishes on the top shelves.

Motion is in deep thoughts, not knowing that his mother is calling his name.

"Motion!"

"Huh?" Motion snaps out of his trance staring at his mother, as she stands in the doorway drying her hands off on her white stained apron.

"I been callin' for you to come in the kitchen and give me a hand with these dishes. I usely have Elliott help me do it, but he's not here right now and I'm tryna get done with this as soon as possible because I'm havin' bible study tonight," she said, turning around making her way back into the kitchen.

Motion tosses the remote on the couch. The plastic covering on the couch crackles as he rises to his feet. He strides into the kitchen staring at his mother reminiscing about the times when he was a kid.

"Mom, guess what?"

"Yes Motion," she said, placing the rest of the dirty dishes in the dishwasher.

"I hate to say it this way, but I'm about to leave the streets alone before it's to late," Motion stated, grabbing the dishes off the square cereamic tiled counter top. Registering what Motion just said, Ms.Hopson remembered hearing those same exact words from his father before he was killed.

"Motion baby, as long as you got that dirty money things will never change." Ms.Hopson said, unwrapping the scarf on her head.

"You oughta have your tail at the Kingdom Hall prayin' for forgiveness." After taking a seat, she rubs her legs from all the standing she has been doing.

"Mom, I'm dead serious. I'm 'bout to make a dramatic change in my life." Motion said sincerely, meaning every word of it.

"I mean, I hate the way you look at me sometimes like I'm not even your son. You b-," Cutting Motion off in the middle of his sentence she says, "Motion, I never will look at you like you're not my son. I just dislike that Satan got to you and your father before Jehovah did." She expresses to him with a solemn look on her face. "Motion son?" She said, lifting up from the chair walking over to him. Embracing his hands, placing them into hers. "Where did I go wrong son?" she inquired, looking him directly in the eyes. Motion is emotional from the fact that his mother is on the verge of crying. He pulls her closer to him, embracing her with a warm and loving hug, whispering in her ear.

"You never went wrong. I chose the lifestyle and now I chose to leave it alone. I'm sorry if I let you down, but I'm gon' better myself. I . . . promise." Kissing her on the forehead, he re leases his embrace. Grabbing his keys off the coffee table, Motion heads for the front door.

"Motion baby."

"Yes mom," he answered, turning around to hear what his mother has to say.

"If you really plan on changing your life, remember these words. Jehovah says in first John Two fifteen. 'Do not be loving either the world or the things in the world. If anyone loves the world, the father is not in him.'" With that being said. Ms.Hopson turns around and return to the kitchen. Standing there digesting what his mother just said Motion hears the front door closing. Elliott stands in the middle of the livingroom.

"What's up big bro?" Elliott greeted, tossing his bookbag on the couch.

"Nothin' much, on my way to go pick up Joy," Motion replied. They embrace each other with a strong brotherly hug.

"Well, I guess I'll see you later." Elliott flops down on the couch blowing out a short breath of air.

"I had a long day."

"I bet you did. I know you been studying a lot more. You finish that business plan for me yet?"

"Yeah, I'm almost finish."

"A'ight cool. See you in a minute bro. Love." Motion closes the door behind him with a lot of things racing through his mind.

* * *

Scotty eases through traffic in his convertible Jaguar, leaning back in the oatmeal leather interior. He twirls the wood grain steering wheel making a smooth right turn. He spots a female prancing to the bus stop in a denim Rocawear skirt. She grips a knock off Coach purse. Scotty plasters his eyes on her ass.

Damn that bitch got a big stupid booty. He eases down on the brakes, pulling up to the curb honking his horn.

"Say baby." The woman ignore his call as he tries to garner her attention. "So it's like that huh?" She doesn't even turn around to acknowledge him. "Fuck you too! That's why you on the bus now." She rolls her eyes at an angry Scotty. He pulls off with his pride hurt. He fumbles between his legs, grabbing his cellphone. He presses speed dial calling Elane. Her phone rings being picked up by the voicemail. Receiving no answer, he calls her house phone and her cellphone repeatedly. **Why this board ain't answering her phone. This ain't like her not to answer her phone.** He hangs up the phone becoming suspicious. He heads to her house with several different thoughts racing through his mind.

He pulls in front of her house rolling to a stop. Her Porche truck is parked in the driveway. Scotty's heart drops in his stomach as he glares at the two tone platinum over black Range Rover parked behind her truck. The huge chrome mirrored rims on the Range Rover accentuates the chrome Ashanti kit. He examines the truck noticing the Minnesota plates.

I'ma fuck this bitch up if she got a nigga in there. Scotty can't believe the crazy thoughts he is having. He never thought that he'd risk his life over a piece of pussy. He climbs out of the car with his heater under his shirt with a dreadful look in his eyes. He rings the doorbell repeatedly. He stands at the door fuming, wondering what is taking her so long to open the door. He can hear the distant sound of movement as someone makes their way to the door.

"Who is it?"

"Scotty." The door swings open, Elane stands in the doorway in a robe. "Heyy baby, what you doing here so early." Before Scotty could reply, he hears a man's voice calling Elane's name. Jealousy kicks in as he makes his way into the house sliding pass Elane concealing his anger.

* * *

Kanisha steers her Cadillac CTS, pulling into the parking lot of Gambino's Italian restaurant. Sonja leans forward in the passenger seat scanning through Kiesha Cole's latest CD. After finding one of her favorite songs, she peers through the windshield recognizing the area.

"Girl, what you know about Gambinos? Me and Scotty come here all the time," Kanisha boasted, parking in between two cars. She never noticed the look of envy registering in Sonja's face.

"You mean to tell me that nigga find time to take you out?"

"Yeah, we do our thang ever now and then. Scotty knows how to be sweetheart when he wanna be. I know he be out taking care of his business. I know he probably be messin' around on the side, but one thing I can say about him is that he makes sure he takes care of home. My car note gets paid, our mortgage gets paid, and he buys me and junior any and everything that we want or need."

"But ask yo' self this question. Are you happy with y'all relationship?" Sonja asked, staring at Kanisha as she sits in the driver seat in silence.

"Naw, I'm not happy," she responded honestly in a low tone. "I'm just hoping that one day he realize how much I truly love him. I know we can make things work out for the best," Kanisha answered, pulling her keys out of the ignition.

"Pul-leeze girl, don't be no fool. That nigga ain't gon' ever change. Once a dog, always a dog. That's one thing my mama always told me." Sonja flips down the sunvisor, gazing in the mirror with her lips pluckered, applying her lavendar purple lip-stick.

Sonja is the only person that Kanisha ever knew to wear that color lip-stick.

"Let me worry about Scotty. That's my man and I'm the one that have to put up with his shit. It's not easy to just walk away from somebody that you're in love with," Kanisha stressed with an attitude.

"I'ma remember that next time you call me cryin' about how he be treatin' you," Sonja said, rolling her eyes at Kanisha.

They always fussing with each other.

They climb out of the car making their way to the front entrance of the restaurant. Kanisha's Fendi low heel pumps claps against the pavement. The smell of italian breakfast sausages grips the air as they step inside the restaurant.

*   *   *

Elane stands in the doorway surprised to see that Scotty came to her house unannounced. "Scotty wait. Let me introduce you to my little brother," Elane said, closing the door behind Scotty. He stops in his tracks, turning around facing her.

"What you say baby?" Scotty asked, playing like he didn't hear a word she said. Scotty didn't want to make a fool of himself.

"Let me introduce you to my little brother. Jaurice! Come in here for a second!"

Jaurice steps out of the kitchen area drinking pineapple juice from the carton. "Boy what I tell you about drinking out of the carton. Next time you get a glass. I don't know where your lips been," Elane stated, standing in front of him with her hands on her curveous hips.

"Stop trippin' sis. You know yo' lil brotha don't get down like that."

"Lil huh, that's what your mouth say. Anyways, Scotty this is Jaurice and Jaurice this is Scotty."

"What up?" Scotty greeted.

"Nothin' much playboy." He checks out the long heavy platinum chain on Scotty's neck, with it's crystal clear diamonds blinging hard. "That's a tight piece you got on. I see my sista ain't messin' with a broke nigga, but I ain't sayin' she's a gold digga," Jaurice said jokingly.

"Jaurice!" Elane jabs him in the rib playfully.

"You know I'm just kiddin' sis." Jaurice glances at the diamond bezel Cartier watch that is wrapped around his wrist. "It's time for me to ride out. It was nice meetin' you cool. Maybe we'll get anotha chance to chop it up on some playa to playa shit one day. Be easy sis, I'll holla at cha as soon as I make it back to the crib."

"Yeah, you make sure you do that and tell mama that I'll be up there next weekend."

"A'ight."

Jaurice grabs his Minnesota Timberwolves fitted cap off the sofa. He slips the cap on, tilting it to the back. His long french braids snakes down his shoulders. Smoothly, he walks across the plush, soft carpet that steals his footsteps, as he heads for the door. The door clicks behind him.

A few seconds later a volcanic sound shakes the walls, rattling the picture frames that are hanging up.

"I told that crazy boy about playing his loud music like that in front of my house. I don't need none of my nosey neighbors complaining about loud music."

The sound of the powerful sound system fades away as he distance himself.

"So, what brought you by this early?

"I just happened to be passing through the neighborhood," Scotty lied. "I tried callin' you on your cell phone and your house phone."

"Oh, I was in the shower. You know I have to go open the shop," Elane replied, walking towards the spiral staircase that leads to the master suite. Scotty's eyes dances from side to side with the rhythm of her rotating hips. Her perfectly rounded ass jiggles under the chiffon robe seeing nothing, but ass and a neatly trimmed mound of pubic hair between her inner thighs. Making it to the top of the stairs, they walk through the long hallway, sinking into the thick carpet. Scotty continues to watch, picturing the two of them in several different positions.

"I know why you came over here unexpectedly," Elane proclaimed, walking into the mastersuite, her ass rocking side to side looking sexy.

"Huh?" Scotty responded playing dumbfounded.

"What you mean huh? Don't play dumb with me Scotty." Elane talks with her back facing him, fishing through the dresser drawers searching for some under clothes. She pulls out a gold satin thong made by Versace.

"A'ight, I'ma keep it real with you. For a minute I thought you had a nigga over here. I thought you was tryna play me."

Elane stares at him through the mirror. She slides out her robe, tossing it on the oakwood canopy bed, putting her Coca Cola bottle shape on display. Bending over, she slips into her thong, letting Scotty's words sink in her head before replying. Scotty gets a good look at the hairy mound, peeking between her thick butterscotch thighs.

"Scotty let me ask you something."

"Go ahead."

"How can I be trying to play you if you're not my man. Can you please make some clarifications, because right now you have me discombobulated?"

"So, you want me to make some clarifications?" Scotty strides in her direction, gazing in her eyes as she slips on her Versace bra. He embraces her tiny waist pulling her against his chest, peppering her neck with warm, moist, kisses.

"Come on Scotty, not now, I have to go open the . . . shop." He ignores her, guiding her to the kingsize canopy bed. Elane tries to resist. Slowly he lays her down on her stomach, kissing all over her back. His hand travels down her spine, he slides her thong to the side, placing two fingers inside her warm pussy from behind, kissing her spine.

"Please Scotty . . . you going to make me late." Her voice falls, growing weak as she succumbs to his tender touch. "Why . . . you . . . doing this . . . to me.?" He buries his face between her bubble shaped ass, eating her pussy from the back. A series of moans escapes her parted lips. The faint scent of strawberry body wash delivers a fresh smell as he savors her juices. Spreading her ass cheeks apart, he grazes her asshole with his tongue. Elane arches her back squirming, gripping the sheets, howling in heat.

"Oooooh baby, w-what you d-doing to me, shit." Elane claws at the sheets, pulling them to her face. Scotty hums as he sucks on her clit, massaging it with his tongue, smacking her on the ass.

"Oh baby please don't stop . . . I'm c-coming," she begged. Her legs tremble, face furrow with pleasure, as she shiver and moan. Each breath taking her to a powerful orgasm.

"Oh shit baby, I'm c-coming again," Elane shouted in gratification. Scotty locks her clit between his lips, spelling each letter of the alphabet with his tongue. He rips off her damp thong, kicking his shoes off, removing all his clothes.

She arches her back cocking her ass in the air on all fours. Scotty holds his fully erected dick in his hand, rubbing his dick against her wet meaty pussy lips teasingly.

"Come on baby give it to me," Elane whined, staring over her shoulder. Scotty slides the head of his dick in her tight pussy. Gently, he spreads her ass cheeks apart, delivering her slow shallow strokes. Her pussy juice glistens on his chocolate pole. Slowly, he eases the other half of his 9 in a half inches in her pussy. Her tight pussy grips his thick mandingo like a fist. She bites down on her lips and let out a wispy moan. Scotty long dicks her, beating the pussy up. She loops her arm around the cherry oakwood column on the canopy bed for support. He smacks her bubblicious ass leaving pink welts on her cheeks. Her mouth drops open, her eyes partially closed.

"Uuh shit Scotty!" she shouted, pounding her fist against the mattress. His arms snakes around her tiny waistline as he drills her from the back, fucking her without mercy. The floral print scarf on her head slides off. She knocks all the pillows on the floor. Their bodies clap rhythmically as Scotty's pelvis and her ass crashes together. She can feel his dick in her stomach. Scotty can feel her insides becoming wetter with each stroke.

Her pussy farts long and hard as he pulls his long, throbbing pipe out of her sloppy, wet, pussy. Her inner thighs is soaked with sex juice.

He lifts her up from the bed. Elane wraps her legs around his waist with her arms looped around his neck. His strong muscular arms flexes, as he cups the bottom of her onion booty. He tosses her up and down, holding her in midair.

"You love this dick don't you?"

"Y-Yes baby. Oooooh this dick . . . is good." Scotty keeps a steady pace as he fucks her, standing flat on his two feet. His body gleams with sweat, her legs overlaps his forearms. Shifting his body weight, he falls back on the bed, allowing her to straddle him and take control. Elane bounces up and down on his dick, her head swerving wildly like she is possessed. Her titties clap together as she rides him like a bull rider.

"Ooh shit, w-what you doing to me?" She screams with her eyeballs rolling in back of her head showing the white. A mind boggling orgasm shoots through her body. Scotty's stomach muscles tightens and a wave of pleasure washes him from his head to his feet. His body shakes involuntarily, as he releases a long nut inside of her. She rolls over, falling off the bed. Her chest heaves as she breathed harder than a woman in labor.

*   *   *

The Jay-Z blue Hummer H2 skates down a side street in Parklawn projects. Its large rims look like huge mirrors, as the dimly lit street lights reflect off of the truck. Its smoked tinted windows only allow you to see the silhouette of two individuals that are occupying the truck.

Slowly, the truck pulls up to the curb, coming to a stop.

"Yeah, it's me, I'm outside," Dirty Red said, hanging up his Nokia N810 cell phone. "Yeah bay, this shit is finally comin' to an end," Dirty Red proclaimed, while adjusting his body to a more comfortable position.

"Bae you straight?" Janette asked, seeing that he is making all sorts of faces, due to the excruciating pain in his feet.

"Yeah, I'm just tryna get comfortable that's all."

"Here let me help you bae," Janette suggested, placing his crutches in the back seat.

"Thanks baby. I wish this little nigga come on." Dirty Red looks to his right, seeing a shadow shifting along the side of the truck. Boom! Boom! Boom!

*   *   *

Loud rumbling bass pumps out of the concert speakers, shaking the dance floor of Club Sensation. The dance floor is packed to its capacity. The DJ shouts into the microphone in between each song.

A dark complexioned man sporting a patterned Prada short sleeve button up shirt, black Prada trousers, and a pair of black suede Prada looafers squeezes through the disorderly crowd. The diamond bezel Bvlgari watch flashes on his wirst, as he adjusts his designer shades. The rotating multi-colored fluorescent lights shifts shadows of light all over the walls and floor. He strides toward the bar and signals for the bartender. The bartender couldn't help but notice the diamonds flashing on his wrist and the crystal clear diamonds in his earlobes.

Six 42 inch Sony Plasma screen televisions overlooks the bar, displaying every area of the crowded dance floor. A Corona sign shines behind the cash register. The man leans over the bar shouting into the bartender's ear, so that he can hear him clearly. The bartender shouts back over the loud deafening music, pointing to an exit sign that is glowing on the far wall adjacent to a closed door. The man nods his head up and down.

After receiving directions, he struts to the closed door. Before the man could reach the door, he is stopped in his tracks by a burly bouncer.

Ricky the bartender peers through the crowd, observing the new security staff, as he stands face to face with the man. Ricky moves quickly, stepping from behind the bar to inform the new security guard of who the man is, so that there will be no confusion.

"This area is off limits my man," the bouncer informed.

"Off limits. Mutha fucka you must don't know who I'am?" the man snarled, balling up his fist. The bouncer senses the man's anger and takes precaution.

"I don't care who you is. My boss gave me instructions not to let anyone come in this area." Ricky can see the tension building between the two men. Ricky moves faster, watching the two men as they knuckle up, standing toe to toe. Ricky knows that with the amount of distance in between him and the men, he will not make it in time to stop the first punch from being thrown.

The man tilts his upper body back like a trained boxer and draws back his arm with his fist clenched. Motion opens his office door greeted by the two men in a boxing stance.

"Eddddieee! What's up cuz?" Motion shouts excitedly captivating Eddie's attention. Slowly, Eddie lowers his fist. With all of his military training, he knows that the security guard is no match for him. The security guard looks at Eddie with a dumbfounded expression glued on his face. Motion makes a gesture with his hand.

"I got this," Motion said to the security staff.

"A'ight boss." He walks away mixing in with the crowd.

"What's up babbbyyy?" Motion said, embracing Eddie with a strong manly hug. "Why you didn't let me know you was comin'?" Motion added.

"I thought it would be better if I surprised you," Eddie replied, dusting off his shirt. Motion notices the crystal clear diamonds glistening on his watch. Motion can't believe how hard they are shining. The quality of Eddie's diamonds got Motion's beat by a long shot. Never in life, have Motion ever seen diamonds with such quality.

"Damn cuz, you blingin' harder than me. What the fuck you done did, struck oil or somethin'?" Motion questioned.

"Naw, I did somethin' better than that," Eddie replied.

"Let's step on in my office baby." Motion ushers him into his luxurious office closing the door behind them.

The loud music that is shaking the club is drowned out by the closed door and the sound proof walls. It seems as if they stepped into another world that is full of peace. The in-wall aquarium gives the office an exotic look. Motion falls back in his leather high back executive chair. Sliding the drawer open on his cherry oak wood desk, he retrieves a blunt stuffed with hydro.

"I see you haven't changed a bit," Eddie stated, watching Motion light the blunt. Motion takes a drag of the blunt and starts coughing with clouds of smoke lingering in front of his face.

"Huh, you . . . wanna . . . h-hit . . . this shit?" Motion offered, holding the blunt in front of him.

"Naw'll, I'ma pass on that today cuz. I came up here to discuss some serious business with you. I got somethin' that can make us filthy rich and take us to anotha level of the game." Eddie proclaimed.

Eddie fishes through his pocket and hands him a tiny ziploc bag. Motion's face crinkles in confusion.

"I 'ont get it. What the hell is this?"

"That's somethin' that can bring you more money than you could ever imagine." Motion continues to inspect the tiny package, as Eddie explains to him every detail.

*　　*　　*

Janette and Dirty Red is startled by the loud knock on the window. Mad as hell, Dirty Red presses a button on the door panel. The window rolls down slowly. A gust of wind pours into the truck.

"Nigga, is you crazy bangin' on my fuckin' window like that?" Dirty Red said in a serious tone.

"My bad," Bernard said, stepping back to admire the monstrous vehicle. "Damn nigga, when you get this?" Bernard asked, placing his hand over his mouth like he is about to throw up.

"I just picked it up yesterday, but anyways let's take care of this business."

Dirty Red unlocks the door letting him inside the truck. Benard opens the door greeted by the customly designed leather interior.

"Man before I say anything, can you please tell me who hooked yo' shit up like this?"

"Listen," Dirty Red said, turning around facing Benard. "Ah shit." A sharp pain shots through his body.

"You okay baby," Janette asked, looking directly into Dirty Red's pain filled eyes.

"Yeah, I'm straight baby."

"What you want me to do?"

"I got it." He reaches into his pocket, pulling out a pill bottle of pain reliever.

"Man, what's wrong with you?" Benard asked, having no knowledge of what happened to Dirty Red.

"Shit." Dirty Red tosses a pill in his mouth, swallowing it with Absolute Vodka Pear.

"Now you know you shouldn't be drinking and doin' business playa. Ain't that's what you told me?" Bernard reminded him.

"You my last stop," Dirty Red said, handing the alcoholic beverage to Janette, who places it into the cooler. "Nigga fuck the bullshit, lets handle this business. I'm ready to smash out of here and lay it down. I'm hurtin' like a mutha fucka."

Bernard reaches in his pocket pulling out a large wad of money and hands it to Dirty Red. Dirty Red leans forward and taps two buttons on the dashboard. A secret compartment pops open underneath the seat. "Grab that shit. You owe me fifteen five," Dirty Red said, leaning. back in the leather interior.

Bernard can't believe his ears heard the right thing. "Did you say fifteen five?" Benard asked, leaning down to pick up the package.

"Yeah, that's a brick. I want you to get yo' money up so you can get out the game. This shit ain't the same no more. It's hard to trust anybody in this game. A lot of niggas out here is workin' for them people. This game ain't like it was in the eighties. It's a lot of watered down niggas out here," Dirty Red stated, speaking nothing but the truth.

Bernard seen the look Dirty Red gave his lady, he senses that something is wrong. Bernard moves hurriedly, placing the bird between his waistline.

"Okay, I'll hit you when I'm done."

"A'ight, later little man." Dirty Red stares at Bernard, as he climbs out of the truck. He dashes back into the house. Janette pulls off leaving the area.

* * *

Traffic moves rapidly as Marco navigates his Lexus down Wisconsin Avenue. Lil Wink leans back in the passenger seat reading a real estate book that Marco gave him to study. The beaming sun seeps through the open sunroof, bathing the interior of the car. Marco pulls up downtown on State Street, parking close to the curb in front of a parking meter.

"What we doin' down here," Lil Wink asked, placing his bookmark between the pages of the book.

"We about to go in the City's Accessor's office and find out who own those houses we was lookin' at the other day. This is where you go when you want to find out information about property in Milwaukee," Marco explained.

Marco presses the power button on the ceiling closing the sunroof. The interior of the car grows dim, as the powered sunroof closes slowly, blocking out the sun. They hop out of the car and drop a couple of coins into the parking meter.

They strut through the large hallways of the Safety building advancing towards the glass doors of the City's Access or's office. Marco looks around in search of the clerk. He spots an older man standing behind the counter shuffling through a folder filled with paperwork.

Marco steps closer to the counter, removing a piece of paper from pocket. The man notices Marco standing at the counter. He makes his way to the window.

"How are you doing today?" The man greeted politely.

"I'm doin' a'ight. What about yo' self?" Marco asked.

"I'm doing just fine young man. What can I help you with today?" He asked.

The man appears to be in his late sixties with a receding hairline and a salt and pepper beard that is perfectly trimmed. Marco slides the piece of paper across the counter.

"I wanna know the assessment on these houses."

"You thinking about buying these houses?" The man asked, punching buttons on the computer. His eyebrows crinkle as he gazes at the screen.

"Bad investment," he said staring at the screen punching more buttons.

"Huh, what you mean bad investment?" Marco shot back.

"Like I said young man, that's a investment, trust me." The man prints out all the information and hands it to Marco. "Here, take this. That's my cell phone number. I'm not tryin' to tell you what to do with your money, but if you want to make some good, profitable investments, give me a ring. I'll be glad to help you out. I'm about to retire in a couple months. You kinda remind me of my son, he's in college down in Atlanta. I've been trying to get my son to get into the real estate, but he's on somethin' else. I admire a young man that has ambition. I'm not suppose to be doing this, but I rather see somebody make it," the man explained.

"I tell you what. How about I give you a call this weekend?" Marco suggested.

"That' s fine with me."

"A'ight, talk to you then."

"You take it easy young man."

Marco and Lil Wink exits the office headed to the car.

*   *   *

"Go head and rack'em. Run that shit back," Nickel said, tilting his head back, drinking the remainder of the Patron, emptying the glass.

"You sure you wanna do that?" D.C asked. This is the third game in the row that D.C won. Nickel met D.C three hours ago and already he feels like that uncle that he always wanted.

"I'm positive old school."

"Well, you gon' and rack'em, remember I'm the winner," he proclaimed, chalking the end of the pool stick. D.C leans against the green padded pooltable positioning himself for the break, rocking the poolstick back and forth. With his derby tilted to the side and a toothpick hanging from the corner of his mouth, he breaks the balls. The poolballs clacks together zigzagging all over the table. Two stripes falls into the side pocket.

"You know what it is," he retorted. Massaging his bushy salt and pepper beard, D.C observes the table contemplating on his next shot.

"Make sure yo' next move, be yo' best move," Nickel chanted, watching him closely, as he angles the pool-stick, leaning forward focusing on his shot with one eye partially closed. Taking his best shot, the white ball clacks against the red striped ball sending it bumping against the side.

"Shit! How the hell I miss that easy shot," he muttered. As Nickel prepared to take his shot, D.C strides over to the jukebox in his Stacy Adams.

"I know what it is. We need some music in here." D.C fumbles in his pants pockets for some change. Dropping two quarters into the machine, he presses number twenty. Isley Brothers' "Choosey Lover" spills out of the sound system. Turning around making his way back to the pooltable, he watches as Nickel drops two balls into the side pocket. Nickel has been undefeated every since he has been hanging out at the MeLro bar slanging his dope. Being that he is now labeled a rat, he can't be seen on the City's Northside.

D.C is the first one to beat him. Holding the pool-stick in his hand, Nickel starts to feel sick. He sits his pool-stick on the side of the pool-table.

"I think I got the shits. My stomach hurtin' like a mafucka. Hold up, I'll be right back."

"Don't be tryna talk yo' way out this ass whoopin'."

"Man I'm fo' real. I think that drink gave me the runs." Nickel rushes to the restroom holding his stomach.

*   *   *

The roaring sound of the 747 crones, as it grips the air, gliding over the clouds, moving like the speed of light. Motion leans back, relaxing on the wide cushioned leather seat with his his hands interlaced behind his head, enjoying the first class flight. His eyes are concealed behind his dark Louis Vuitton shades. Many thoughts flood his mind as he lay back pondering. Motion can't get his mind off of what was inside the tiny zip-loc bag.

Toon and Eddie just finished eating an order of lobster tails. A half empty bottle of Louis Thirteen sits on the table in front of them. The flight attendant removes all of their dirty dishes replacing them with a fresh dessert.

Man I hope Eddie know what he is doin'. I hope his connect ain't on no bullshit. It's a lot of money to be made. If everything goes as planned, my player days is over with. I can take off my jersey and retire from the game for good. The sound of the P.A system snaps Motion out of his trance.

"Attention passengers, we are now about to land in Freetown. Tempatures are ninety eight degrees, very humid. Please make sure you are seated and please fasten your seatbelts. Thank you for choosing U.S Airline and I hope you enjoyed your flight."

Toon and Eddie return to their seat fastening their seatbelts. Motion scopes his twelve time zone Jacob & Co watch and says, "That business should be gettin' handled right about now."

*   *   *

Nickel sits on the toilet taking a drag from his Newport cigarette. The tip of it shines a bright orange color, as he continues to inhale the cancer stick. He blows out a billow of smoke, staring at all the nicknames and gang literature scratched in the walls inside the stall. The faint sound of music trapped behind the bathroom door grows louder, as someone opens the door, stepping into the bathroom. Slowly, the door swings closed drowning out the music, being replaced by the clacking sound of footsteps. Nickel locks his eyes on the shadow that is shifting along the floor nearing his stall. The footsteps echo throughout the bathroom. The unknown individual slows his pace, stopping in front of Nickel's stall. Seeing the pair of blue Stacy Adams, Nickel nervously asks, "D.C is that you?" Nickel waits a few seconds for a response, but the only response he receives is a clicking sound that he is very familiar with. The door swings open and his face flashes with terror. Sitting on the toilet with his denim Enyce pants crumpled around his ankles, he drops the burning cigarette on the floor. The man shoves the barrel of the Nickel plated 357 Mag into his hanging mouth knocking out Nickel's front teeth. "Aaaw," Nickel groaned in excruciating pain with blood leaking from his mouth.

"This is what I do to rat mafuckas like you, who can't keep their fuckin' mouth closed," the man said in a raspy voice. Biting down on his lower lip, the man squeezes the trigger. Blocka! Nickel's head jerks back crashing against the ceramic tiled wall. Brain fragments disperses from the back of his head sticking to the walls. Leaning forward, the man towers over Nickel's slumped body. With the same look of terror still plastered on his face, Nickel leans against the bloody stall lifeless.

Smoke lingers from the barrel of the man's 357 Mag, as he glimpses around, tucking the gun into his waistband. D.C looks in the mirror adjusting his derby, shielding his eyes. Twirling a toothpick around in his mouth, he makes his way out of the bathroom in a casual mannerism like nothing ever happened. The loud music playing in the bar overpowered the barking sound of the gunfire. No one notices him as he exits the bar.

D.C jumps into an old model Cadillac that he has registered in an alias name. The Visine that he slipped in Nickel's drink worked out perfectly, giving him the shits just as he planned.

Through his reliable sources on the streets, he found out that Nickel was on parole and followed him from the parole building, after attending to a visit with his parole officer. Now that he is a nice distance from the bar, he snatches off the fake bushy salt and pepper beard. Gazing in the rearview mirror rubbing his face, he says, "I did it again. They don't call me Dog Catcher for nothin'. People must don't believe that saying that "every dog gets their day.""

*   *   *

After 14 hours of flying, Motion, Eddie, and Toon arrives at Freetown International airport. Freetown is the capital of Sierra Leone and the largest city and main port. The city was founded in 1787 as a settlement for freed slaves.

They exit the plane right on the runway. The blazing heat attacks them as they make their way into the airport. Toon adjusts his Louis Vuitton visor, blocking his eyes from the beaming sun.

"Damn it's hot as a mafucka down here," Motion complained, wiping his forehead with the back of his hand.

"You ain't seen nothin' yet. This is nice compared to how it normally be," Eddie proclaimed, escorting them inside the airport.

Eddie is no stranger to Africa. Being stationed in Africa over the years has allowed him to become very familiar with his surroundings.

They walk inside the terminal to what appears to be a welcome party. Motion and Toon scans the sea of unfamiliar faces. They notice signs hanging up allover that warn the guests of robbery and theft. They suggest that the visitors leave all of their valuable possessions at the front desk.

Sierra Leone is ranked the world's poorest country by the United Nations for the past 3 years out of 177 countries, with about 70% of its people living on a dollar a day. Corruption by government officials and police is widespread. Bribes are the norm and expected. Although, Toon and Motion is no stranger to poverty, they are seeing another level of poverty.

Slowly, they adjust to their surroundings. After grabbing their Louis Vuitton luggage off of the carousel, they strut towards the exit.

Flight schedules are electronically posted on television screens in easy view. The roaring sound of airplanes coming can be heard over head. The terminal is busy with ticket agents checking reservations on computer screens. Passenger service agents are selling tickets and taking baggage, giving out claim checks.

They exit the terminal greeted by a large flag with three horizontal stripes, green, white, and blue on a pole rippling from the hot wind. People are in front of the terminal hustling, trying to sell any and everything.

A man jumps out of a dusty jeep wearing a dingy shirt, and a pair of sandals, exposing his ashy feet, and a pair of denim shorts that was once a pair of pants. He approaches them with a friendly smile. The man can tell that they are Americans by their attire.

"You look for ride?" he asked in a heavy accent. The man has a rubber black complexion and short kinky hair. It looks as if he has never used lotion in his life. If they didn't know any better, they would've mistaken him for a heroine addict.

"Yeah, we on our way to Sierra Leone," Eddie answered.

"C'mon, me take you to Sierra Leone," he replied, showing his brown and yellow stained teeth. He helps them throw their luggage in the jeep. Bringing the engine to life, he pulls down the dusty, unpaved road. A trail of dirt lingers behind them as they move about, bouncing around in their seats on a four hour ride to Sierre Leone.

The streets are filled with litter and garbage everywhere. There are no traffic lights. Motion and Toon observes the many modern buildings taking in the site. Looking at the poor people in the rural area, living in the mud houses with corrugated iron or thatched roofs made them appreciate what they have at home.

Eddie glances around at the scenery, after an hour of riding down the unpaved road. It doesn't look like the same route he took the last time he went to Sierra Leone.

Maybe he's takin' another route? Eddie notices a large cloud of dust moving in their direction from ahead. Looking to the back, he spots another large cloud of dust approaching them from the rear. *I think this muthafucka set us up. Fuck! I don't even have my pistol. I should've known this muthafucka was up to somethin'. I can't believe I got caught slippin'.* Their bodies jerk as the man steps on the gas speaking a local African language that they can not understand.

Toon's and Motion's instincts tells them that something is wrong. "Man, what's goin' on Eddie?" Motion asked, glimpsing over his shoulders at the vehicles closing in on them.

"It look like we about to find out," Eddie said. A group of men are positioned in the bed of a dented up pick-up truck, clutching AK47's with long extended banna clips, aiming the deadly weapons in their direction, barking in their native tongue. A topless Jeep Wrangler full of armed men moves closer, giving them no where to go. The man stops the jeep in the middle of the sandy feild, following their command. The armed men pour out of their vehicles surrounding them. Eddie, Motion, and Toon places their hands in the air feeling defeated. They have no where to run. A Sierra Leonian man with a gleaming bald head snatches the driver out of the jeep, shouting in his deep accent. Motion, Toon, and Eddie can't understand what the angry man is saying. Two of the men assist the bald headed man by gripping the driver's arms with a tight firm hold restraining him. The bald headed man glares into the man's fearful eyes in silence, flexing his jaw muscles. He pulls out a long, shiny, sharp machete. Grabbing a fist full of the man's kinky hair, he runs the machete along his neck. Blood oozes from his neck, squirting all over the two armed men that are gripping his arms. The man tussles with the machete, as he saws through the man's neck bone, cutting his head clean off. The headless corspe tumbles to the ground with blood oozing from it's limb. In Sierra Leone, murder is the way of life.

Toon vomits in the back seat of the jeep, after witnessing the vicious assassination. One of the armed men kicks the head out of their path, making his way to the jeep, gripping the high powered semi-automatic with its curved clip.

Motion's body is drenched with perspiration. Not only from the blazing hot climate, but in fear for his life.

*　　*　　*

Shasha parks her Benz truck in front of fourth District police department. She steps out of the truck in firm fitting Akademik jeans and a red, white, and black Akademik halter top exposing her pierced navel. Her red, white, and black number 23 Air Jordans coasts across the pavement, as she nears the main entrance of the police department. Tired of receiving so many parking tickets, she decided to get a parking permit.

She locks her eyes on a Pepsi blue BMW 760, that is resting on chrome 24 inch Lexani rims. The car is parked a few cars down from hers. *I like that Beamer. I never seen that car in traffic before.* Busy admiring the car, Shasha isn't paying any attention to where she is going. She bumps into a man that is exiting the police department. Her car keys and her cell phone falls to the ground.

146

"Ooops, my bad baby," the man apologized, kneeling down helping her recover her belongings. The smell of his Usher cologne lingers in the air, delivering a pleasant scent.

"I should've been watching where I was goin'. I just got a lot on my mind. I had to file a police report because some body busted my window out and stole my car system. They was givin' me a hard time in there. You know how it is dealin' with them lazy ass cops," he said, handing Shasha her car keys. Shasha looks up at the man after picking up her cell phone.

"Don't . . . worry about it . . . papi," Shasha replied. She remember the man from Elane's shop, when she was getting her hair done. One thing she never forgets is a face. A smile pulls at the corner of his mouth putting his gold teeth on display.

"You take care. Once again I apologize for my clumsiness."

"A'ight papi."

They walk off going their separate ways.

That's one of the dudes I seen leavin' out of Elane's office in that Cadillac truck. Somethin' ain't right about papi. Shasha stands motionless as she peers through the glass doors. The man hops into the BMW and dips into the heavy traffic on Sliver Spring Drive.

I thought he said somebody broke in his car. I didn't see no damage done to his car. Somethin' ain't right. I betta call Scotty as soon as I leave here. Shasha steps up to the counter waiting for someone to assist her.

*   *   *

The afternoon sun shimmers, bathing the earth as Scotty and his female companion exit Gambino's Italian restaurant. They hop inside a Grand Cherokee that Scotty rented in a dope fiend's name. Scotty's black Paul Smith loafers eases down on the gas pedal, as he zips out of the parking lot onto the highway.

"Scotty I really enjoyed myself. Next time we come up here I got a big surprise for you."

"Oh yeah, and what's that?" Scotty asked.

"You'll have to wait and see," she smiled seductively, watching him as he focuses on his driving.

"I wanna come in yo' house and give you some of this thug passion, but I gotta handle some business first," Scotty said, gazing at the green and white signs on the side road. He glimpses at his female companion, who is leaning over in his seat unzipping his pants. She tucks her hand into his boxers fondling his mandingo. The warmth of her soft hands caressing his manhood gives him a throbbing erection. Pulling out his hard throbbing dick, she grazes,it with her moist tongue. Slowly, she engulfs half of his long, thick 9 in a half inch dick in her tiny, tight mouth, with her eyes partially closed. Scotty tilts his head back, leaning against the headrest, enjoying her juicy mouth. No longer able to take it, he pulls over to the side of the highway. He cups the back of her head, sinking deeper into her mouth. A warm fire runs under his skin. He grabs her arm guiding her into the driver seat. With no resistance, she climbs into the driver seat. Scotty pushes the power button on the door panel sliding the power seat back. She sits on his lap, gripping the steering wheel, with her back facing him. Scotty raises up her beige sleeveless Dolce & Gabbana dress staring at her plump ass. Scotty can't believe how a woman so slender got so much ass. Scotty notices that she doesn't have on any panties. Her shaved, meaty pussy stares him in the face screaming fuck me, as she cocks her ass in the air, guiding his dick in her pussy. His mushroom shaped dick head brushes against her clit making her hiss.

The continuous sound of automobiles hum, passing by them. Knowing that some stranger maybe watching them excites her. The warm soft summer breeze pours through the open windows. She bites down on her lower lip, as she slowly lowers her body. Scotty watches as his whole dick disappear inside her deep, wet pussy. Her fat pussy lips are wrapped around his dick. The rhythm of their breath quickens, as she bounces up and down, gripping the steering wheel, moaning to the rhythm of her movement. Scotty balls her dress up in his fist, slapping her wiggling ass with the other.

"Yeah baby. You like this good pussy don't you?" she said, swerving her head wildly. He squeezes her juicy ass cheeks. The smell of sex lingers in the air.

"Shittt, you know it. Uuuuh shit you ridin 'the hell out of this dick."
This little bitch know she can take some dick.

"Yo' bitch can't . . . ride this big dick . . . like this could she?"

She rides him harder like he is the last piece of dick she will ever have. He looks at his shiny dick as she rides him, watching it go in and out.

"Ooh baby . . . I'ma 'bout to . . . cum." She speeds up her pace as she nears her orgasm. The truck bounces up and down as if it has hydralics. Scotty's stomach muscles tighten, his mouth drops open, as he explodes inside of her. She continues to ride him having a long powerful orgasm. Scotty's cell phone chimes garnering his attention. He fishes between the driver seat and the console searching for his cell phone. Grabbing the phone, he answers just in time.

"Yeah, what up?"

"It's me Elane baby. My brother dropped that money off to me already. I need you to hurry up and bring that, because he trying to jump back on the highway."

"A'ight, I'm on my way."

"Why you breathing so hard?"

"I had to run and answer the phone," Scotty lied.

"Well, I'll be at the house waiting for you."

"I'll be there in a minute."

"Okay bye baby." Click! Scotty tosses the cell phone to the side with his female companion still on his lap.

"Come on, get up, I gotta hurry up. That's the call I been waitin' on." She climbs out of his lap into the passenger seat. Scotty grabs a hand full of napkins out of the glove compartment and cleans himself off. Quickly, he jumps back onto the highway, making his way to drop her off and pick up the dope he has stashed at her house.

They dip into the driveway. "Grab that bag for me so I can go handle this business," Scotty instructed, watching her fix her lipstick.

"Why you always wear that ugly ass lipstick?"

"You know this is my trademark baby," she replied, climbing out of the truck. "I'll be right back." She closes the door and prances to the side door of her residence. Scotty stares at her slender frame as her dress clings to her shapely body. Scotty loves the way she walk.

She returns with a bulgy Louis Vuitton duffel bag, struggling on her way to the truck. She opens the back door, placing the duffel bag into the back seat.

"Whew, that bag kinda heavy."

"Good lookin' baby, I'll catch you later," Scotty thanked her as he pulls out of her driveway.

Scotty stops at a red light leaning back in the rental truck. He spots a Pepsi blue BMW on 24 inch rims, traveling Northbound headed in the same direction he is going.

Damn, that mutha fucka wet ass hell. He thinks to himself, watching the luxurious automobile maneuver through the bustling traffic. The chiming sound of his cell phone captivates his attention. Scanning the glowing screen, he recognizes Shasha's number. He presses send answering the phone.

"Yo, what up famm? . . . Hello . . . Hello . . . Shasha you there?" Scotty can't hear anything but static. He hangs up the phone. ***Somethin' must be wrong with her phone. She'll call back. Maybe her battery goin' dead.***

* * *

"Damn, I must've broke my phone when I dropped it on the ground," Shasha muttered. She makes her way to the nearest payphone.

* * *

Scotty rounds the corner pulling up to Elane's house. ***Why the hell her truck ain't in the driveway like it usually be? Maybe she parked her truck in the garage?*** Scotty has a key to get in the house. She gave him a key to her house as they grew closer to each other. Scotty spends more time with Elane than he do with Kanisha.

Scotty's cell phone ring again. He looks at the illuminating screen, seeing an unknown caller. He doesn't answer the call. ***Whoever that is they know I don't answer unknown calls.*** Scotty climbs out of the truck grabbing the Louis Vuitton duffel bag that contains 10 kilos of uncut cocaine.

As he struts to the front door, he notices the curtains to Elane's mastersuite dancing like she was just peeking out the window.

Scotty sticks the key into the door and turns the door knob. Upon stepping inside Elane's house, he looks around with a searching gaze, noticing something strange. Seeing that the house is empty, containing no furniture, he reaches for his Glock .40 that is tucked in his waistband.

150

Before he could draw his gun, he hear the clicking sound of multiple guns followed by loud shouting.

"Freeze DEA! Don't move!" A group of angry law enforcement officers barked, pouring out of every room in the house. Scotty drops the duffel bag on the floor, tossing his hands in the air, staring at the muzzles of all the high powered handguns pointed in his direction. ***Damn, I can't believe this bitch set me up. I'ma kill that bitch.*** A tall slender built officer restrains Scotty, placing him into handcuffs. The silver badge around his neck gleams as he faces Scotty.

"I don't know if you know about me Scotty, but they call me Bodo," he introduced himself. Scotty tilts his head looking into Bodo's blue eyes.

"And what that suppose to mean?" Scotty retorted with a smirk on his face.

"That mean you have two choices. You either hire yourself the best attorney and go to trial, or you can make a wise choice to help yourself."

A dark complexion officer in plain clothes unzips the Louis Vuitton duffel bag, dumping the 10 kilos onto the floor in front of Scotty.

"Yeah we got us one red handed. I don't think it's an attorney on the face of this earth that can help him right now," the dark complexion, officer proclaimed, as he counts the book shaped packages. Scotty observes the gold teeth that are gleaming in the man's mouth. The man doesn't look nothing like an undercover police officer. He places the kilos back inside the bag.

They escort Scotty out of the house, guiding him to an unmarked van. Scotty sees the same Pepsi blue BMW he saw earlier, parked in the drive way behind his rental truck. Scotty peers through the windows of the van in deep thoughts.

*   *   *

With expanded eyes, Motion and Toon stares at a group of shadows shifting around on the sandy pavement. Eddie shields his eyes like a soldier saluting his commander, looking skyward at the group of sinister looking white headed vultures, gliding on almost motionless wings and soaring in wide circles. The vultures can smell the stench scent of death lingering in the atmosphere.

The bald headed Sierra Leonian sits in the back of the jeep with Motion and Toon, holding on to an arching bar for support, as they travel down the bumpy road.

"Ye have ta be careful out here Amer'dicans. Displace is verdi dangerous. Shabba send me ta come get ya. When me pull up, I see ya get in dis jeep wit' da theft. Him plan ta kill ya and and rob ya fa ye goods. Me and mi men follow ya and wait fa rite time ta stop ya," the bald headed Sierra Leonian man explained in his broken English.

"What's yo' name?" Eddie asked.

"They call me Tula," he answered, looking into the sky like he is trying to find the heaven. "It's a storm comin' our way," Tula informed. "Move faster." Tula ordered for the driver to speed up.

Reaching into his pocket, Tula pulls out a stone with human like figures curved in it. Looking at the stone, Toon asks, "What's that Tula?"

"Dis is a Nomoli. Here in Sierra Leone we believe da it bring ya good luck. Possessin' one of dese bring an abundant yeild of crops."

"Where it come from?"

"No one knows fa certain where it come from. No one even knows who carved it. Dis stone is found in the soil. It's a mystery behind dis stone."

Motion observes the mountainous view as they make their way to their destination. They pull up in a small village with sheltering made of clay and some made of tree limbs and cardboard. The lights are run on fuel operated generators that very few of the natives can afford. Because of the lack of electricity, there is no hot water, heat, or refrigerators. The natives shop each day only for food they will eat that day.

A group of Sierra Leonian kids with their ribcages pressing against their skin surrounds the jeep, staring at the visitors in admiration.

"Amer'dicans," they said in unison. One of the teenagers stands in the dirt barefooted, checking out Motion's shades and his Jacob & Co watch. The loud chanting sound of the kids voices captivates the attention of their superior. Eddie displays a white smile glad to see Shabba.

"Come my friends. Make ye selves at home," Shabba greeted. Motion and Toon scans the scenery finding that to be a hard thing to do, seeing the conditions that they are living in. All of the men climb out of the jeep.

"Yumi," Shabba called out. A woman breaks through the group of kids wearing a bright colorful dress with a thin piece of fabric covering her full sized breasts.

"Yes papa," she answered in a soft innocent voice.

"Get me friends somethin' da drink." The woman fixes her ebony brown eyes on Toon. The two of them gazes at each other in a daze.

"Yumi now," shabba demanded.

"Okay papa." Yumi flashes a child-like smile, batting her long eyelashes before walking off. Toon can't believe how beautiful of a creature Yumi is. Toon has never seen a woman with such natural beauty in his life. Yumi is what you consider to be a diamond in the rough.

Shabba limps with his wooden cane taking calculated steps, as he escorts them to an area with a group of people pushing wheel barrels.

"Ya see da over there?" Shabba points his handless arm at a man cleaning pebbles. Shabba's hand was chopped off by a squad called the "Cut Hands Commando." The rebels killed some of his people when they came to his mine trying to take over.

A couple of Shabba's men are pacing back and forth gripping high powered assault rifles. One of the children are carrying a wooden pot on his head, supporting it with his limbs. Unfortunately, his hands were hacked off with a machete. Most of the Sierra Leonians that are bustling around the mine is topless.

Motion never thought that he'd be in Sierra Leone, Africa trying to smuggle uncut diamonds into the U.S. Sierra Leone is a small country that provides a large portion of the world's most valuable treasures-diamonds. It is among the leading countries in production of diamonds used in the industry. The diamonds used for gems and also diamonds used in the industry. The diamonds lie in gravel deposits along riverbeds and swamps in Eastern parts of the country. About 70% of the diamonds are used to make gemstones and the rest are less expensive.

Most men in Sierra Leone are farmers. But many grow only enough food for their families and work during the season mining diamonds.

"Him is cleanin' uncut diamonds. The average person would not know they have value," Shabba informed.

Yumi returns with two water jugs containing sanitized water. The sun kisses her cinnamon skin tone. Her long thin spaghetti braids shadows her face. Toon is eyeing her from head to toe. His eyeballs shifts as he scans her curveous frame. *I never knew the women in Africa was this beautiful.* Toon thinks to himself, watching a smiling Yumi. She hands him a jug of water.

"Thank you," Toon said, looking in her deep brown eyes.

"You welcome Amer'dican," she replied, snickering at Toon as she struts away. Toon tilts his head back with his eyes partially closed, guzzling down the water. That is the best water he has ever tasted. Maybe that is because he is so thirsty he thought.

"Me know ya probably tired. Me'll have mi daughter and wife fix ya a place ta sleep. Later me tell ya about diamonds," Shabba said, limping away with his cane in front of him.

After taking a long nap, Motion, Eddie, and Toon gather around the fire listening intently as Shabba share his wisdom. The fire crackles, dancing with the cool midnight breeze. The silohuette of the fire reflects in their eyes. Yumi leans against her father with her head resting on his shoulder, watching Toon the whole entire time.

"Da word diamond is a corruption of da Greek word adamas, which means unconquerable. Da first discoveries of diamonds were in ancient India. Da full beauty of the stone was not really recognized until da development of the gem shape called the "Brilliant cut" towards the end of da seventeenth century, by da Italian lapidary Vincenzo Peruzzi. Da Cullinan, da largest diamond yet found, it weighed three thousand, one hundred, and six carats when discovered in da Premier mine in ninteen o-five. It was cut into nine large stones. It's now part of da British crown jewels and nearly one hundred gems. Da only way ya can cut a diamond is wit' a diamond."

Shabba pauses as he opens a small pouch, pulling out one of the largest diamonds Motion has ever seen.

"Ya see dis precious stone? In da Amer'dica dis stone sybolize wealth, love, and prosperity. But here in Sierra Leone, Africa diamonds is da symbol of greed, corruption, and . . . death."

A white tree of light arces across the sky followed by a sharp detonation of thunder. Shabba struggles to his feet in silence making his way into his house made of clay that he calls his home.

*   *   *

Motion unzips the Louis Vuitton bag retrieving his walkman. Motion places the headphones over his ears. Slowly, he drifts off into another world. Motion has very big plans for his rough diamonds. He can't wait to launch his own line of watches. But at the same time, he plans to make Shabba a rich man.

Feeling something rubbing against his shoulders, Motion turns around staring at the young teenage boy that has both his hands hacked off. The little boy smiles at Motion.

"What is dat?" the little boy questioned.

"This is a walkman."

"Walkman."

"Yep."

"Can me see?"

"Anytime lil' man." Motion puts the headphones over his ears adjusting them. The little boy flashes a toothless smile. He bobs his head to the music.

"Me like. Who is dis?"

"That's Tupac."

"Tupac. Me heard of him. Him get killed in Amer'dica."

"Yeah, that's him."

The little boy removes the headphones with his limbs. "Thank ya."

"No problem. Hold on, you know what?" Motion puts the headphones around his neck. "You keep those. It's a gift from me to you."

"Whoa, thank ya Amer'dican."

"You don't have to call me American. I'ma African just like you. Call me Motion."

"Okay."

"What's yo' name?"

"Costa."

"Well, check this out Costa. I'ma get me some rest and call it a night. I'll talk to you in the mornin'."

"Okay Motion. Me talk ta ya ta morrow. Mi thug nigga." Motion chuckles at Costa's statement as he struts to the mud house to get some shut eye.

Motion's eyes jerks open to the sound of what seems to be hysterical laughter. Never in Motion's life have he ever heard a laugh so weird. The laughing gets louder and louder, but he doesn't hear anyone talking. It sounds like a group of drunkies.

Motion eases up off the blanket, making his way to the doorway. Toon and Eddie are sound asleep. As soon as Motion reaches the doorway, the loud barking sound of gunfire sends him to the ground taking cover.

Dat! Dat! Dat! Dat! Dat! Dat! Dat! Dat! A group of yellowish gary animals with black spots scurries pass Motion's view.

"Man what the fuck was that?" Toon asked, awakening from his sleep startled.

"Man, I 'ont know what the fuck that was," Motion replied, laying on the ground, gazing through the doorway. One of Shabba's men walks to their sleeping quarters carrying his chopper.

"Sorry about dat. Me had ta get rid of dose hyenas. Everything is under control. Ya can go back ta sleep." The man walks away leaving his footprints in the dirt.

The next day arrived quickly and Motion is prepared to conduct business. They stand on the sandy surface watching Shabba's men put the rough diamonds together. Costa sashays with his new headphones on that Motion gave him.

"Westside ta da day I die, thug life, m-o-b," Costa recites Tupac's lyrics. He loves when Tupac says "Westside" considering that Sierra Leone is West Africa. Shabba looks at the happy little boy.

"Thug life. M-o-b," Shabba repeated, shaking his head, smiling at Costa.

"Well, me guess it's time fa us ta do business. Costa come, bring me da diamonds," Shabba waves his limb, garnering Costa's attention.

Costa retrieves a large wooden pot, carrying it on his head. Kneeling down, he carefully places the pot on the ground.

Eddie, Motion, and Toon looks into the pot analyzing all the various size pebbles. The rough diamonds looks like they are worthless.

"Ya see dose? Dose are worth a fortune in ya country. All me won't is seven hundred and fifty thousand dollars in Amer'dican money. And me gaurantee they pass through the U.S Customs and make it ta de Amer'dica safely. Me send one of mi men wit' ya," Shabba bargained.

Motion looks at the diamonds in silence before responding to his offer.

"And if they don't make it to my country?"

"Me give ya money-back, ya have mi word."

"Well, I tell you what Shabba. I'm gon' show you how we do business in our country. Aye Toon, grab that package," Motion said. Toon strolls to the mud house and returns with a large, heavy, Louis Vuitton luggage. Toon sits the luggage on the ground. He wipes his sweaty forehead with the back of his hand, blowing out a short breath of air. Motion crouches to the ground, unzipping the luggage exposing large bundles of Leones. Costa whistles at the site of the money.

"That's equivalent to a million dollars in U.S currency. I had it converted into Leones, so that leaves you with an extra quarter mill. I want you to take that and look out for your people," Motion stated. "Do we have a deal?" Motion added.

"Deal." Shabba shakes Motion's outstretched hand.

"Thank ya Eddie. Without ya, dis wouldn't be possible," Shabba thanked.

"No problem Shabba. Anything for you my man," Eddie replied.

Motion has major plans for the diamonds. The line of watches that he are going to launch is called "Vonoti." Eddie has a connection with a diamond cutter in Belguim. Motion already made reservations to fly him into Sierra Leone. Motion's plans are slowly coming together.

*　　*　　*

The illuminating computer monitor reflects off Elliott's pecan complexion. His fingers moves rapidly, tap dancing on the keyboard. It has been a long strenuous day for him. All of the research and typing has him exhausted.

A creaky sound seizes his attention. Looking over his shoulder, he sees his mother standing behind him in her nightgown and slippers, with a scarf wrapped around her head.

"Baby cut that computer off and get you some rest. You been on that internet all night. It's four o'clock in the mornin'. Care yo' tail to bed and stop over workin' yo' self. You oughta be gettin' some rest. You suppose to be on summer vacation," Ms. Hopson stressed with her hands planted on her big hips.

"I know mama. I was just tryna finish this project I'm workin' on for Motion," Elliott stated, massaging his temples. He flicks the computer off and rises to his feet.

"Motion bet not be gettin' my baby wore out before he make it to college."

"It's alright mama. I'm just glad he's leaving those streets alone. I don't know what I would do if I loss my big brother. We already loss daddy to the streets."

"I know . . . I'm glad he's talkin' about doin' somethin' legit. We had a long talk the other day. Now you gon' and get you some rest baby. When you get up mama'll have a nice breakfast waiting on you."

"Alright mama." Elliott kisses his mother on the forehead and hikes up the long flight of stairs, making his way to his bedroom.

*   *   *

Toon squirms in his sleep. He feels something crawling under his shirt. His eyes flicks open to the site of a beautiful African Goddess. She touches her lip with her indexfinger pointed upward. "Ssssh. Come."

Yumi grabs his hand guiding him out of the mud house. They creep through the small village ducking off in the grassy area.

Yumi gazes in Toon's eyes, watching him for a moment in silence They are facing each other with their fingers interlaced. Staring in each other's eyes, they slowly lock lips in a moment of passion. Breathing heavily, they peel off each other's clothes. Yumi's garments are crumpled on the ground by her feet.

Feeling the warmth of Toon's breath on her nipples send a warm sensation traveling under her skin. Toon lay her down in the grass. Toon slides between her silky thighs with impatience and a solemn expression on his face. Yumi's chest heaves as she burn in anticipation. She raises her hips, howling in pain, as the peak of Toon rushes into the dampness of her, spreading her open, stretching her walls out. Her face twists with pain and pleasure. Toon peppers her neck with moist kisses. The scent of her skin smells like berries.

Yumi holds his head, raking his hair, crying a soft love song, a melody that reassures him that he is pleasing her. Pulling out of her wetness, he turns her around, putting her in the doggy style position. She cocks her plump booty in the air, howling like a wounded cat, craving more of him. Sliding between her warm moist folds, he goes for the kill. His long, thick soldier sinks inside of her. Gripping her tiny waist, he drills her from the back whipping her with his dick. Her face winces in torment, her large wooden looped earrings is bouncing to their love making, and her full sized breasts are clapping together.

"Oooh mandin-go. Ooooh me love Amer'dican mandingo," Yumi cried in her heavy accent. Pussy juice squirts allover Toon's pelvis, glistening like honey on his pubic hair, as she cums over and over. Her pussy becomes looser and Toon's body jerks involuntarily, as he releases his juices inside of her womb. He folds up, laying on her smooth back. Yumi has the meanest pussy Toon has ever had. He never seen a woman cum like Yumi.

The couple lay in the grass in silence. Yumi lies on his muscular chest, as he stares at the sky, watching the the shimmering stars.

"Ya made me feel good. Dis was me first time doin' dis," Yumi admitted, listening to the sound of Toon's heart beat.

"You mean to tell me your a virgin?" Toon asked.

"Yes. Me father tell me I have ta wait 'til I get married. Me just turned twenty one years old last month. If me father find out you sleep wit' me, he'll kill ya."

"Huh. For what?"

"Here in our country, a father-" Yumi stops in mid-sentence, looking to her right.

"What's wro-" Toon stops in the middle of his speech in fright. He never seen a set of eyes that look so wicked. His body trembles allover.

"Be still, don't move," Yumi whispered, locking her focus on the black venomous snake with its yellow streak. The snake hisses, inching its way to Toon's face. His eyes widen in terror, as the venomous reptile springs back. Toon is no fool, he can sense that the snake is preparing for attack. It's fangs pops out slowly. Toon thinks about making a run for it. He knows that he isn't faster than the snake. Moving with great speed, the snake moves towards Toon's neck. Yumi's hand moves swiftly, gripping the snake by its neck, flinging it into the grass.

"Shit!" Toon shouted, climbing to his feet. Yumi laughs at a frightened Toon, finding it amusing. She has never seen a man afraid of a snake.

"Ya don't have ta be afraid. Me want let nothin' harm ya."

They put on their clothes and head back to the village while everyone is still sound asleep. The couple kisses each other before returning to their sleeping quarters.

Morning arrived in no time. Eddie, Motion, and Toon are preparing for their long trip back home. Shabba, Costa, and Yumi watches as they load their luggage into the Jeep Wrangler. Motion walks up to Shabba with his hand extended in front of him.

"I want to thank you for your hospitality. I really got the chance to learn more about your country. This is one experience that I will never forget as long as I live," Motion stated while shaking Shabba's hand.

"Hope ta see ya again sometime," Shabba said. Motion climbs into the jeep. Yumi gives Toon a hug and a kiss on the cheek.

"Me gon' miss ya," she whispered in his ear. Toon doesn't want to release her.

"I'ma miss you too baby. Maybe we will see each other one day in the future." They gaze into each other's eyes that are filled with sorrow.

Toon and Eddie jumps into the jeep joining Motion, the driver, and Canton. Canton will make sure the diamonds make it to the United States of America safely like Shabba promised.

The driver turns the key, bringing the engine to life. Shabba and his wife waves at them. Shabba says, "Hold on." He limps to the jeep staring at Toon. "Me never seen man afraid of snakes." A smile pulls at the corners of his mouth. Costa cuts in between them.

"Aye Motion," Costa shouted.

"What's up lil' man?"

"Westside 'til I die, thug life mi nigga."

"West world baby." Motion bumps his fist against his limb.

They pull off on their long journey, traveling down the bumpy unpaved road.

*   *   *

Traffic moves rapidly, as Scotty paces back in forth in front of the pretrial services department on Michigan Avenue. Running out of patience, Scotty makes his way up the block.

A silver Dodge Durango screeches, as it turns the corner, garnering Scotty's attention. The truck pulls up to the curb and the tinted window descends.

"Get in," the driver said, his face barely visible behind the half open window. Scotty glimpses over his shoulder making.sure that no one notices him. He opens the door and hops into the truck. The truck dips into to the bustling traffic.

The unmark vehicle is basically empty of all it's usual police equipment. A small radio crackles on the dash board, with the sound of a dispatcher. A strobe light sits on the dashboard in plain view.

"So Scotty, let me make this clear to you," Bodo said, turning down the volume on the scanner. "You know what I want right?" Bodo asked, watching Scotty out the corner of his eye.

"Naw, I don't know what you want," Scotty replied sarcastically, peering out the tinted windows of the Durango. The truck jerks, as Bodo maneuvers from one lane to another, pulling up to the curb. His reckless driving made his anger evident. He throws the truck into park and slams his hand on the dashboard.

"Look here damnit! I don't have no time for this bullshit!" Bodo snapped, unlocking the doors. "I'm not about to waste my time with you. It's a lot of motherfuckers that need my help. If you want to help yourself that's on you. I don't have to do the time, you do. I will go home to my family every night, while you are in prison rubbin' booty holes and elbows in the shower with a bunch of other convicts. Now, we're either going to do this or I can have your signature bond terminated and have you place back in custody," Bodo said, making himself clear. He watches the facial expression on Scotty's face, hoping that his words will have a positive influence on his decision.

"What is it that you want from me?"

"You know who I want," Bodo said, leaning closer to Scotty cracking an evil smile, staring in his eyes. "Motion that's who I want." With that being said, Scotty turns his head facing the window in deep thoughts.

"I don't know if I want to do that." Scotty continues to stare out the window, avoiding eye contact with Bodo.

"Get out," Bodo said, breaking the silence.

"Wait . . . Wait, if I give you Motion," he pluses for a moment, having flash backs of all the pussy that him and Motion shared, the things they use to do together, the way Motion treated him good, and the good food that Ms. Hopson used to cook for them.

"What can you do about this case?" Scotty asked, praying that Bodo can save him from doing a lot of time behind bars.

"Have you ever heard that I walk on water. I'm like Jesus, I can make a lot of miracles happen," Bodo proclaimed.

"Well, I heard that you can keep a muthafucka from going to jail."

"As long as you give me what I want, I'll give you what you want," Bodo stated with a wicked smile growing on his face.

Still in deep thought, Scotty knows that his freedom is at steak. Scotty replies, "What is it that you want me to do?"

"Now we talkin' business." Bodo removes a cigar from his shirt pocket. "This is what I need you to do."

CHAPTER NINE

Miami Beach, Florida

Motion stands behind Ayesha with his arms looped around her small waist, occupying the private balcony of the beach front home that he purchased in Florida. They are enjoying the beautiful, colorful, tropical sunset.

Tall palm trees are swaying, being pushed by the gentle breeze. Emerald green water ripples, slapping against the sandy white shore. Ayesha's long, thick, wavy, jet black hair flutters, being teased by the wind. A cool soft breeze whispers in her ears. The breeze picks up the edge of her skirt, fluttering it aside, unveiling her smooth, silky, muscular calves. The powerful scent of her erotic perfume lingers in the air. Her high heeled fuck me pumps makes her three inches taller, matching Motion's height.

"Just look at the beautiful site baby. This is what I call livin'. I told you from day one that I was gon' take you to the top. Pretty soon I'll be out the game for good."

"I hope so baby," Ayesha said, gazing at the panoramic views, caressing Motion's hands.

"You know I have always been a man of my word. Every promise that I made to you I kept. I'm just ready to live life and grow old with you. I know I can't keep livin' this lifestyle. I ain't met nobody that had longevity in this game. Once you make a career out of the dope game it leads to only two things, either jail or death. I don't wanna be just another statstic. I wanna be a father to our daughter and protect her from this dog eat dog world. I wanna be there for you, the woman I love with all my heart. You made so many sacrifices for me and tolerated my shit over the years. It's nothin' in the world that I wouldn't do for you. Out of all people you been there for me through thick and thin. You never once turned yo' back on me. You was there when I didn't have shit, I'll never forget that baby. It's until death do us apart . . . I mean that baby." Motion expressed himself with heartfelt words.

"I'm going to always be down with you baby no matter what you choose to do. I got your back forever. You can always count on me. I'm glad that you finally see the light. I can't afford to lose you to the streets. Your the only one that I have in this world besides our daughter." Ayesha responded. Motion brushes her hair to the side, kissing her neck.

"Mmmm," she purred. His breath is like a tender brand against her delicate skin. Placing a hand on her hip, he nestles her against his pulsing erection. Motion tugs her earlobe into the warmth of his mouth, biting gently with his teeth. His dick twitches. He wants to fuck the shit out of her badly. He whispers against her heated flesh, feasting on the long column of her neck. Slowly his hand slips under her skirt, climbing between her luscious thighs. Her limbs tremble as his touch glides over her clit. Motion palms her breast with the other hand massaging it. She signs, a long, slow, satisfied breath of air.

Placing her hand on top of his, she controls the pace. Her other hand massages him through the fabric of his pants. A massive erection tents his Prada trousers. The clink of his belt buckle and the rasp of his zipper commingles with their simultaneous moans. Ayesha's panties fall to her heels. Motion's crumpled trousers rests at his ankles. His shoes and trousers sails across the private balcony hitting the floor with a thud. Pulling her skirt to her hips, she spreads her legs inviting his throbbing erection. He rubs his hard dick between her ass cheeks. The crown of his dick rubs against her moist pussy lips teasingly. Her hips dances in the rhythm of his touch. Heat soars inside her belly, then down her thighs. Motion sinks inside her hot pussy rotating his hips. She utters a suffocated little cry, gripping the banister for support, arching her back. Motion pulses inside her. Her warm pussy melts around him like liquid heat. She climaxes in a frantic, seething orgasm. An explosion erupts inside her and spreads like wild fire. Ayesha's moans ars close to being frantic as he drills her with no remorse. Creamy rivulet are sliding down her thick, flawless thighs, an indication of her feverish arousal. His balls slaps against her ass cheeks. Growling like a wild beast, he moves faster and faster. She moans a super sexy sound driving him crazy.

"Oooooh baby, I-I'm about t-to . . . come shit," she cried in estascy. Motion's mouth drops open, as he releases his juices inside of her wetness. Panting heavily, he spins her around, leading her to the leather lounge chair. He spreads her legs, her crisp bush opens to him. A hint of pink glistens. Droplets of moisture gleams on her curly pubic hairs like dew. Her chest sucks in and out, as she pants. The warmth of Motion's tongue grazing her thighs, ignites a fire deep inside of her. His mouth closes over her throbbing clit. With his face buried between her legs, he licks her half hidden little clit that is peeking out her fat pussy lips. Her body reacts with a rush of moisture.

Tucking his hands under her, he squeezes her two firm globes. Her ass cheeks are warm and slippery with her sex juices. She squirms and wiggles her butt, trying to escape his gratifying touch. Watching him through her eyelashes, she sees the reflection of their bodies on the sliding glass patio doors.

Ayesha explodes with another powerful orgasm. A loud orgasmic whimper pours from her vocal cords, as he whips her clit with his tongue. She falls into an orgasmic daze, shaking involuntarily. Motion's magic stick rises again, hearing the sound of her cries.

They switch positions. Ayesha straddles him, placing his towering dick inside her hot pussy. Her french manicured fingernails drags across his muscular shoulders. She rides the hell out of him, moaning, tossing her head, rotating her hips, moving wildly in a zone. Her lengthy hair cascades over her shoulders and down her back. After long hours of love making, they retire in the luxurious master suite.

The early morning sound of the birds singing their soft melody crones. The warm early morning breeze leaps into the mastersuite through the ajar sliding glass doors. A warm soft compassionate breeze kisses Motion's and Ayesha's naked bodies, as they lie in the circular, cushy bed that Motion had imported from London.

Quietly, Motion climbs out of the bed. He pads across the plush carpet, heading to the walk-in-closet.

Stepping out of the closet, he tosses on his heavy robe with his initals embroidered in it. Ayesha is sprawled on the bed sleeping peacefully. Motion creeps out of the mastersuite.

After returning from Sierra Leone, Motion met Ayesha at O'hara International airport in Chicago and they made a one way flight to Florida. Motion made a promise to Ayesha that he refuses to break.

Ayesha tosses and turn under the satin sheets. Rome's "I belong to you" flows out of the surr6und sound system. Ayesha's eyes flicks open to the site of Motion standing in front of her, holding a bed-tray, situated with two plates. Both plates have stainless steel covers over them, making what's on the plate invisible.

Gazing into Ayesha's slanted eyes, Motion says, "Good morning baby." A smile spreads across her face.

"Good morning to you," she replied, "What is this, breakfast in bed?"

"You can call it that my love," Motion responded, placing the breakfast onto the bed-tray on her lap. He climbs into the bed joining her. Ayesha sniffs the air anticipating the pleasant smell of freshly cooked breakfast, but she is disappointed. Motion removes a small remote from the pocket of his robe and presses a button. The revolving round bed with its remote control movement rotates, spinning like a carousel, facing the sliding glass doors, giving them a panoramic view of the sparkling water, being touched by the rising sun.

Ayesha lifts the stainless steel plate cover. Her eyes expand as she studies the plate in admiration, expecting a hot breakfast to appear.

"Awww, how sweet, a teddy bear. Thank you baby, but I don't think I can eat this," Ayesha responded, trying to figure out what he is up to.

"I know that baby," Motion chuckled. "Gon' and squeeze it baby."

Ayesha squeezes the teddy bear and a recording comes to life.

"Will you marry me?" the mouth on the teddy bear moves. Ayesha shifts her head, staring at Motion in shock. She never expected for Motion to purpose to her so soon.

"Yes baby. I've been waiting for you to ask me that for years. I never thought this . . . day would come."

"Since the answer is yes, I want you to lift the other plate cover."

Lifting the plate cover, Ayesha is blinded by a huge diamond ring. The early morning sun rays are beaming through the glass doors striking the exquisite princess cut diamond, making it sparkle unbelievably hard.

Motion had the diamond cut in Sierra Leone. He flew a diamond cutter in from Belguim, when he was in Sierra Leone. The diamond is so big and flawless that it would make Kobe's wife jealous.

Ayesha has a lot of diamonds that Motion bought her, but she has never seen an engagement ring or any other ring with so much clarity.

Her eyes becomes misty, as she stares at the ring in a hypnotic trance. Motion removes the ring off the plate and places it on her left hand.

"From this day it's just me and you. I'll never let anything come in between us. Your love is a touchstone of my existence. Your love breath life into me each and everyday. From the first day we met, I knew that our friendship would blossom into somethin' everlasting. Our love is a union of two spirits destined for eternal happiness. Baby you have become the star of my life that brings me warmth in this cold world. I'll cherish you and love you for eternity. I wish I knew of another way to express the love I possess for you, but words can't express the true essence of my love that I have for you.

Each time I gaze into your eyes, I'm drawn into the farthest reaches of your mind's inner world. There, I find a land of compassion, of understanding and of love. Without you Ayesha, my life would be empty of all inspiration. There wouldn't be no work of art for me to gaze at, no one to share life with, no one to share my treasures with, and no timeless melody to listen too. You mean the world to me baby. I promise you nothin' but happiness. The love that I have for you will continue to live even when death do us apart. No matter what . . . it's me and you until the end."

*   *   *

The crystal clear sound of Mary J. Blige's voice floats from the factory sound system. Shasha rocks her head to the rhythm of the music. Sitting behind the steering wheel of her Benz truck, she waits patiently at the busy intersection for the light to turn green. Peering through the front windshield, Shasha spots the Pepsi blue BMW 760 that she seen a couple of days ago.

The foreign whip is parked in the parking lot in front of Walmart. Shasha notices something strange going on. Scotty's Jaquar is parked next to the BMW. Shasha has been trying to contact Scotty for the last couple of days. She never known Scotty not to answer his phone.

Shasha puts on her blinker and dips into the turning lane. She guides the Benz truck into the crammed parking lot, watching the two cars closely from a distance. Scotty climbs out of the BMW, glimpsing over his shoulders nervously. The BMW pulls out of the parking lot. Its chrome rims flickers, as it mixes in with the heavy traffic. Shasha rolls down her window calling Scotty's name. Scotty turns around, startled by the sound of her voice.

"I been tryna get in touch with you for the last couple of days papi. Where you hidin' at?" Shasha queried, watching a paranoid Scotty. He walks up to her truck.

"I was spendin' some quality time with my family," he lied.

"You know papi with the blue Beamer?"

"Yeah, I know 'em. I met him through Elane. He brought some weight from me a couple of times."

"Are you sure papi straight?"

"Yeah, he good. Why you asked me that?"

"Because I ran into him the other day comin' out of the police station. He said he was filing a police report because somebody broke in his car, but I didn't see nothin' wrong with his car. It's somethin' strange about him. I don't trust him papi. You make sure you be careful," Shasha said.

"He straight, but I'ma have my man check him out," Scotty said, scoping his watch.

"Make sure you do that. I'm tellin' you papi, somethin' is not right about him."

"Thanks for lettin' me know. Where you headed to?"

"I'm on my way to my mother's house. She been cryin' about me not comin' to see her."

"I feel that. Well, you gon' and check on yo' moms. I gotta get out of here. Just hit me up if you need somethin'. Motion and Toon should be back in a minute."

"A'ight. I'll call you and let you know if I hear anything about papi."

"A'ight cool."

*   *   *

It's a bright sunny day in June. The sun shimmers, bathing the large grassy field behind Madison High School. Families and friends are gathered around at the large ceremony supporting the graduates. The trees crackle being pushed by the soft spring breeze. Standing in silence, the audience watches as the common cement speaker announces the names of the graduates.

"Unfortunately one of the graduates is not in attendance. So I would like to give a round of applause to Donald Crumb for doing an outstanding job."

The large throng of supporters comes to life, breaking the silence by clapping their hands. Some of the people in the crowd are holding banners in the air that says, "Happy Graduation." Faces gleam with triumphant as they cheer. The commencement speaker stands on the stage beside the principle and the Valedictorian, holding the microphone. The principle hands the commencement speaker another diploma. The audience waits in silence for him to read off the next name. One graduate stands in between his parents nervous, chewing on his fingernails. The graduates that where already called stands on the stage, holding their diplomas, with their green graduation hat's covering their skulls. Their green robes cover the attire that they are wearing.

"This graduate here has been very outstanding and has stayed on the honor roll through the entire year. This is a very unique kid. Give it up for Elliott . . . Hopson."

The audience erupts, whistling, and hooting as Elliott approaches the stage in his tailor made Palzileri suit with matching gators. The principle's shiny bald head gleams as the sun bathe him. Elliott stares at his signature handlebar mustache, as he shakes the principle's hand.

Flashes of light dances around in the crowd, as the supporters snap pictures. Motion stands in the crowd beside Ayesha, Joy, Ms.Hopson, and Dirty Red. The Tiffany diamonds on Motion's platinum pinky ring twinkles, as he puts his hands to his mouth cheering for his little brother.

Ms. Hopson gazes through misty eyes, watching Elliott receive his diploma. This is the day that she has been anticipating has finally arrived. She stands there proudly, dashing the tears away from her eyes.

"My baby finally made it. He's going to college," Ms. Hopson whispered to herself. Ayesha embraces Ms. Hopson's hand, sharing the joyful moment with her.

A light wind tosses Ayesha's long silky hair. She brushes it out of her face, squinting from the beaming sun. Tears spill over Bridget's eyelashes, coursing down her unblemished skin. Elliott and Bridget are standing on the stage holding each other, with their diplomas clutched in their hands. The commencement speaker prepares to announce the final graduate.

"Uut uum." He clears his throat, unwrapping the manilla envelope. "Now, I would like t-" A loud booming sound overpowers the loud speakers, shaking the earth. Everyone divert their eyes to the advancing 71' Buick Riviera Boattail. Its cherry red, candy paint shines like a wet Jollyrancher. Its loud chrome tail pipes growls, sounding like a baby jet. Tall polished chrome rims flashes under the candy painted frame, sitting high. The driver of the monstrous old school automobile sticks his hand out of the window slapping the stop sign. The stop sign wobbles, making a metallic sound. Under the microscope of attention, he presses his feet down on the gas pedal, pulling onto the grassy surface.

Elliott focuses on the car as it parks in the grass. The driver jumps out of the old school looking like a midget, as he stands next to it. With the music still blasting, he pulls off his dark stunner shades, glimpsing around, scanning the large crowd of supporters. Three other occupants in the vehicle bob their head to the music.

All the graduates standing on the stage recognizes Donald Crumb. He is the most popular kid at the school. It is rumored that he is a drug dealer. He had some of the finest girls in school. His crispy braids zig zags on his head parted to perfection. The VVS1 's in his earlobes sparkles uncontrolably. All of his threads are made by Argyle. Throughout the entire school year, never once did he wear the same pair of shoes.

Donald always envied Elliott because he has the finest girl in school. Everytime he caught Bridget by herself, he would try to game her. He knows that Bridget is dedicated to Elliott. Donald considers Elliott as his only competition in school. Donald made a promise to himself that he will one day have Bridget by any means.

Donald's right hand man Rip jumps out of the old school dancing to the rhythm of the blaring music, doing the crip walk, with his lips folded in his mouth, resembling Snoop Dogg. A security guard breaks through the crowd making a gesture with his hands, signaling for them to turn the music off. Donald fiddles in his pants pocket, pulling out a small electronic device. Aiming it at the car, he pushes a button shutting the music off. His lips curve into a smile, as he stares at the security guard.

"Anything else I can help you with?" Donald asked. Glaring at Donald, the security guard doesn't respond to his sarcasm. The security guard turns around and they resume with the ceremony.

The commencement speaker calls the last graduate. The audience hoots and hollers as they stand on the stage in their graduation gowns. They all fall into formation with their hats in hand.

"At the count of three."

"One! Two! Three!" they count together, tossing their hats in the air. Graduation balloons floats in the air, being released by the cheerful supporters. All of the graduates steps off the stage joining their families and friends, celebrating victory. They huddle around in groups embracing each other.

Elliott and Bridget embrace Ms. Hopson and Bridget's parents with a warm loving hug. Ms. Hopson looks into Elliott's deep brown eyes in tears.

"Baby I'm so proud of you," Ms.Hopson said in a motherly tone.

"I told you I wasn't gon' let you down mama. This mean a lot to me." Elliott was accepted to Harvard University.

"Come here lil bro," Motion said. Elliott steps up to Motion, Ayesha, Dirty Red, and Joy, gripping them with a firm hug.

"Mommy, Uncle Elliott gra'wait," Joy blurted, flashing her almond shaped eyes. Bridget and her parents film her on the camcorder. Ayesha takes pictures of Ms. Hopson, Motion, and Elliott with her camera phone.

A spanking brand new pearl white Mercedes Benz CLS550 equipped with 22 inch chrome shoes pulls next to Donald's old school glistening. Donald's jaws drop as he observes the foreign machine. Eyes expand as the onlookers admire the luxurious whip. A man hops out of the Mercedes with a large smile on his face. He tosses the keys to Elliott. Motion smiles, seeing the glow in his little brother's eyes.

"Uncle Scotttyy!" Joy shouted excitedly, running up to him. Scotty scoops her up, holding her in the air. He kisses her on her dimpled cheek.

"Aye lil mama."

Scotty always gives Joy anything she want. Scotty's sister always baby sits Joy and Scotty Jr.

Elliott clutches the keys in his hand. "What's this?"

"That's you lil' bro. Happy graduation," Motion replied.

"What! You fo' real?"

Motion chuckles at his facial expression. "Of course I'm fo' real." Elliott gives Motion and Scotty a hug.

"I'm proud of you famm. You know I'll do anything for you," Scotty proclaimed. Scotty always accepted Elliott as his younger brother.

"Thank y'all."

"Give those keys back, I don't want you drivin' that car," Ms. Hopson cut in.

"Come on mama, don't be like that. This is my graduation gift from my big brother. I did good, so let me enjoy myself for a change. I'm on my way to college, I'm not a kid anymore," Elliott pleaded.

"Yeah mama, let him enjoy his self," Motion added.

"I don't want my baby to get in any trouble behind this car."

"Mama he ain't gon' get in no trouble. Besides, he won't be in Milwaukee too much longer," Motion advocated.

"Yeah mama," Elliott said, looking at his concerned mother.

"Okay," Ms. Hopson said, feeling sorry for her baby boy.

"You make sure you be careful in that car." *Maybe I need to loosen up on him a little and let him enjoy this special day.* Elliott grips his mother with a tight hug.

"Thanks mama."

Elliott hops into the car sinking in the oatmeal leather interior. Gripping the steering wheel, he admires the car. Bridget climbs into the passenger seat joining him.

Donald's facial expression changes, as he figures out what just occurred. Jealousy is written allover Donald's face.

Elliott sticks his head out of the window. "Y'all ready to roll? My stomach is in my back."

"Lets go," Motion said. Dirty Red limps behind Motion, as they make their way to Motion's Bentley coupe Ms. Hopson follows behind them in her PT Cruiser. A strange feeling travels through her body, as she watches Elliott bend the corner in the Mercedes.

* * *

Vegas brushes imaginary wrinkles out of his Giorgio Armani blazer, that coordinates with his chocolate colored David Eden shoes. He grabs a small box off the concrete table that contains all of his important paperwork and makes his way to the steel doors that read "Receiving & Deliver". Pushing the intercom button next to the door, a officer speaks through the intercom.

"Are you ready to go Mr. Hawkins?"

"What you think?" Vegas replied sarcastically, staring at the small square tinted window that hides the officer's face.

"Well, you take it easy out there. I heard it's kinda fucked up on them streets," the officer stated, pressing the button, unlocking the doors. Walking through the door, Vegas says, "Yeah, heard that too, but it's only hard for those that make it hard on themselves. And like the old saying goes, 'The world makes way for a man who knows where he's goin'" With that being said, Vegas exits through another door, making his way down the corridor. As he gets closer and closer to his freedom, his David Edens glides across the pavement with a smooth clacking sound.

He spots Shakedown and some of the other officers that are against everything he stands for. He can read the envy in their eyes as they try their best to conceal their true feelings. ***I'm glad I'll never see any of these racist mutha fuckas ever again in life.***

"Vegas buddy, I hate to see you go so soon. I was just about to get me a new car with all that little extra money I was making off of you," Shakedown said, walking towards Vegas, twirling his keys in his hand.

"Sorry to say, but that fake ass jailhouse hustlin' we had goin' on is over wit'," Vegas said, peering through the windows of the front lobby.

"If you really wanna make some real money walk with me outta this mafucka." Vegas struts through the gated pathway that has shiny razor wire spiraling along the top of the fence. Running closely behind Vegas, Shakedown slowly comes to a stop and says,

"Well, I'll be damn!!" He stares at a stretched Hummer H2 with gigantic chrome wheels.

"Now that is how a real businessman get down," Vegas stated, standing in front of the entrance holding the small box in his hands. The Hummer pulls up closer to the entrance. The shiny rims glistens, being kissed by the shimmering sun. The back door slowly pops open. A pair of red Jimmy Choo Merrit pumps digs into the graveled surface, as a woman slowly climbs out of the luxurious vehicle with the door concealing her upper body. Vegas stares at a beautiful Elane, hypnotized by her presence. He never thought that this day would come. She prances in his direction in a red Dereon cat suit with her arms open welcoming his embrace. They've been longing for this moment for seven years.

"Heyy baby." Elane greets him with misty eyes, rushing over to Vegas, embracing with a warm firm hug and a passionate kiss. Vegas drops the box that was in his hands, as he grips the love of his life inhaling the fresh sweet scent of her perfume. Vegas can't believe that he is a free man.

Elane whispers in his ears, "Don't get scared now baby, grab that ass, it's all yours." He lifts her in the air gripping her bubblicious ass kissing her allover her neck. She encircles him with her strong muscular legs.

"Mmmm, I misse'd you so . . . much," he proclaimed.

"Uh hmmm, excuse me," Jaurice interrupts the entwined lovers, sticking his head out of the door.

"I know my man been gone fo' a minute, but can't y'all do that shit later?"

Vegas hear Jaurice's voice and becomes excited, pulling away from Elane's embrace, as he guides her back to the doors of the stretched Hummer. Vegas has always treated Jaurice like his son. Vegas taught Jaurice the game at a young age. Jaurice has always looked up to Vegas.

"My nigga, you know it's on right?" Vegas said, holding Elane's hand, helping her inside the truck.

"Hell yeah it's on. M-" Before Juaurice could finish his words, Shakedown yells out.

"Vegas you forgetting something." Shakedown bends over retrieving the box. He heads towards the Hummer. He extends his arms, holding the box in front of Vegas.

"Naw, that's you. It might come in handy for you one day. I know you tired of workin' this bullshit ass job. So, just follow the directions inside the box and you might become very successful one day." Vegas close the door leaving Shakedown standing there motionless, holding the box in his hands puzzled. The streteched Hummer pulls off slowly exiting the parking lot.

Standing in the middle of the lot, Shakedown rips open the box. He scans a bunch of papers with numbers and graphs on them. In the corner of the box, he sees a tiny piece of paper that reads, "Directions." He reads the piece of paper.

"I really don't get down like this by helping the police do their dirty work, but since you made my time easy, I'm gon' make yo life a little easier. I left a cell phone in my old cell with my roommate. Give him a new one and take that one. Press speed dial 2 and you will get E-Trade stock market. Ask for Mark and tell him your one of Vegas' boys. He's going to open you up an E-Trade account. I already gave him ten thousand dollars for you to start off with. In the next six months or so, that ten thousand dollars will shoot up to three hundred thousand. How I know? I made over 6 million dollars in the last seven years of my incarceration and I couldn't have done it without you. So enjoy your wealth and make the best of it. I'm out."

Shakedown stuffs the piece of paper into his pocket and hurries back inside the prison.

The lights dances all inside of the truck making it look like a ballroom. Elane cracks open a bottle of Ace of Spade and pours the three of them a glass.

"To my man who stayed strong and held his grounds," she proclaimed, passing everyone a glass.

"To a real stand up dude," Jaurice said, leaning back in his seat, having no knowledge of Elane setting up Scotty.

Vegas leans forward with his elbow on his knees.

"First I like to thank myself for being who I am and gettin' paid while I sat in that fucked up ass place they call prison. Now that I'm free, I have bigger plans. The streets better be prepared because I'm about to shit on the city. Let's toast." They all raise up their glasses. "At the count of three we gon' say money." Vegas said, knowing that he got $11.2 million waiting on him in an offshore bank account. "One, two, three," he counted.

"Money." They said in unison tapping glasses. The clinking sound of toasting commingles with the sound of Shorty Low "They Know" escaping the sound system.

Vegas was granted immediate release after going back to court on a Rule 35 motion. He had Elane assist his agents on his behalf. Vegas feels like a lucky man to have Elane on his team. Elane has earned the title of a down ass bitch.

Marco leans back in his drop top 72' Chevy Caprice, gripping the woodgrain steeringwheel. He flicks on his blinker, switching lanes traveling down Wisconsin Avenue. His girlfriend Titianna relaxes in the passenger's seat with roving eyes, taking in the scenery. Her long curly hair dances in the wind as they jump on the expressway.

Marco took Titianna to a play at the Riverside Theater entitled "Love Street." They had a good time and enjoyed each other's companionship. He fell in love with her over the four months of them dating. She is everything that Marco could ever want in a woman. She has an unblemished vanilla complexion, full sized breasts, thick full lips, and naturally curly hair. It looks like she is mixed with another nationality, but she is full blooded African-American. The thing that Marco loves most about her is her personality and sense of humor.

The 572 big block growls under the hood as Marco presses down on the gas pedal, dipping in the turning lane. The 26 inch flat face rims chop, as he slows down, exiting the expressway, bending the corner. After bending a few corners, Marco pulls up in front of Titianna's house. The illuminating street lights casts shadows of light on his lemon lime paint job. Usher's "Move Mountains" floats out of the sound system. Marco can't help but notice Titianna's long pretty eyelashes, as she rumbles through her Chanel tote bag for her house keys.

Marco hops out of the car, opening the passenger door for Titianna. He is the first man to ever open doors for her. Every time that they're together, he treats her like a queen. Their shadows shift on the pavement as they strut to the front door. He towers over her as they stand face to face on the porch. She tilts her head back, as they study each other's eyes in silence. The bushes move with a soft crackle being pushed by the warm summer breeze. Her mouth parts as she continues to gaze into his eyes. His mouth moves intently against her lips, tasting them with delicious slowness. She curves her arm around his neck pulling him closer. Lingering in each other's arms, they kiss long and passionate.

An unknown man is parked down the street in a dark blue Dodge Magnum, observing the two lovers engaging in a compassionate moment. The man sits an electronic communication device in his lap. He watches them closely as they go their separate ways. As soon as Marco pulled off, disappearing around the corner, the man slowly pulls up to Titianna's residence.

*　　*　　*

Gambino's Italian restaurant is packed with a large throng of customers. Silverware clinks together and the clattering sound of the gossiping customers fills the atmosphere. Waiters and waitresses bustle from table to table, assisting the customers. Large chandeliers shine brightly hanging from the hand carved ceiling, reflecting off the tall champagne glasses making them sparkle. Red table cloth drapes over each neatly organized table, ruffling on the sides touching the floor, hiding the table base on each table.

Scotty and his mistress are seated across from each other in the midst of the other customers, who are predominantly German.

"Did you make those arrangements for us to take that trip to the Bahamas? You know I'm really lookin' forward to it. And you know we have to be careful, I don't want to get into it with that crazy ass bitch you got at home," she said, twirling the ice around in her glass with her long artistic fingernail.

"Don't worry about that baby, let me handle this. I got it under control," Scotty said with confidence, looking into the woman's eyes.

"Let you handle it huh?" She slips her finger inside her mouth and pulls it out slowly, staring at Scotty with a seductive look burning in her eyes. "You sure you can handle it baby."

"I can handle anything baby."

"Oh yeah." She fishes an ice cube out of her glass, placing it inside her mouth flirtatiously with her eyes partially closed. Scotty swivels his head, diverting his eyes to the older white woman, who has long burnette hair and brown eyes. She is seated next to an older white man that is much older than her. Scotty shifts his eyes staring at the now empty chair that his mistress was seated in. He glimpses around with searching eyes. *Damn, where the fuck she go that quick?* Scotty's question is answered as the smooth ripping sound of his flyer being unzipped cuts through the air. He can feel the gentle touch of her silky hands, as she fondles his rock hard throbbing erection.

Scotty loves his mistress adventurous side. She knows how to keep him curious and interested. He likes to take risk and live on the edge. Scotty doesn't have any intentions on leaving the dope game, especially since he has a license to sell dope.

He can feel her warm hot breath, as she slowly swallows his dick inch by inch. A low groan emits from him. "Mmmm." He scans the faces of the customers, who doesn't have any idea of what is going on under the table.

He places his hand under the table, cupping the back of her head. Having a hard time keeping a straight face, Scotty fixes his eyes on the older white woman with the burnette hair who continues to gaze in his direction. The lady winks her eye at him holding her thumb up with a smile on her face. Scotty returns a smile, pretending like he is reading the menu.

His mistress is bobbing her head sucking his dick like a pro. A warm sensation travels around under his skin. A waitress prances over to his table in her white apron, carrying a tray in her hands with a stack of dirty plates on it.

"Excuse me sir," the waitress said politely with a warm friendly smile on her face. "Are you enjoying your meal?" she asked.

Scotty is in the middle of busting a nut.

"Y-Yes . . . It is . . . I mean was good," Scotty stuttered, his face crinkling up.

"Sir, are you okay?" she asked, towering over him with a look of confusion. His mistress swallows every drop of his cum.

"Yeah . . . I'm okay. I just had somethin' on my mind," he lied.

"Well, if I can help you or your companion with anything just let me know."

"A'ight." Scotty smiles at the waitress as she walks off. Scotty's mistress peeks from under the table cloth before coming from underneath the table, returning to her seat.

"You crazy as hell," Scotty stated, watching her as she pulls out her tiny personal sized mirror out of her purse, fixing her lipstick.

"You ain't seen nothin' yet baby. Just make sure you arrange for our trip next week."

"I'm looking forward to it," he said, placing a fifty dollar tip on the table. "I guess we betta get out of here, it's gettin' kinda late. I know the baby mama gon' be blowin' up my cell phone in a minute."

"Well, lets ride than baby."

They exit Gambinos after paying for the meal.

*   *   *

The shiny 72' Chevy Caprice glimmers as it moves through traffic. Marco rocks his head to the rhythm of the music that is escaping the powerful subwoofers. Heads turn as the heavy deep, bass drops hard, sounding like a stampede of dinosaurs running down the street shaking the earth.

The indigo blue screen on Marco's cell phone flashes, attracting his attention. Picking up the phone, he recognizes Titianna's phone number on the screen along with her picture. He turns down the volume on the powerful sound system and answers the call.

"Hello." Titianna cries on the other end.

"Marc-" He hears a loud crashing sound and the line goes dead.

"Titianna!" Marco shouts into the phone receiving no response. His heart drums' against his chest, he drops the cell phone in his lap and smashes down on the gas pedal making a U-turn in the middle of the street. The screeching sound of his tires startles the onlookers. The needle on the speedometer bounces, as he storms down Appleton Avenue, heading to Titianna's house. The 572 big block engine growls like an angry pitbull. Turning the corner, he spots three police cars in front of Titianna's residence. The 26 inch rims under his candy painted frame glides across the pavement, as he comes to a screeching halt in the middle of the street. He notices her front door knocked off it's hinges. He jumps out of the car jogging to her front door. Before he is able to make it to her door, he is blinded by a flash of light.

"Freeezeee!" An officer in plain clothes aims a black 9 millimeter at Marco. "Get on the fucking ground!" the pale face officer bellowed.

"Man what's goin' on?" Marco asked, disregarding the officer's orders.

"I said get on the fucking ground now!" he snarled, watching Marco as he gets on the ground slowly.

"Man I'm just comin' to check on my fiance."

"Shut the fuck up you woman beater!" The officer shouted, planting his knee in Marco's back. He grimaces in pain as the officer handles him rough.

"Wait officer! You got the wrong person!" Titianna exclaimed in tears, standing in the doorway. The officer was in the middle of placing Marco in handcuffs. The officer holsters his gun and help Marco off of the ground.

"Sorry about that sir," the officer apologized. The sound of his police radio crackles with the voices of dispatchers. Marco dusts the dirt off of his clothes. The only thing that he is concerned about is Titianna. If it wasn't for her, he would've cursed the officer out.

He wraps his arms around a crying Titianna. She lays her head on his chest, hiding the bruises on her face. Marco grips her chin with his thumb and index finger.

"Look at me sweetheart," he said. Reluctantly she looks into his eyes that are broadcasting genuine concern. He observes the purple and black bruises around her eyes that doesn't have much of an effect on her beautiful facial features.

"Don't feel embarrassed baby. No matter what, you'll always be beautiful in my eyes. You don't have to worry no more as long as I'm here. I won't let nobody ever hurt you again . . . I promise," Marco sincerely expressed. Tears blur her vision as she studies the face of the man that she grew to love dearly. Wiping the tears from her eyes, he eases her frantic worried mind.

"Ma'am, we have all the information we need for now. Just come to the station to file for a restraining order." An officer said, walking out of her house with a pad of paper and a camera in his hand.

"Okay."

"Are you sure you going to be okay here by yourself?" Marco cuts in answering the question for her.

"Yeah, she gon' be a'ight. I'ma stay here with her."

"Oh well, if you have any more problems out of that maniac just call us back."

"A'ight." The officers make their way back to their patrol cars, leaving Marco and Titianna standing on the porch.

"Come on baby, let's go inside. You get some rest and I'll take care of this mess."

"Thank you baby."

"You don't have to thank me baby, this is my job to take care of my queen. Now, gon' and get some rest." Titianna smiles through all the pain, stepping inside the house feeling secure.

*   *   *

The soft humming sound of the dryer twirling crones, as Kanisha leans over sorting out the dirty clothes, placing them in individual piles. Usually she be sleep at this time, but for some reason she is tireless. Digging through the half empty hamper, she notices a stain on Scotty's wifebeater. Kanisha holds the white garment close to her face examining it carefully. Her heart drops to the bottom of her stomach, as she plasters her ebony brown eyes on the lavendar purple stain in the state of turmoil. A sting of tears are pricking behind her eyes. *I can't believe that dirty bitch been fuckin' my man behind my back. I'ma kill Scotty and that trifling ass bitch.* Kanisha sprints up the stairs heading to the kitchen. Grabbing a knife out of the drawer, she makes her way to their mastersuite with several different emotions racing through her head.

Kanisha steps inside Scotty's walk-in-closet, snatching all of his designer clothes off of the framework of bars in rage. Flinging his shoes out of the closet, she knocks over the ceramic lamp that was sitting on the nightstand. The lamp crashes to the floor bursting into shards of pieces.

The bedroom door swings open gaimng Kanisha's attention. Her eyeballs roll setting on the doorway.

"Mommy why you cryin'?" Scotty Junior asked, looking into his mother's tear stained face. Her hands are trembling as she clutches Scotty's sabotaged Prada blazer.

"Mommy just a little upset Junior," she admitted.

"Daddy make you upset again?" he questioned, his round gleamy eyes blink, as he waits for a response. He stands in the doorway in his Spiderman pajamas. Kanisha thinks about lying to him, but decides to tell him the truth.

"Yeah, it's your no good ass daddy."

"You catch him in bed on top of Aunt Sonja?" With a hanging mouth and eyes the size of headlights, Kanisha questions him.

"Where you get that from Junior?"

181

"Me saw daddy on top of Aunt Sonja when me wake up. Me hear her cryin'," Scotty Jr. replied.

Kanisha can't believe what she is hearing. His words slap her in the face like a bucket of cold water. A wave of nausea courses through her body.

"Junior go put on yo' shoes."

"Where we goin'?" he asked in curiousity.

"Don't question me, go put on yo' shoes," she snapped.

"Okay mommy."

Scooping up an arm full of Scotty's attire, she hurries to the master's bathroom tossing the clothes into the jacuzzi. Running back and forth, she piles half of his favorite outfits in the jacuzzi pouring bleach on them. The strong breath taking smell of bleach hugs the air.

Slipping on a pair of sweats, t-shirt, and house shoes, she rushes out of the house with Scotty Jr trailing behind her. Scotty Jr climbs into the back seat of the Cadillac CTS.

"Wait right here baby, mama'll be right back." Scotty Jr. sits in the dark peering through the window at an angry Kanisha.

She enters the heated garage with a wicked look on her face. Air spits from the tires of Scotty's Ferrari, as Kanisha kneels down slashing each one of the tires. Scanning the tools hanging up on the wall, Kanisha grabs a crowbar. She swings the crowbar with all of her strength busting out all the windows on the Ferrari and dents up the frame. The car is not insured because Kanisha forgot to go pay the bill for the month.

Stepping out of the garage, she prances back to her car opening the driver's door. The interior lights glow, shining on the charcoal gray leather interior. Slowly, the interior lights dim as the door closes.

"Mommy what took you so long?"

"Mommy had to take care of some business," she replied, sticking the car keys into the ignition. The engine comes to life. So many devious thoughts has her occupied as she smashes down on the gas pedal making her way to Sonja's house.

Turning the corner, she spots a car in front of Sonja's house. Its tail lights are shining with a soft glow. Her roving eyes lock on what appears to be the silhouette of a man and a woman from the faraway distance. Moving closer to the car allows her to get a better visual. The couple turns around aware of her presence. Fuming, Kanisha pulls up recklessly bumping the rearend of Scotty's Jaguar blocking him in.

She leaps out of the car rushing the passenger side of the Jaguar with the crowbar in hand. Glass rain on Sonja's lap, as Kanisha strikes the passenger window.

"Bitch, I'ma kill you! You triflin' ass hoe!" Kanisha shouts, swinging the crowbar repeatedly catching Sonja on the shoulder. Sonja jumps in Scotty's lap screaming, dodging the fierce blows. Kanisha leans inside the car with half of her body in the window.

"Get that crazy bitch!" Sonja shouted, her trembling fingers reaching for the door handle. Gripping the door handle, Sonja manages to open the door and climb out of the car running off. Scotty wraps his hand around Kanisha's wrist dragging her out of the car.

"Have you lost yo' fuckin' mind?" Scotty barked. The heavy platinum chains dangle on his neck clinging together, as he restrains a hysterical Kanisha, removing the crowbar from her hand.

"Let me go motherfucka! You sorry ass nigga! How you gon' fuck my bestfriend?"

"What you talkin' about? I was just givin' her a ride home," Scotty lied.

"Nigga save that shit! Junior told me he seen you . . . on top of Sonja in our bed! How c-could you do m-me like this. H-How you gon' disrespect me and fuck my bestfriend in our house, our bed and in f-front of our damn son. I'm done with yo' ass this time. I-I can't believe you," Kanisha cried. Scotty rubs his fingers through her hair. "Just leave me alone! I hate you!" She breaks loose from his embrace jumping in her car.

Her intense love and hate for him leaves her with conflicting emotions. Scotty stares at her dumb founded. It seems as if his whole life is falling apart.

Pulling up beside Scotty, Kanisha rolls down her window.

"Here you can have this back! Give it to that bitch!" She snatches the five carat diamond engagement ring off her finger and tosses it out of the window. The ring lands by his feet, sparkling on the pavement.

"Kanisha! Wait . . . I love you!" Scotty proclaimed, watching her, as she peels off.

*   *   *

The moon shimmers from the heavens, descending brightly upon Lake Michigan. The water sparkles, slapping against the base of the graffiti stained concrete slabs that Elliott and Bridget are sitting on. A cool, moist, fresh breeze of air melts against their skin. Bridget snuggles into the warmth of Elliott's arms. His arms tighten around her. Taking a deep breath, he inhales her intoxicating scent, as he does every time she's in his presence. Her hair brushes against his chin. Moving her lengthy hair to the side, he plants a soft, tender kiss on her naked shoulder.

"Elliott," Bridget whispered.

"Huh."

"I can't believe that were accepted to Harvard University."

"I can't believe it either. Maybe that is God's way of tellin' us we are meant to be together."

"That's the same way I see it. So have you decided if we are going to live on campus or find us an apartment?"

"Naw, I ain't decided, it ain't nothin' to decide."

"What you mean by that?" Bridget questioned, her eyebrows forming into check marks.

"Like I said baby, it ain't nothin' to decide. My brother already bought us a house one mile away from the campus." Bridget's mouth drops open in surprise.

"Are you for real?"

"Yep." A smile spreads across Elliott's face, hearing the sound of excitement lingering in her voice.

"Why you just now telling me?"

"I wanted to surprise you baby."

Hearing the word surprise come out of his mouth reminds her of what she been waiting to tell him.

"Speaking of surprise, it's something I need to tell you."

"I bet it's about the talk we had the other day, ain't it?" he guessed.

"Nope. It has nothing to do with that." Her facial expression changes. Elliott senses that something is wrong.

"Well, what is it baby?" Elliott gazes in her eyes with a questioning look.

"I'm pregnant." Looking at her in silence, Elliott forgets about the surprise that he has for her.

Studying her for a long moment, he finally says, "So what we gon' do baby? How we suppose to finish college with a baby on the way? We have to come up with somethin'."

"I thought about having an abortion," Bridget informed sadly.

"What! Baby we can't do that. I don't believe in abortions, that's takin' a life. We gotta deal with this another way."

"I already came up with a solution."

"And what's that?" Elliott asked.

"I'm having our baby. I had a long talk with my parents and they don't believe in abortions either. They said that they'll take care of our baby until we finish school. At first I thought they was going to be mad at me, but they was very understanding about the whole situation," Bridget explained.

A rush of happiness sizzles through him, as he studies her crystal brown eyes. He covers her hand with his in an enveloping caress, kissing her hand. Bridget twines her arms around his neck, as he lowers his lips to hers. The kiss turns into a series of moans, a languorous exploration. Elliott loses himself in Bridget's arms, surrendering to her fire, even as he exulted in his victory. Bridget clings to him with all her sleek strength, drawing him into her, he feels as if he'd stepped into another universe.

"I guess it's time for us to celebrate baby. Let's get out of here."

The headlights on Elliott's brand new Mercedes Benz blinks and the alarm chirps, as he presses a button on the keychain. Elliott opens the passenger door, letting Bridget inside the car. She melts in the leather interior of the luxurious whip, inhaling the fresh smell of pine and brand new leather.

Switching on the Mercedes' ignition, the engine purrs to life, instruments on the dashboard begins to glow a fluorescent orange. Leaning over, he activates the custom sound system. Keyshia Cole's "Sent From Heaven" spills out of the speakers. Bridget bobs her head rythmically, snapping her fingers, singing along with the song.

Sitting at the crowded intersection, waiting for the lights to turn green, Elliott gazes in Bridget's eyes as she sings to him.

"I wanna be the one you believe in your heart was sent from, sent from heaven. I wanna be the one you trust. I wanna be. I wanna be the one you need."

Studying the windows to her soul, Elliott can see the happiness and the joy gleaming in them. Bridget brought so much meaning into his life. He can't image what life would be like with her to share it with. A bright smile appears on his face, as she traces his lips with her finger. "I wanna be the one you believe in your heart. Sent from heaven." With his gentle touch, Elliott grabs her finger tips and kisses the back of her hand.

Carefully, he navigates the Benz through the congested traffic.

Bonk! Bonk! Car horns blare, as they ride bumper to bumper, hanging out of their windows, banging their music.

Elliott travels Westbound on Wisconsin Avenue, making a smooth right turn on 35th street. The Mercedes stands out, sparkling under the city lights. Elliott guides the foreign automobile into the gas station, with its fancy imported glimmering rims.

The gas station is cluttered with various automobiles. Elliott and Bridget is stealing all of the attention. A candy painted monstrous looking old school is parked across the street with two occupants in it, leaning back, observing Elliott and Bridget parked at the gas pump.

"Look at that nigga, frontin' like he ballin'. That nigga ain't never hustled a day in his life. If it whatn't for his brotha he wouldn't have shit. I got somethin' for that nigga," Donald said, displaying a wicked grin. Rip looks at Donald with a "why you hating" look.

"Man, what ol' boy do to you?" Rip questioned.

"He got somethin' that suppose to be mine," Donald replied.

"Man it's plenty bitches out there, nigga you trippin'."

Donald is speechless, he doesn't even truly know what he have against Elliott. Donald have always been jealous of Elliott.

Donald reaches into the console with a sneaky smile on his face and hops out of the car.

"Man you trippin'. That nigga ain't did nothin' to you," Rip said, watching Donald make his way across the street.

"Here baby. I'll pump the'gas and you pay," Elliott said, handing Bridget a fifty dollar bill.

"You want me to get you something to drink?" Bridget asked.

"Yeah, get me a Sprite." Bridget steps out of the car sporting her Rocawear skirt and a pair of high heeled tennis shoes. She prances into the gas station with her Tad's purse clutched under arm. Opening the cooler, she grabs an icy cold Sprite, and a kiwi strawberry juice.

The Arabian behind the bulletproof booth standing in front of the cash-register is eyeing her from head to toe. Like most of the Arabs, he watches her with lust buried deep in his eyes. *I wouldn't mind fucking her young tight pussy.* Bridget drops the money under the window and fumbles through her purse for coins.

The clapping sound of gunfire followed by the ear piercing sound of screeching tires cuts through the atmosphere, gripping Bridget's attention. Peering through the large glass windows, she notices that the lot is empty. Elliott's Mercedes is no longer in sight. Bridget's heart drums against her chest, as she trots to the door with a worrisome look plastered on her face. She sees the tail lights on Donald's old school as it rounds the corner.

Unbeknowst to her, a set of eyes are watching from the darkness. An unknown man is standing on the side of the gas station. He vanishes without being noticed.

Ms. Hopson's body jerks forward, as she awakes from her sleep. It feels as if someone had just kicked her in the heart. She is experiencing the same feeling that she had when the father to her boys was killed.

Climbing out of the bed, she puts on her robe and house shoes. Moving through the hallway, she makes her way to Elliott's room. Opening the door, she sees no signs of him. All she see is his neatly made bed. *Where this boy at? His tail should've been back by now. Please good lord, let my baby be alright.* Ms.Hopson picks up the cordless phone, dialing his cell phone number.

*   *   *

A cocaine white BMW 745 pulls up to the crowded front entrance of Club Sensation banging Young Jeezy. The powerful car system over powers everyone's conversation.

"I got that white girl, that Christina Aguilera." It's rose gold Asanti rims and rose gold grill flickers, being slapped by the street lights.

Tonight is a special night for Motion and his boys, who are celebrating their success in the game. V100's radio station van is parked outside the club.

Everybody that is standing in the long winding line has on several different designer clothes. Short skirts, cat suits, high heel pumps, gators, fat booties, big hips, thick thighs, slim, fat, meduim built men and women are all over.

A Mexican and black man with "414" tatted on the back of his shiny bald head steps out of the BMW dressed in a white mink wife beater, white mink shorts, and a pair of white hard bottomed Airforce ones. The rose gold candy around his neck and wrist is flooded with VVS1's.

Pulling out a thick wad of money, he drops a few bills in the extended hand of a valet attendant.

"Don't spend it all in one place playboy," he said, approaching the sidewalk.

A thick Russian girl with thick blond hair climbs out of the passenger seat of the quarter to eight in a white Chanel cat suit. The tight fitting outfit compliments her perfectly curved body, gaining the attention of men and women.

"God damn!" A man shouted from the line, admiring the Russian girl's flawless figure. The steady sound of her Roberto Cavalli pumps meeting the concrete is all that can be heard, as she strides across the sidewalk, looping her arm around her man's muscular biceps, that is tatted from wrist to shoulder with various artwork. Pushing her cat suit to the limit, she puts a majority of the sisters to shame.

"What's crackin' Twin?" the security staff greeted. They shake hands and snap fingers.

"You know what it is baby. Drivin' foreign and fuckin' foreign. They don't have to worry about spittin' at my bitch cause she don't speak they language." Twin and his Russian dime piece steps into to Club Sensation. Loud thunderous music shakes the dance floor. A large throng of people dances under the strobe lights. Large plasma screen televisions are hanging up behind the the L-shaped bar, displaying the crowded dance floor, looking like a scene on Soul Train.

The D.J mixes the music chatting on the microphone. "Are y'all having a good time out there? Let me hear y'all make some noise. This is Reggie Butler from V-100 live on the radio inside of Club Sensation. All the ladies free up until midnight. Come and enjoy the party of a life time. Free drinks all night long. Excuse me, how are you ladies doing tonight?" D.J Reggie Butler asked, staring at a group of woman.

"Fine," they replied in unison.

"What's your name sweetheart?" Reggie Butler asked.

"Nika."

"Are you enjoying yourself at Club Sensation?"

"Yeah."

"You have anybody you want to send a shot out too?"

"Yeah. My mom and my little sister Na-Na. I love y'all."

"Once again this is Reggie Butler live on the radio inside of Club Sensation. Ladies get in free up until midnight. Free drinks all night long. You must be twenty one years and older to get in. Whoa, look who just stepped into the building. It's Moe a.k.a the black Escobar and Mikie entering the building. They fresh out the fed joint. Lets give it up for them for holding it downnn!"

The crowd begins to shout as they make their way through the threshold of party goers. Flashes of light dances on the bezel of Moe's iced out Franc Vila watch with its titanium band. The candy that is draping down his chest reflects off the strobe lights.

Moe is a known legend in the Westlawn housing projects. Once upon a time he regulated the flow of drugs on the city's westside.

"This is Reggie Butler live inside of Club Sensation. We have Moe live on the radio. How does it feel to be back at home?"

"It feels better than pus-' Beep!' Words can't explain how I feel at this time," Moe answered.

"Is it anybody you would like to send a shout out to?"

"Yeah. I'd like to send a shout out to all my homies in the Westlawn projects. My man Rudy Best, Corey a.k.a Fatbrains, Sean Pitner, John Burkes, Cowboy, Kim Spinks, Rell, Ricky Allen, Day-Day, Joy, Maurice James rest in peace, Melvin Cooper, Kevin Cooper, Alice Burkes, Kee-Kee, Tosha, Aaron, Silk, rest in peace. My nig-' Beep!' Bruce Jackson much love, Bruce Brown, Sam Brown, Tywon, Wallee, Munk, June, Virg, Moonie, Antino Spinks, Charcol, Poohca, Poohca Slim, Corey Armstrong, Sugar, Bay, Coo Coo Cal, Rob, Mike Swan, Travis Swan, Freddie Riley, Sweethands, My cousin Deanagelo Hawthorne, rest in peace, love famm and I'll meet you at the crossroad. Any of my other Westlawn peeps, if I didn't mention yo' name I apologize. Also I can't forget about my nig-' Beep!' on lock down. My main man Deon Applewhite, much love. My man Ralph Briggs a.k.a Snoop, Anthony Robinson, Michael Taylor, K.P, Binghi Mannix from the Virgin Islands,

Paul Moore a.k.a Smalls, Alfonzo off 45th, Lamont Stokes, Sterling Daniels, Corey Hudson, Robert Chambers, Tree Chambers, Walter Brown, C-low, Alfred Trice, Will out of the Zoo, Perrish Cannaday, Wayne Ingram my crazy rasta from, Jamacia, Jerod Harris, Green eyed Nu-Nu, Lil Rab, Stacy Dodd, Baldhead, Tiny Tune, Peanut, Fingers, X Love, Tone-Tone, Lil Ernie Jackson, West world, Shawn Mitchel, K.Mitchel, J.R, West world, the list goes on and on. If I forgot about anybody don't take it personal. Last but not least I would like to give a shout out to all those brothas in the game. Watch out for those haters and those feds because they playin' for keeps. I'll holla, love."

"There you have it, Moe live on the radio. What about you Mikie? How you feel about being a free man once again?"

"Well, first of all I like to give a thanks to the man above, God. With out him none of this would have ever happen. I also like to give a shout out to my little brother Keith "Butter" Smith, Tyrone "Fat Dog" Simmons, Twin, Fat Mac, Twist, Taz, Boo, Lil Tone, Amanda, Gee, Baseball even though you a sucka, Quick, Cash, Peggy, Pony Tail for all that hot shit he use to bring me, Lil Johnny, E, Rico, Shake, Chris, and everybody else from the tray nine. Little, Ken, Brain "B" hang in there my nigga this shit is almost over, Lil Shitty, Joesph and James the twins out of Berryland "What's up", their brother Black, my nigga Black off Hopkins doing a bid, Quo Quo nice looking my nigga Chem stay up boss man, Lil Keb, Qo City, Greg Mac, Junior, M.J., Tada, Ghost, Lil Kev, A.D., Steven "Eastside" Cheeks, Ford, Alan "Deaky" Simmons Jr. keep ya head up nigga you in a big man world now little homie, and the rest of the Terre Haute USP and FCI. Star, Muff, Aisa Al, Precious, Antino Goodwin, Marco, Deville, Big Baby, and everybody in the Milwaukee County Jail. To my family Lil Keb thanks for holding me down that bid you know you straight for life my nig, to Ean, Big Keb, both my mom's, I love ya'll dearly, to Pop's for accepting all my collect calls when I didn't have no money Kenneth Smith Sr. R.I.P., much love, Kissey Man Christopher, my sisters, Tammy, Tiffany, and Keela, much love, and last but not least, my future wife Loretta a.k.a "My Love", and my beautiful daughter's Michelle, Camille, and Aniyah daddy love y'all with all his heart. And my two little soldiers Brenden and Jaidion and to the rest of the world, if I forgot y'all on this one, I'll damn be sure to catch y'all at the next party and I'm out peace."

"There you have it live on the radio, two of Milwaukee's finest. Once again all women get in free up until midnight. This is the party of a life time. Well, it's time for us to pay the bills so we'll be right back after this commercial break. This is Reggie Butler live from your favorite radio station V100 point seven."

The dance floor is packed inside of Club Sensation. Men and women are gyrating to the sounds of Young Jeezy's "I put on." Motion strides out of his office clutching a stainless steel case, approaching D.J Reggie Butler. He leans over and says something in his ear. Reggie Butler nods his head and agreement as Motion makes his way to the V.I.P section. Sasha is seated in the exclusive section wearing a burgandy sleeveless dress by Dolce & Gabbana and burgandy and gold Louis Vuitton high heel pumps. She is looking down in her champange glass, holding it with her french manicured hands.

"What's up babyyy?" Scotty said with enthusiasm. Sasha tilts her head locking eyes with Motion. She inspects his attire from head to toe. Although Motion is like a brother to her it doesn't stop her from looking at him in a sexual way. She shoots him a seductive smile.

Motion tosses the case on the table leaving his cronies in suspense, as he slowly opens the case. With perfect timing Lil Flip's "Game over," erupts from the high powered sound system. Motion removes a frosty platinum chain and medallion that reads "Game Over" in flawless diamonds. As he loops the heavy chain around his neck the crystal clear rocks glistens, blinding everyone's sight. A waitress prances over to Motion carrying a bottle of Louis Thirteen Black Pearl. He Reaches over and grab the bottle.

"This is a cause for a celebration. We finally made it baby!" Motion shouted, holding the bottle in the air. Plop! He cracks it open. Foam floats from the bottle, pouring onto the floor.

"We poppin' bottles like we just won a championship game." Lil Wayne spits from the concert speakers vibrating the floor. The massive group of party goers go ballistic, hearing the classic song flow throughout the club. "We bottle poppin', we, we, bottle poppin'."

"Well, lets get it poppin' than!" Dirty Red added, pulling out a pound of hydro.

"That's what I'm talkin' 'bout. Roll that shit baby," Scotty said, staring at the brick shaped package.

Dirty Red passes the blunt around the semicircle. Motion tilts his head back, taking a swig from the Louis bottle. The orange tip glowing on the blunt illuminates the silhouette of Toon's face. Blowing out a billow of smoke, he sits the blunt in the ashtray. Scotty fondles with his waistline, retrieving a triple stack. He swallows one of the X-pills and flushes it down with a glass of Incredible Hulk. Knowing that he is about to break the rules of the game, he begins to get nervous. Sasha glimpses at Scotty occcasionally, as she tries to figure out why he has been acting strange. ***Somethin' just don't feel right about papi. Lately he been doin' some strange shit.*** Shasha ponders as she sips on her drink. Sasha brushes a strand of her hair behind her ear, shifting her attention on Motion.

"You look nice today papi," Shasha complimented.

"Thank you mami," Motion replied.

"Man what kind of suit is that any way?" Toon inquired.

"It's an Italian cut suit made by Paknoci. I found it when I was out in Florida with Ayesha."

"That's a bad muthafucka, I gotta give you that," Dirty Red stated. Scotty rises out of his seat.

"Aye y'all, I'll be right back. I gotta piss like a muthafucka," Scotty lied.

Scotty steps inside the bathroom. The door closes behind him drowning out the loud music. He glimpses around sneakily and flips open his cellphone. He presses speed dial and waits patiently for someone to answer.

"Hello," a male voice answered.

"Yeah, what's up?" Scotty said.

"Did you take care of that yet?" Bodo asked.

"Yeah, I'm workin' on that right now."

"You have to hurry up we runnin' out of time. If you don't take care of this soon I'ma have to lock you back up. So, I suggest that you put a move on it buddy." Click!

"Muthafucka," Scotty said aloud, flipping his cell phone closed. The X-pill he popped is starting to take its effect.

Stepping out the bathroom he struts through the crammed dance floor brushing up against all the beautiful women. Peering through his designer frames, he affixes his focus on a thick red bone. Her skirt is so short that you can see her ass cheeks wiggling with each move. She spins around in a circle, causing her tiny skirt and long dark hair to spin in the breeze.

"I'm tellin' y'all it's about to go down. Everybody gon' be a part of this operation. I'ma make sure our families live comfortable for the rest of their lives and our kids," Motion announced. Scotty walks back to the V.l.P section to join the crew. Before he is able to take his seat, Motion notices a beeper attached to his waistband.

"When you start wearin' beepers?" Motion inquired.

"Aaw, I just picked this up the other day. I thought it'll be a good idea to work off of this instead of my phone," Scotty lied.

"Man you takin' it back to the old school," Dirty Red blurted.

"Let me check that out for a minute," Motion asked. Scotty hands it to Motion.

Twirling it around, he examines it from every angle.

"Damn, I ain't seen one of these in a long time," Motion proclaimed, handing it back to him.

Scotty wipes his forehead with back of his hand.

"You a'ight famm?" Motion asked, looking at Scotty with genuine concern.

"I'm straight. I think that X got me trippin'."

"Man you need to leave that shit alone."

"This shit be havin' me feelin' good as hell. You need to try this shit one day. I'm tellin' you. Once you get some of this shit in yo' system I guarantee you will punish the hell out of some pussy."

"Naw, I'm straight."

"Well, since we all congregated here today. Tell me what we suppose to do after we move the rest of the dope we got stashed? And what we suppose to do if yo' plan fail. Legit money is different from this dope money," Scotty questioned.

"Don't worry about that. I already put everything together. We about to make more money than ever before . . . trust me."

"So, that's it, trust you huh? So we just suppose to rely on you. I'm not feelin' that Motion. All this game over shit is a bunch of garbage. You got enough money to last you for the rest of yo' life. This shit ain't right. We helped you built this shit!"

"Hold up Scotty you trippin'. It ain't like that. You had the same opportunity as me. I kept tellin' you to invest yo' money. It's time for us to leave this shit alone and go legit. Our luck is about to run out. I don't wanna be like the rest of those niggas sittin' in the federal joint with a hundred years because they was tryna make a career out of this shit. I'm only tryna do what I think is best for the team," Motion explained.

"You always had all the answers . . . Mr. Big Shot. I remember when you didn't have shit! I was the nigga there with you puttin' my life and freedom on the line to help you make this shit happen! Me Motion!" Scotty barked, banging his fist against his chest.

"Chill out famm," Toon cuts in, "We suppose to be havin' a good time. We made it to far for this shit."

Motion takes another sip from the bottle. He ignores Scotty, knowing that he is not in his right state of mind.

"Come on papi, lets go dance," Sasha said, grabbing Motion by the wrist. "Maybe when we come back papi will have his mind right."

"Maybe you right mami. Come on lets go." Motion and Sasha walks off mixing in with the massive crowd on the dance floor.

Scanning the empty lot, Bridget sees no sign of human life. Her heart pumps with trepidation. A nozzle dangles from the gas pump. The strong smell of gasoline leaking on the pavement makes it hard for her to breath. She covers her nose and mouth with an open hand. Hearing the sound of someone grimacing and dragging their body on the graveled ground steals her attention. Whoever it is, is on the other side of the gas pump.

Without hesitation, Bridget eases toward the gas pump. Her heart drops to her stomach, shock to see the figure lying up against the gas pump in a sitting position holding his bloody chest. The site of Elliott's bullet riddled body cuts into her heart like a machete.

Bridget begins to feel dizzy. Screaming hysterically, she drops to her knees, embracing Elliott's convulsing body. Her world starts to feel gloomy and dark.

"Please b-baby, d-don't leave me," Bridget cried. Tears are flowing from her misty eyes, glistening on her cheeks. Elliott studies her pain filled eyes, as he gasps for air.

Sirens wail in the background becoming louder and louder. Elliott's lips tremble as he struggle to say something. His hand shakes as he uses the last of his strength to hand her a piece of paper that is balled up in his fist. Bridget clutches it in her hand. Resting her head on his chest, she listens to the drumming sound of his heart playing a soft love song. It's a song that she never wants to end. But, unfortunately the song she is listening to slowly fades away coming to an end. Elliott's eyes slowly close as the world that he once shared with the love of his life grows dark and cold. All his dreams, goals, and plans to marry Bridget and be a father to his unborn child is no longer a reality. Bridget's body is numb. She doesn't even notice the authorities and the paramedics approaching them. Holding his lifeless body in her arms is all that matters to her at this moment.

* * *

Motion, Dirty Red, Toon, and Sasha are in the V.I.P section cracking open more bottles of champange. Scotty is seated in a secluded area of the club popping X-pills, getting some mean head from the red bone he spotted on the dance floor. The volcanic sound of the music pumps out of the huge speakers shaking the floor. Globes of light are rotating throughout the interior of the club.

A tall chocolate complexion woman wearing a DKNY dress with gold straps and a pair of gold Cole Haan pumps is on the dance floor. Motion studies the woman's long muscular legs that look like they belong on a race-horse. Making eye contact with Motion, she turns around rocking her bubble shaped ass. She pulls her dress up to her waistline, exposing her smooth hersey brown ass. Her round juicy ass hides her gold thong. Bending over, she grips her ankles, watching Motion through her parted legs, with her lengthy weave touching the floor. She wobbles her ass working every muscle in it. She gives Motion a flirtatious look enticing him. His manhood rises, creating a tent underneath his trousers.

Sasha watches Motion as he admire the chocolate Goddess. Sasha is not attracted to women, but she has to admit it. The woman does have a banging body. If she was a man her dick would be hard too. For some reason she is finding herself feeling a little jealous.

Sasha taps Motion on his shoulder, snapping him out of his lustful moment. She couldn't wait for Scotty to leave so that she can talk to him about the suspicious activity that has been going on concerning Scotty. It has been bothering her for quite a while.

"Hold up Sasha," Motion said, holding his index finger up with his eyes plastered on the woman, as she continues to entertain him. He know that he can no longer touch, but in his eyes their is nothing wrong with looking.

The front entrance of the club is cluttered with people waiting to get inside the club. A fire engine red porsche pulls up to the curb gaining everyone's attention. A woman steps out of the exotic sports car rocking a pair of red open toe Jimmy Choo pumps, a red skirt, red lipstick, and red fingernail polish. The parking attendant hops inside her car pulling it around the back.

The pleasant smell of her perfume wafts the air, as she prances to the front of the line. Some of the females that are waiting impatiently to get inside turn their noses up with envy. One girl even says aloud, "That's some bullshit. That bitch can wait just like everybody else!" The woman ignore the foul remark.

A man dressed in dingy jeans is running up behind her out of breath. The slender built man appears to be homeless. He tries to rush into the club behind the woman dressed in red. She glimpses over her shoulder with a disgusting look on her face. Security stops him right in his tracks.

"Where you think you goin' partna?" the security staff barked.

"I-I need to get inside it's an emergency," the man replied, trying to catch his breath.

"An emergency."

"Yeah, an emergency. I need to talk to my man Motion."

"Motion." He looks the man up and down.

"Man get out of here. Motion don't know you." The security staff snatches the man by his collar escorting him off the premise.

Sasha and Motion steps inside his office to have a talk in private. They close the door behind them.

"What's wrong Sasha?" Motion asked, with a look of concern.

"It's Scotty. Somethi-" Motion's cell phone chimes interrupting their conversation.

"Hold on for a minute Shasha." Motion answers the phone. "What's up?" As Motion listens to the caller crying on the other end, his whole facial expression changes from happy to sad.

"What?" Motion hangs up the phone with a worried look on his face.

"Come on lets get out of here."

"What's wrong Motion?" Sasha questioned.

"Just come on." Out of all the years Sasha has known Motion, she never seen him like this before. Something really has to be wrong. They storm out of the office.

*   *   *

Motion emerges through the doors of the hospital with his entourage trailing behind him. They bypass the receptionist desk heading to Elliott's room.

"Doctor Harrison you have a call on line three," announced a receptionist over the loud speakers.

Scurrying down the long crowded hallway, Motion makes his way to the elevators. Motion presses an arrow shaped button pointing upward. The button lights up and the elevator slowly descend. Running out of patience, he presses the button repeatedly.

"Hurry the fuck up!" he barked. The door slides open and they barge into the small crammed elevator. They exit the elevator on the sixth floor. Motion pushes two janitors out of his pathway making his way to Elliott's room.

"There go Bridget right there," Scotty said, pointing a jeweled finger.

Bridget is sitting on a bench outside of the room. Tears are escaping the confines of her eyes. Ms. Hopson walks out of Elliott's room with tears spilling from her eyes, ruining her mascara and clothes. Motion looks in her direction, seeing an expression on her face indicating that she just received the bad news.

Motion struts towards Ms. Hopson to embrace his mother with a hug. As he tempts to loop his arm around her, she pushes him away rejecting him.

"Get away from me!" she snapped, eyeing him coldly.

"Mama, what I do?" Smack! Ms.Hopson slaps him across his face.

"It's all your fault my baby is gone! I told you I didn't want him to have n-nothin' to do with yo' dirty money! Gone, just get away from me!" Ms. Hopson cried, her voice angrily escalated.

Motion cups the side of his face, staring at his mother in disbelief. Ayesha prances down the hallway in her high heel pumps. She witnessed the altercation from a distance. She has her long wavy hair in a bun. Diamond earrings are hanging from her ears like miniature chandeliers, swinging gently above her shoulders. The smell of her rich perfume grips the air, as she comfort Motion with a warm loving hug.

"Baby please be strong. I know you love your little brother. Right now your mother is grieving. No matter what baby, I promise you I'll be here through all of this. We'll make it through this," Ayesha promised, rubbing his arm. Sasha sits beside Bridget massaging her back.

"It's gon' be okay mami. Elliott is in a better place now. I know it ain't easy, but you have to move on with your life. We all have to go some day. You know we all gon' miss him mami."

Bridget dabs underneath her eyes with the sleeve of her shirt.

"I-I don't . . . understand." The muscles in Bridget's face tremble as she struggle with her words. "Why would somebody want to hurt him?"

"Those the kind of people that we have to deal with in this world mami. All we can do is live our lives and keep our love ones in our hearts," Sasha consoled, thinking about when she loss her brother.

Motion, Dirty Red, Toon, Ayesha, and Scotty join Sasha and Bridget. Motion leans over and gives Bridget a tight hug.

"We gotta be strong Bridget. I know this is hard on you too, but I want you to know that you'll always be my little sister. If you need anything . . . I mean anything. Don't hesitate, just give me a call. You hear me sis?"

"Yeah."

A tear roll down Motion's face screaming revenge. Slowly he's growing stern and cold. He whispers in her ear in an eerie tone.

"I promise you somebody is gon' pay for this." With those words being said, Motion struts off with revenge burning in his eyes.

They enter the elevator leaving Bridget sitting on the bench all alone. With her head buried in her lap, she realizes that the paper Elliott gave her before he died is still in her hand. Slowly she unfolds the paper. Gazing at the paper, she reads it carefully.

Love's True Definition
Every morning when I awake you are my first thought,

The love that I possess for you could never be bought,
Your beautiful smile sets my heart on fire and light up my soul,
Your tender, soft, kiss makes my heart beat out of control, It seems as if you were perfectly molded by the hands of the most high,
But it was more than your exquisite features that caught my eye,
It is your personality, characteristics, and inner self,
That's what make me want to grow old with you and love you until my day of death, My only purpose on this earth is to please you, So don't you ever doubt my love, baby it's true,
I never knew that I could love someone this much, And I want you to know, through all adversities I'll be your crutch, I know sometimes love can become very complicated,
No matter what I will always remain dedicated,
Through all the struggles baby I will be right there,
You are my soul mate, we are the perfect pair, For you I will climb the highest mountain and swim the deepest sea, And I can't wait until that day I propose to you down on one knee,
Our love is what I consider to be the ultimate blessing,
I hope you understand these words I've been expressing,
This love we have for each other is heaven made,
It's a love so profound that will never fade,
Now if you don't know what love is let me explain,
Love is when one loses their balance and the other half is the kane,
Love is when two people's thoughts and spirits connect, When one is down and the other one have your back, Love is two hearts that beat as one,
Love is a life time, until God say our job is done, I crave for your love like a drug addict craving his next high,
It's the truth baby I can't lie,
The day that we went on our first date love was planted,
And never in life will I take you for granted,
Whenever you need someone to talk to I'm here to listen,
Now this is what I call "Love's True Definition."

Bridget sits on the bench motionless, staring at the poem in a daze. Rubbing on her stomach, she starts talking to her unborn child in a motherly tone.

"Baby, we gon' make it through this."

199

*   *   *

P. Diddy's "Missing you" flows out of the powerful surround system. Motion sits behind the bar drinking a bottle of Patron. It has been four days since he changed his attire. His neatly trimmed goatee is turning into a full beard. The strong stench smell of alcohol clings to his body. If someone could see him right now, they would think that he became his own best customer.

Motion's bartender Ricky finishes wiping off the countertop.

"Yo' Motion! I'ma 'bout to go out front and sweep up the sidewalk. If you need anything just holla for me," Ricky said.

"A'ight." As Ricky struts away, Motion picks up a framed picture. Tears spill down his face, as he studies Elliott's graduation picture. *I should've never bought him that car. If I wouldn't have bought him that car he'll still be alive. Why the hell they had to kill him over a car? They could've just took the car.* Motion flings the bottle of Patron across the bar with all his strength. Crack! The bottle bursts open. Shards of glass rain all over the floor. His nose flared so wide that you can see the hairs inside his nose.

It's all your fault my baby is gone!
It's all your fault my baby is gone!
It's all your fault my baby is gone!

Ms. Hopson's voice echoes through Motion's head over and over. He still can't believe how she treated him at the hospital.

"Somebody gon' pay for this shit! I promise!" Motion barked. He twirls around staggering, knocking over all the bottles of liquor that is situated behind the bar. The clinging sound of glass penetrates the atmosphere, crashing against the floor, as Motion loses his temper. The alcohol and marijuana has his mind clouded.

Ricky stands in front of the club sweeping the sidewalk. A man approaches him from behind startling him. Turning around, he acknowledges a slender built man. Ricky looks the man up and down.

Every now and then homeless people would catch Ricky in front of the club and beg for change. He would always give them money. It wasn't because he has a kind heart, but he was instructed by Motion to give the homeless money anytime he or any of his employees run into them in front of the club. Motion would reimburse them at the end of the day.

"Don't bother with the speech, I heard it all before. I already know what you want," Ricky stated, pulling out a five dollar bill. "Here you go," Ricky offered, extending his hand in front of the man.

"What you handin' me that for?" the man asked with a puzzled facial expression.

"This is what you want ain't it?"

"Naw, I need to talk to Motion."

"He ain't here," Ricky lied.

Motion told him to say that if anyone come looking for him. All Motion wants to do is be alone and mourn his brother's death.

"Well, when you see him tell h-" A loud crashing sound coming from inside the club captivates their attention. Ricky dashes inside the club with the broom clutched in his hand. Stepping inside the club, Ricky stares at a crying Motion. Motion is seated behind the bar with his head buried in his arms, gripping Elliott's picture. Ricky's eyes dances around, as he scans the sabotaged bar. Broken bottles and liquor is all over the place.

"Motion, are you a'ight?"

"Yeah, I'm straight man. I'm just going through a thang right now," Motion replied, lifting his head. To Motion's surprise he recognizes the slender built man standing behind Ricky.

"Poochie, what you doin' here?" Motion inquired.

"I need to talk to you about somethin' important," Poochie answered, with a serious look.

"What is it? You know I'm not really in a mood to talk. I just loss my little brother."

"That's what it's about," Poochie informed.

Motion locks his focus on Poochie, paying full attention to him. Ricky stands there sweeping up glass fragments.

"You mind if I talk to you in private?"

"Yeah, come on in my office." Motion escorts him to his office. Falling back in his leather executive high back chair, Motion listens closely to his every word.

"I know who killed yo' . . . brother."

*   *   *

A candy red old school changes lanes, traveling down Fond Du Lac avenue. Loud volcanic bass pumps out of the high priced car system shaking the earth. It's 30 inch chrome wheels gleams, as the sun kisses them.

The driver of the car is leaning back in his seat, peering through his Roberto Cavalli shades. He doesn't notice the black Dodge Magnum trailing behind him. His rearview mirror is bouncing hard, making everything in it a blur. He makes a right turn pulling onto a side street, parking in front of a tattered duplex. Grabbing the small device in his lap, he turns down the volume on his car system. He punches a number into his cell phone.

"I'm outside yo'." A young man steps out of the house sagging in a pair of Coogi jeans. A white gold chain with a small charm attached to it bounces against his chest, as he strides across the pavement in his Coogi gym shoes. Hopping into the passenger seat, he greets the driver with a strong handshake.

"What up Donald?"

"Same ol' shit just anotha day. What up with you though?"

"Mann, I'm just tryna make it out here and feed my three kids. I'ma 'bout to move my family up out of this dump. I promised my girl that we're movin' in a couple of weeks. I just gotta bust a couple more moves."

"I hear that. So what you got for me?" Donald asked. Cliff reaches inside his pocket and pulls out a thick wad of money.

"I got three stacks for you." Cliff tosses the money in Donald's lap.

"Reach under the seat and grab that." Cliff fishes under the seat, removing a jar of X-pills. "That's a thousand pills. Next time you holla at me I got you for two dollas a pill."

"Cool, I can work with that."

"Just h-" Donald stops in mid-sentence, staring out the passenger window intoxicated with fear. Donald locks his focus on the man that he remember from his graduation ceremony, aiming a large nickel plated revolver in the interior of his car.

Cliff shifts his gaze on another man standing in front of the driver's window clenching a large semi-automatic handgun that resembles the one seen on the movie "Dirty Harry."

Donald and Cliff swivels their heads looking in the window, feeling like two trapped animals with nowhere to run. Donald thinks about reaching on the side of the seat for his gun, but he knows that he will be no match against two armed men.

"Open the door!" Toon barked. Donald unlocks the door following his instructions, hoping that the man will spare his life. Toon opens the passenger door, climbing into the back seat. Cliff is contemplating on making a run for it. Toon closes the door behind him.

Dirty Red received information that Donald Crumb was seen running from the scene with something in his hand. Dirty Red's little homie gave him the 411. Dirty Red and Toon remember Donald's face from Elliott's graduation. But the one thing they remembered the most is his flashy old school.

"Man, I'ma ask you one time and one time only. Who killed my little man Elliott?" Toon questioned in a raspy voice.

"Man I-I don't know," Donald answered in a trembling voice. Toon fixes his eyes on Dirty Red and nods his head.

"Put yo' hands on the steering-wheel," Dirty Red ordered.

"Come on man, I swear I don't know w-who killed him," Donald exclaimed. Crack! "Aaw!" Toon struck him in the back of his cranium with the heavy revolver.

"Put yo' hands on the steering wheel!" Reluctantly, Donald places his hands on the steering wheel. Dirty Red leans through the window handcuffing him to the steering-wheel. "You was seen runnin' from his car, but you don't know who killed him huh?"

"I was there, but I swear I didn't see who killed him?" Donald cried. Bloc! Bloc! Dirty Red shot him in both his thighs.

Contemplating long enough, Cliff moves swiftly, making a run for it. Toon fires two rounds from the baby canon, hitting Cliff in his leg. Cliff falls to the ground grimacing in pain, squirming, gripping his wounded leg. Toon hops out of the car staring down at a frightened Cliff.

"Please don't kill me man!" Cliff begged, looking in Toon's eyes. Toon pulls back the hammer, biting down on his lower lip. With the eyes of a cold blooded killer, he glares at the man. Click! A familiar sound garners Toon's attention. Slowly he turns around with his gun still aimed at Cliff's dome.

*   *   *

Homicide Detective Jeffrey McCormick relaxes in his office, leaning back in the swivel chair behind the desk. The rich smell of hot coffee lingers in the air, floating out of his ceramic coffee mug. For the last two hours he has been analyzing a video tape, investigating the latest homicide that took place at a gas station on the City's Northside.

Lately, Detective McCormick has been under a lot of pressure. The Chief of Police has been receiving numerous complaints from the community about all of the unsolved murders. Noticing something on the video tape, he leans forward. He points the remote at the television screen, rewinding the tape over and over. Two young black males walked pass the surveillance cameras looking suspicious. One of the young men had a shiny object in his hand. Detective McCormick can't identify the object in the man's hand. The second individual that crossed the surveillance cameras was carrying a large revolver, with a hoodie over his head.

Maybe it was two gunmen? Naw, than that would mean that the witness's statements are inconsistent. Detective McCormick thinks to himself becoming frustrated. He rakes his fingers through his short, honey blond hair and blows out a long breath. In the middle of him sipping his coffee the phone rings. *I hope that isn't the chief about to get on my ass again.* He sits the coffee mug down and pulls his necktie loose before answering the phone.

"Hello, Detective McCormick speaking, how may I help you?"

"Hello Detective McCormick. This is Dan Winston from the forensic lab. I did a bullet comparison like you requested and I come to find out that the bullets match the bullets that were at the other crime scenes. The making of the gun is a Colt Anaconda .44 Magnum. Also I have two serial numbers restoration. If you would like to come to the lab and examine everything I can assist you further in this matter."

"I'll be there in the next hour. Thank you, I really appreciate it."

"No problem Detective McCormick. I'll see you then." Detective McCormick hangs up the phone. That is the best news he has heard all week. Finally he is getting closer to solving the cases. A smile creases his pale white face. *That means most likely the same person is responsible for killing the young man at the church, and at the dice game. So that means the same person that committed those murders*

is the same person who did the murder at the gas station. Detective McCormick tosses his gray blazer over shoulders and storms out of his office.

*   *   *

"Everything happened real quick. I was on the side of the gas station takin' a leak and I seen somebody with a hoodie on creep pass me carryin' a pistol. I damn near pissed on myself. Within seconds after that, all I heard was shots being fired and a lot of screamin'. I peeked from behind the gas station. I seen the man wearin' the hoodie pull off in Elliott's Benz. I only seen the car parked one time in your mother's driveway. I got a good look at ol' boys face and I recognized him from the neighborhood. I even bought dope from him a couple of times before. Everybody in the hood call the young nigga Coupe. He suppose to be part of the murder squad. He's the same one that killed that shortie over a dice game from what I hear. They say the young nigga is wild and quick to bust that thang," Poochie informed.

Without saying a word, Motion slowly rises out of his seat. Poochie looks up at Motion in silence, trying to read his facial expression. Sliding the drawer open to his desk, he retrieves a remote. He struts pass Poochie and moves a large plant to the side.

Kneeling down on the floor, he peels back the carpet, exposing a small safe that is mounted in the floor. He punches a code into the remote and the safe makes a beeping sound followed with a soft click. Motion flips the safe open and returns to his desk standing in front of Poochie. With his eyes stretched open, Poochie plasters his eyes on the two bricks of hundred dollar bills that Motion slid in front of him.

"What is this for?" Poochie questioned, shifting his gaze to Motion.

"That's the twenty thousand dollar reward for your information." Poochie picks up one of the crispy stacks of money. He fans the money with his thumb, fantasizing on how much dope he can buy with it.

"I ain't seen this much money in a long, long time," Poochie proclaimed, placing the money back on the desk. "I appreciate the reward, but I can't accept that youngin'."

"What you mean you can't accept it?" Motion questioned, finding it hard to believe that a junky like Poochie would refuse some money.

"It just wouldn't be right. This is not about money. It's about findin' the man that's responsible for killin' Elliott. That was my little man. He really made me proud of him. He was on his way to doin' somethin' that I always wanted to do with my life. And also, I have too much respect for yo' father."

Motion falls back in his seat and says, "Man you just don't know how I feel right now."

"I do know how you feel Motion . . . believe that. I been through a lot myself. I'ma share somethin' with you that I never shared with nobody, but yo' father when he was livin'." Poochie pauses for a second, taking a deep breath. Blowing out a short breath of air, he begins to speak.

"Back in the days I used to run with this cat by the name of Vegas. Vegas was my right hand man. When I came up I put him on and did everythang I could for him. Whenever I ate, he ate. I introduced him to my plug. Once the money started rollin' in I started seeing the changes in him.

One day he called me and asked me to bring him three bricks because he was out. So, him being my man that I trusted, I brought him three bricks with no problem.

On my way back home I started gettin' this strange feeling that somethin' whatn't right. When I made it back home, I noticed a trail of footprints in the snow leadin' to my front porch. I found that strange because I never brought anybody to my house where I laid my head at. That's when I upped my strap. I really knew somethin' was wrong when my front door was unlocked. With caution I opened the door. All I kept thinkin' about is my fiance and my six year old son.

I eased up the steps after checkin' the lower floor. As soon as I made it to the top of the stairs, I ran to our bedroom. The whole room was tore a part. Still I didn't see no signs of my fiance and my son. That's when I ran into my . . . son's room . . . and found my . . . fiancé and my son." Poochie takes a deep breath and continue. "They were layin' in the bed lifeless . . . tied up with one to the head execution style. That's when I realized the nigga that I trusted to the fullest set me up." Poochie puts his head down for a moment, fighting back the pain that he feels deep inside his heart, as he relives that day.

"At that very moment, my life didn't mean nothin' to me. I felt like I didn't have nothin' to live for. I even contemplated on committing suicide.

I put a loaded gun to my head, but I didn't have enough courage to pull the trigger. That's when I gave up and became my own best customer. I couldn't cope with the reality of my son and fiance being gone . . . forever. I was blaming myself for a long time. Just when you think that life is good, somethin' unexpected happens to make you realize that life ain't fair. You just gotta adapt to the pain, hurt, and disappointment that comes with life, than figure out a way to keep goin' in spite of it all. Yo' father was the only one there for me. He never turned his back on me. It wasn't long after that before he got killed. Right then and there I knew it was over with for me," Poochie expressed, rubbing his hand over his face.

"How come you didn't kill that muthafucka for doin' that to yo' family?" Motion asked, his blood boiling.

"Because yo' father suggested that we wait at least a year until the heat die down. During that time Vegas took the ten bricks of coke and eighty five stacks that he robbed me for and blew up over night. At that time I was so high that my mind stayed cloudy. Vegas started dealin' directly with my connection. When the time came for me and yo' father to go through with our plan, that's when he got killed. A few months later Vegas got indicted in a big drug conspiracy. I was left without a way of gettin' next to him.

After four years of fightin' his case, he was acquitted on all charges and released back on the streets. Several more years pasted by and he got indicted again. He ended up gettin' a life sentence and that was the last I heard of him," Poochie explained.

"Man that's fucked up. I'm sorry to hear that. I probably would've did the same thing."

"You know what Motion?"

"What's that?"

"People used to tell me that time will heal my wounds. I never agreed with that. The only thing that heals wounds is understandin'. I realized no matter how much I stress, it's not goin' to bring them back. I know I have to move on. We get one shot at this game called life . . . one shot. And we have to take that one chance and live it to the fullest. The streets is infested with snakes and rats. Greed and jealousy will make a man lose his common sense. All you have to do is go back to biblical times. Whenever you get the chance get a bible and read Gensis Chapter four. It talks about how Cain deceived and killed his own brother Abel. It's always the closest person to you that will bring you down." Motion thinks about what Sasha told him about Scotty the other day, as he continues to listen to Poochie.

"Before an enemy becomes an enemy, he was once a friend. In our times of prosperity we can't recognize our true friends. When a man is successful even his enemy will speak friendly to him. An enemy will cry with you, bust that pistol with you, and pretend to help you. With his lips he speaks sweetly, but in his heart he's plottin' against you. I don't want you to ever forget that youngin'. Take all your wounds and turn them into wisdom. The world makes way for the man who knows were he is goin'. The man who is prepared for the battle has half of the battle fought. You know what the difference is between 'Money And The Power'?" Poochie asked, staring at Motion waiting for a reply.

"I never thought about it."

"This is the difference. Money represents comfort and power represents control." With those final words, Poochie rises out of the chair and exits Motion's office. Motion has a whole new respect for Poochie. Motion retrieves his cellphone dialing a number.

"Please mister, don't hurt my daddy." Toon looks into the eyes of an innocent little boy standing in the doorway. He shifts his focus back to a startled Cliff, dragging his body, groaning in excruciating pain.

"Please man, d-don't kill me in front of my son. My boys need m-me. I'll give you everything I-I got," Cliff pleaded, staring into the barrel of death.

Looking into the little boy's round, baby brown eyes, Toon decides to spare the man's life. He thinks about how much pain he suffered growing up without a father.

Leaning over, he searches through Cliff's pockets pulling out his I.D. After scanning the name on it, he says, "Today must be yo' lucky day. Usually I kill all witnesses, but this time I'ma spare yo' life. If you give the police any information, I promise you I'll find you and kill everything you love, then you." Toon places the I.D back into his pocket.

Dirty Red pops open a bottle of 151 Bacardi. He tilts it, emptying the alcoholic beverage allover Donald's body.

"Please man, I'm tellin' you I didn't have nothin' to do with Elliott gettin' killed, I swear!" Dirty Red doesn't pay any attention to his plea. He lights up a cigarette, taking a long pull from it. Donald looks up at him, as he blows out a cloud of smoke revealing a wicked smile. Dirty Red flicks the burning cigarette into Donald's lap, setting his clothes and the interior of the car on fire. Donald yanks his arms in vain, trying to break loose from the handcuffs.

Dirty Red and Toon saunters away, cutting through the neighbor's yard. All they can hear is Donald screaming hysterically. Toon heard several people die before, but he never heard a man scream like that in his life. It sounds like something that is inhuman. Dark clouds of smoke lingers in the air. A chiming sound gains their attention, as they make their getaway. Toon picks up his cellphone seeing Motion's number flashing on the digital screen.

"Yo' what up?"

The rumbling sound of traffic embraces the atmosphere, as vehicles travel up and down Lisbon Avenue. Toon and Dirty Red parks the Dodge Magnum on 31st street in a secluded spot. They step out of the car scanning the scenery. Sauntering side by side, they make their way to a garage, which is known as a chop shop.

Toon knocks on the door, hearing the faint sound of machinery. Within seconds someone peeks through a slot.

"What's up? Can I help you with somethin'?" a masculine voice barked from behind the door.

"Yeah, I need to talk to Clearance about some business. A friend of mine by the name of House sent me down here," Toon lied, using the information he received from a close associate of his. The eyes behind the door dances, as he appraise the two well dressed men. Being convinced that they are legit, the man opens the door ushering them inside.

They look around with a searching gaze. A slender built man in his mid-forties is operating a metal grinder, dressed in an oily khaki suit is stationed underneath a late model Lexus. Seeing that he is the only other person in the shop, lets them know that their job is going to be easy.

"So what can I do for y'all?" Clearance asked, his eyes bouncing from Toon to Dirty Red.

"I need to know if anybody came through here tryna sell a pearl white Mercedes Benz CLS 550?" Toon asked.

"Naw, I don't recall nobody tryna sell me a car like that," Clearance lied. Toon brandishes a Dan Wesson .41 Magnum. Dirty Red snatches the mechanic from under the car at gun point. Clearance shrinks back in fear, staring at an angry Toon.

"Now I'ma asked you again, but this time I'ma say it slower, maybe you'll understand me better. I . . . need . . . to . . . know . . . if . . . anybody . . . came . . . through . . . here . . . tryna . . . sell . . . a . . . pearl . . . white . . . Mercedes . . . Benz . . . C-L-S five fifty?" Clearance trembles in fear. He is reluctant to answer the question. Toon pulls the hammer back, pressing the barrel of the gun against Clearance's temple.

"Okay, okay. A young cat came through here and tried to sell me that car, but I wouldn't do business with him. I sensed that something wasn't right about the car. I seen dried up blood on the door panel. He l-left me a number in case I changed my mind," Clearance confessed, hoping that Toon will put the gun down.

"How long ago was this?" Toon questioned.

"It was a few hours ago." Toon glares at the old man coming up with an idea. He makes Clearance place a call to Coupe, telling him that he is interested in the car. Toon makes a call on his cellphone.

*   *   *

Coupe travels down several side streets, after taking the Mercedes Benz out of his stash spot. He drives with caution, trying to avoid the police.

Running low on money, he can't wait to make the transaction with Clearance. He reveals an evil grin, as he pulls up to the garage. With the honk of the horn, the electric garage door ascends, allowing him to pull inside. Coupe caresses his banger taking it off safety. Seeing that Clearance is by himself, he becomes a little relaxed. Clearance directs him inside the garage, making signals with his hands. He throws an open hand in the air, standing in front of the car. Coupe stops the car and climbs out of it.

"So, I see you changed yo' mind huh ol' school?" Coupe said, handing him the car keys.

"Yeah, I got somebody that's interested in this fine automobile." Sensing that something isn't right, Coupe attempts to reach for his gun. Toon and Dirty Red rises out of the seats of the Lexus with their guns drawn.

"Don't even think about it," Dirty Red warned, stepping out of the car, gripping a nickel plated 10 millimeter semi-automatic. Toon removes the .44 Mag from Coupe's waistband disarming him.

Toon pops open the trunk on the Lexus, ordering Clearance into the trunk. Climbing into the trunk, he joins the mechanic that Dirty Red knocked out with his gun.

"Come on baby, I 'ont got nothin' to do with this," Clearance pleaded, as Toon slams the trunk closed.

"I'ma let you back out," Toon promised.

No longer than fifteen minutes later, the chiming sound of Toon's cellphone captivates his attention. After glancing at the number on the screen, he answers the call.

"Yo' . . . A'ight." Toon struts over to the wall adjacent to the garage door. He presses a green button affixed to the wall. Coupe sits in a chair with his wrists bound with duct tape. Coupe locks his focus on the ascending garage door. A large polished chrome grill gleams, obscuring Coupe's vision, as a car pulls into the garage slowly. Coupe squints as he studies the extravagant automobile halting in front of him. His heart lurches, hammering against his chest at the sight of two men climbing out of the car dressed in transparent raincoats. Lines of anger traces the men's forehead, as they make their approach.

Toon and Dirty Red stands in the corner conversing with the driver of the car. Coupe can't interpret anything that they are saying, as they speak in a low tone. The low cut waves in the driver's hair dances, as he swivels his head locking eyes with Coupe. Grabbing a chair, he walks over to Coupe. He twirls the chair around sitting it with the back-rest against his chest.

"So, you the one that killed my little brother huh," Motion stated, with a scorn look burning in his eyes. Coupe sits there in silence staring at Motion. "You took somethin' very valuable from me. Somethin' that can never be . . . replaced. I guess it's time I take somethin' away from you that can never be replaced. You wanna playa gangsta' s games, I' ma show you how . . . real gangstas get down."

Motion cracks his knuckles and rises out of the chair walking to the trunk of his car. Motion stretches a pair of latex gloves over his hands. A metallic sound breaks the silence, as he removes a heavy duty chain out of the trunk. Coupe is frozen in the chair paralyzed by fear.

Standing in front of Coupe, he swings the chain with all his strength, striking him across the shoulder. Coupe falls to the ground groaning, as a sharp pain courses through his entire body. Motion swings the chain haphazardly, striking him repeatedly, allover his frail frame. Blood squirts from his head, splattering on Motion's raincoat.

"You . . . bitch!" Whip! "Ass . . . mutha." Whip! "Fucka!"

The veins in Motion's neck bulges, as he shouts in between striking him. Motion beats him brutally with the chain. Coupe squirms on the ground in a puddle of blood. His swollen head has him looking deformed. Warm blood pours down his gashed forehead blocking his vision. All of his wounds are burning.

Swinging one last time, Motion slips in Coupe's blood losing his balance. Catching his balance, Motion drops the chain on the concrete pavement. It looks like someone slaughtered a pig.

Coupe is lying on the ground motionless, struggling to see through his swollen eyes. At this time Coupe's own mother would not be able to identify him. Reaching under his bloody raincoat, Motion removes a Mauser Bolo 7.63 millimeter from his waistband. With an diabolical look on his face, Motion cocks it back. Using a great deal of force, he jams the barrel of the gun in Coupe's mouth, busting his lip, knocking out all his front teeth.

"You live by the gun . . . You die by the gun," Motion said in a raspy voice before squeezing the trigger.

The deafening sound of gunfire, barks, reverberating throughout the garage. Coupe's head jerks back from the impact of the gun, bouncing against the pavement. Brain fragment is leaking out of the back of his head. Imminent death gripped him with one squeeze of the trigger.

Motion and Eddie stares at his bloody corpse in silence. He finally realize what Tupac meant in his lyrics, "Revenge is like the sweetest joy next to gettin' pussy."

"Hey, let us out of here!" Clearance's muffled voice and the sound of feet drumming on the trunk brings Motion back to his senses. "I thought you said you was gon' let us out of here!" Clearance whined.

"Oh yeah, that's right. I did say I was gon' let them out the trunk," Toon said, walking over to the trunk.

Toon pops the trunk open letting them out. "You right. I did promise to let y'all out. I have always been a man of my word," Toon said.

Clearance and the mechanic climbs out of the trunk. Clearance leans over, dusting off his pants leg. They watch as Toon struts away, lingering behind Dirty Red, Eddie, and Motion.

Stopping in his tracks Toon turns around aiming two handguns at the men. A red dot shines between their bulging eyes.

"I-I thought you said you was gone let us out?" Clearance stuttered.

"I did say I was gon' let y'all out the trunk, but I never said I was gon' let y'all live. You know the way the game go old head. A dead man can't talk." Toon pulls back on the triggers, introducing them to death. The last thing they seen was flashes of light.

Shifting clouds are blocking out the sun, making it gloomy. Rain is pouring down from the heavens, drizzling on the earth. A procession of automobiles are moving along the winding pathway in a formal fashion, pulling into Graceland cemetery. A black Drop-Head Phantom with it's platinum hood is leading the group of luxurious vehicles. It's brake lights glow bright red, as it stops along the dusty pathway. The suicide door on the Phantom coupe pops open slowly. It has been over two weeks since Elliott was muredered.

Motion climbs out of the Phantom wearing a pair of Roberto Cavalli shades and a black double breasted Ermenegildo Zegna suit. Motion flicks open his black umbrella, shielding himself from the rain. Gravel crunches under his Eastsayeren shoes, as he strides to the passenger door. He opens the door for Ayesha and Joy, helping them out of the car.

Glimpsing around, Motion scans the names that are engraved on the various tombstones, as he walks in the direction of the large crowd, that is gathered around Elliott's coffin. Ayesha peers through her Tiffany

& Co shades, reading the names on the tombstones. The name Willie Bean sounds very familiar to her, but the name Bryan J. Hawthorne she remembered from being on the news. He is the 18 month old boy that was killed in an attempted car jacking. *It's a shame how our people are killing each other for materialistic items,* Ayesha thinks to herself.

Ms. Hopson stands in the front row listening to Pastor Allen deliver his sermon. Julio is in the crowd laying low. He came to pay his respect to Motion and Eddie. Standing next to Ms. Hopson is Eddie and Bridget. Ayesha greets Ms. Hopson with a hug. Motion chose to keep his distance from his mother at this time. Scotty, Dirty Red, and Toon walks up behind Motion and embraces him with a brotherly hug.

"What up famm?" Scotty greeted, while comforting Motion with a strong brotherly hug.

"Just tryna make it through this," Motion replied, his voice sounding weak.

"Don't worry, you know we got yo' back," Scotty proclaimed, standing beside Motion in a tailor-made Giorgio Armani suit. Marco struts toward the mourners, as the pastor delivers his eulogy.

"It's said that the face of God are on his people, but the fool can't see it. For those of us that knew Elliott, who love Elliott, or even just talked to Elliott knew that he was an acceptional man. For those of us that knew Elliott, who love Elliott, or even just talked to Elliott knew that he love poetry and spoke with a poetic flair."

Ms. Hopson listens to the words that are escaping Pastor Banks' mouth. For some reason she feel like she met him before. She studies his facial features closely, but can't figure out why he look so familiar.

Arriving to the cemetery late, Poochie mixes in with the crowd of mourners. Dressed in a freshly pressed, white button up and a pair of creased trousers, Poochie looks more like a hardworking citizen instead of a junky. A look of surprise registers on his face, as he stares at Pastor

Banks. It has been a long time since Poochie seen Pastor Banks, but he could never forget his face.

"Today we didn't come here to mourn, but to celebrate Elliott's going home party. His return to the hands of the maker. This is a day to rejoice. The sheep is going home to the shepherd. Some may say that an evil man took the life of Elliott, but I beg the differ. The only thing he took was the car, but Elliott has been delivered into the hands of the lord. What comes from God, must return to God. With that being said, I would like to end this with Mathews chapter twenty two, verse twenty." Pastor Banks shuffles through the pages of his bible and begin to read.

"And he said to them who's image and description is this. They said to him Ceasars. And he said to them render therefore to Ceasar the things that are Ceasars. And to God that things are Gods."

Scotty leans over next to Motion whispering in his ear in a conspiratorial tone. "Did y'all find those niggas who killed Elliott and murk they ass yet?" Scotty asked, keeping his eyes on the pastor. Motion doesn't reply to him. ***With his lips he speaks sweetly, but in his heart he's plottin' against you. I don't ever want you to forget that.*** Poochie's words of wisdom floats through Motion's head, as he contemplates. Everything that Sasha told him is starting to.make a lot of sense to him.

"Motion what's up? You heard me?"

"Yeah . . . I heard you," Motion replied, his blood boiling.

"Let's bow our heads and have a moment of silence," Pastor Banks said, preparing to say a prayer. Cock! Cock! The mourners that are gathered around Elliott's coffin gasps, as they witness Motion aiming a chrome .45 automatic at Scotty's chest. Sasha can not believe the scene that is unfolding right before her eyes. Ms. Hopson cups her hand over her mouth.

"Oh . . . my . . . God," Ms. Hopson blurted, watching the anger gleaming in Motion's eyes. Some of the mourners backpedal, easing away from the scene.

"Take off yo' clothes Scotty!" Motion barked, gripping the large handgun.

"Man, what's up Motion you trippin'."

"I said strip Scotty!" Motion snarled, his trigger finger trembling.

"Man I thought we was family. Are you forgettin' we started this shit together," Scotty said, peeling off his clothes piece by piece.

Motion notices the beeper clipped to his trousers. Hearing the roaring sound of car engines, Motion glances around spotting a convoy of black unmarked vehicles with tinted windows. Motion snatches the beeper from his waistband.

"You mean to tell me you been settin' me up all this time! I thought we was boys Scotty! Family remember! I treated you like a brother!"

Motion flings the beeper across the grass. It crashes into a tombstone and bursts into pieces. A river of tears flows from his eyes. The reality of betrayal comes rainning down on him.

"I can't believe this shit! Out of all people in the world, Scotty you! What happened to the love Scotty! What happened to the honor in this game!" Motion's jaw muscles and temple flexes as he grips the gun.

"They made me do it Motion. I swear I never meant for it to be like this. They threatened to put me away for life. What was I suppose to do Motion?" Scotty cried, standing in the middle of the cemetery in his boxers.

"So you give me up! Yo' own brother! The nigga you grew up with!" Motion shouted. Beads of sweat pour down Scotty's forehead.

"Freeeeeze! Put down the gun!" screamed a D.E.A agent, aiming his gun at Motion.

"Come on baby, please don't do this," Ayesha begged, standing beside Motion.

"This is your final warning! Put down the gun!" Motion stands there still gripping his gun.

"Wait, give me a second with this young man before y'all pull the trigger," Pastor Banks requested, taking control of the situation. "Before you decide to squeeze that trigger, just listen to me for a minute young man. I know now is not the time you want to hear a bunch of religious talk. So, allow me to speak to you man to man. Everything in life have an opportunity cost. Are you willing to pay the price of this here action? When once face with this similar situation, I thought I was willing to pay. The long fourteen years of being away from my family, missing my children, denied of every conceivable freedom. Young man, young man, trust me . . . it's not worth it. You may be able to close your eyes and pull the trigger on his life, but can you close your eyes and pull the trigger on your own? 'Vengeance is mine' says the Lord. My son . . . please put the weapon down."

With reluctance, Motion kneels down slowly, placing the gun on the ground. Scanning the faces of angry D.E.A agents, Motion puts his hands in the air. Officer Bodo takes the pleasure of slapplng the handcuffs around Motion's wrists.

"It's going to be a very long time before you see the streets again." A smile of victory grows on Bodo's face. "Good job Scotty," Bodo said, patting Scotty on his back.

"You rat mutha fucka! I should've killed yo' bitch ass!" Motion snapped. More D.E.A agents steps on the scene with indictments. They also place Toon and Dirty Red into handcuffs. Ayesha stands in her tracks, watching them escort the love of her life away. Tears drop from her eyes, sparkling on her unblemished face.

"Mommy, why they takin' my daddy away?" Joy cried, looking at Motion, who is now sitting in the back seat of an unmarked car.

Motion locks his eyes on his precious little girl. His heart is beating painfully under his chest. This was his worst nightmare, being taken away from his daughter. *I can't believe you Scotty. Why would you take me away from my family? I would've never did you like this.* Motion glimpses around and notices a green Tahoe driving pass the cemetery. *Damn, that's the same truck I seen a few months ago trailing behind me. I should've known this was comin'.* The truck vanishes from the scene, turning down Sherman Boulevard. Toon, Dirty Red, and Motion is being driven away in separate cars.

Ayesha prances to Motion's Drop-Head Phantom. Before she reaches the driver's side, the D.E.A pulls up behind it in a tow truck. The agent jumps out of the truck strutting towards Ayesha.

"I'm sorry ma'am, but this vehicle is being seized by the federal government." Dropping her head, Ayesha walks away aimlessly. She can't believe what is happening to her.

"Mami where you goin'?" Sasha asked.

"I don't know. I'm just confused right now," Ayesha answered.

"I seen what just happened mami. You and Joy can ride with me mami," Sasha offered. Ayesha and Joy climbs into Sasha truck and pulls off. Julio vanished before he was noticed. Marco jumps into his car. Pulling out of the cemetery, Marco begins to get nervous. He is wondering do they have anything on him. Two more tow trucks pulls up and tows away Toon and Dirty Red's cars. Slowly everyone evacuates from the cemetery.

*   *   *

The repetitious sound of playing cards, smacking the table, cuts through the atmosphere. A group of inmates are huddled around a table playing a game of spades.

"Let yo' next move be yo' best move. If you do the wrong thing I'ma set that ass!" said an inmate, staring at the inmate seated on his right side. His eyes bounce back and forth from his hand to the three cards that are laying on the table. He hesitates, weighing out his options.

Motion enters the pod dressed in an orange uniform carrying a bedroll, being escorted by a female deputy. She hands Motion's face card to the deputy that is seated behind the deputy's work station, who is punching buttons on the computer. After scanning the face card, the deputy points his indexfinger at the upper tier.

"You'll be living in cell twenty six." Motion glimpses around analyzing his surroundings, as he strides to the cell. Feeling the sea of eyeballs watching him makes him feel uncomfortable.

Stepping inside the cell, he notices that it is two or three times smaller than his walk-in-closest. This is the first time that he has ever been inside of a jail cell.

Motion makes up the bed and organizes the cell before joining the other inmates in the dayroom. The only thing on Motion's mind is Ayesha, Joy, and bail. He still can't believe how Scotty deceived him. Motion thinks about the conversation that he had with Poochie. Everything Poochie said made a lot of sense to him. A man never knows what he would do under pressure until his faith is tested. But one thing Motion promised himself is that he will not go out like a coward. Being a true hustler, he understands that this is all a part of the game.

Motion finds a seat in front of the television. He sits beside three inmates that are watching the news. Motion doesn't recognize any of the inmates. Most of them seem like they are young enough to attend highschool. A majority of the inmates housed in Milwaukee County Jail are facing state cases. Only a few of the inmates have federal cases.

Leaning back in his seat, Motion watches the television closely, straining his ears trying to hear over the noise. Just when Motion was getting into the news, a tall, frail, inmate no older than twenty years of age steps out of his cell. He struts pass Motion with his orange pants sagging. Reaching above his head, he switches the channel to B.E.T. Seating next to Motion, he crosses his legs. He never acknowledged Motion one time. Several of the other inmates gather around to watch 106th & Park.

Motion rises from his seat, turning the channel back to the news.

One thing Motion does not tolerate is disrespect.

He returns to his seat, leaning back in a calm mannerism. ***These young niggas got me fucked up.*** Motion locks his eyes on the news, paying no attention to the other inmates.

The tall, frail inmate seated next to him rises out of his seat slowly with a devilish look in his eyes.

"I take it that you 'ont know da rules around here?" he stated, glaring at a fearless Motion. Receiving no response from Motion is starting to aggrevate him. "Nigga you must don't know who I am? We runnin' dis shit around here. I was tryna be a playa about dis, but now I think it's time to get into some gangsta shit."

A group of inmates starts inching their way in his direction, towering over him, coming from every different direction. Still Motion sits there showing no sign of fear.

* * *

Scotty lounges in his lavish livingroom sinking in the plush leather sofa, surfing through the channels on the massive plasma screen television. It has been over a month since Kanisha packed her things and moved out of town with her mother. Scotty feels empty without her in his life. ***Damn baby I miss the shit out of you. I never meant for it to be like this. Now I see what they mean when they say, you never miss what you have until it's gone.*** The chiming sound of the doorbell captures his attention. Rising from the leather sofa, he struts to the front door shirtless. Peering through the peep-hole, he sees the woman that he has been waiting for. A short smile fills his face. Opening the door, he ushers the nerdy looking female into his palace.

"What's up baby? I been missin' the hell out of you," Scotty greeted with a lie.

"I've been missing you too honey," Becky said seductively.

"You know our routine baby," Scotty said, unbuckling his belt. Becky wraps her hair in a long ponytail. She gazes at Scotty through the lenses of her bifocals. Pinching his zipper, Scotty unzips his pants letting them fall to the carpeted floor.

"Holy shit honey. You have a dick big enough to choke a horse," Becky blurted, admiring his solid six pack that is complimenting his thick, snake long dick.

Dropping to her knees, Becky gently grips his long throbbing pipe. She grazes it with her warm tongue licking up and down his shaft. To intensify the sensation, she gently massages his balls while deep throating him.

"Mmmm, that's it baby," Scotty groaned. It looks as if he is standing in front of a urinal. One hand on his hip and the other palming the back of her head. His crisscut diamonds in his platinum pinky ring sparkles with the movement of his hand, as he cups her bobbing head. The saliva on his chocolate rod glistens, as she holds it in her tiny hand. Becky swallows half of it, bobbing her head in a steady rhythm.

"Mmmmm . . . cum . . . in . . . my . . . mouth," she moaned in between sucks. A warm sensation travels down Scotty's spine making him feel like he's in paradise. Her warm saliva trickles down his balls. She swirls her tongue around the head of his dick. Inch by inch, she swallows the full length of his manhood like a certified pro.

"Uuh shit!" Scotty groaned, his knees buckling as she quickens her pace. Scotty's body jerks involuntarily, as he explodes inside her juicy mouth. "Shiiit baby! I love the w-way you suck this dick!" Some of Scotty's sex juices leaks out the corners of her mouth.

Becky swallows all of Scotty's warm, creamy juices. The X-pills that Scotty popped earlier have him hard as a rock. With his thumbs resting on her hips, Scotty begins to roll down her plaid skirt. She peels off her white tank top, allowing her surgically enhanced titties to spring loose. Her red pubic hair accentuates her olive thighs. Scotty fingers the petal of her pussy and begins to play with her clit. He looks at his shiny fingertips, admiring the juices that are coating them. Becky grabs his hand and sucks the juices off his fingertips.

"Mmmm," she purred, licking her lips.

Placing her in the doggy style position, he slides his hard, throbbing, long dick one-third of the way inside her pulsating pussy. Becky trembles with convulsions, as her pussy muscles throb along his shaft. She reaches between her thighs massaging his nutsack. He plunges deep inside of her on the in stroke and then slides out until the rim of his head kisses the opening of her V-spot. Spreading her ass cheeks apart, he stares at the creamy juices shining on his pipe. Scotty starts drilling her from the back, beating up her hot, pulsating walls.

"OOOOOO, yessss, baby, that's it, that's it," Becky sings in ecstasy. He plunges her pussy repeatedly as hard as he can until they are both dripping in salty sweat. Her pussy is suctioning hard. The blood in her veins sizzle. The dimples in the sides of Scotty's ass deepens with every powerful stroke. "00000, you, f-fucking the hell out of me!" Becky cried, whimpering like a baby. Scotty smacks her flat, firm, white ass, leaving pink welts on it. "Honey I'm about t-to c-cum!" Becky moaned hysterically.

Cum squirts out of her gushy, wet, pussy moistening Scotty's pubic hair. Her face winces in torment and her moans for him not to stop becomes louder and louder. Becky is in a hypnotic trance. Gripping her around her tiny waist, he nearly lifts her off the carpet with each thrust. Scotty slides his creamy dick out of her and spits his saliva in her ass crack lubricating her asshole. Her inner thighs are soaked with pussy juice. Gently Scotty eases inside her pink wrinkled elastic like asshole, reaching his hand around her hip, massaging her clit. Arching her back, Becky gives him easy access.

"Uuugh! Baby it feel gooddd!" Becky shouted. Her ass is warm and slippery with her sex juices. Scotty drives her crazy, as she goes into an orgasmic daze. She moans loudly tossing her hair, as Scotty pounds deep inside of her tight asshole. She bucks him back. "Fuck me harder! Fuck me harder!" Becky screamed, throwing her ass against his pelvis. Her bifocals fall off her face, bouncing on the plush carpet with a soft thud. The clapping sound of flesh mingles with their moans of pleasure.

"Uuuuh shit! I'ma 'bout to nut baby!" Scotty shouted, pulling his long, thick dick out of her wet ass. He squirts his creamy white liquid allover her spine and her pink ass cheeks. Becky's asshole looks like a gaping baby mouth. Juices glisten around her open asshole. "Shit that was good," Scotty said, squeezing the rest of the cum out of his dick.

"I love it when you fuck the hell out of me honey," Becky proclaimed.

They ascend the sprawling staircase in Scotty's 3,000 squarefoot three story house, making their way to the shower.

The agreement Scotty made with the feds allowed him to maintain ownership of all his asset.

After taking a shower, Scotty and Becky gets dressed. Stepping into the walk-in-closet, Scotty returns with a leather suitcase containing 6,000 X-pills.

"Here you go sweetheart. I need you to make this last run for me. My man is goin' to pick you up at the bus station. Make sure you be careful. After this we about to start a family. I'm ready to give this up and walk you down that aisle. I'm ready to give you the life that you deserve. I'ma pay your tuition and have us a house built from the ground. I never . . . knew that love was so strong. I . . . promise from this day . . . it's just you and me," Scotty lied, putting on his best performance. Becky stares into his eyes believing his every word. Her heart skips a beat.

"Honey I-I love you so much," she said in between tears. "I've been waiting for you to say that for a long time. You know I-I'll do anything for you honey." They are interrupted by the sound of a car horn in the driveway.

"Damn baby that's the cab. I wish I could spend more time with you," Scotty lied.

"Don't worry honey we have a lot of time to spend together," Becky said, standing on her tippy toes, kissing Scotty on his tender lips. "Bye honey. See you soon."

"Bye baby."

Becky exits the house jumping into the cab. Scotty locks the door behind her and flips open his cellphone with a devious smile. "Bye, bye, baby," he said aloud.

*　　*　　*

Leaning back in a calm mannerism, Motion continues to watch the news. A picture flashes across the screen gaining the attention of all the inmates. Recognizing the face of the man causes them to stop in their tracks. Everybody in the dayroom listens closely to the news.

"Earlier this afternoon federal authorities arrested three men at Graceland Cemetery after a six month investigation. The three are alleged to be responsible for operating a mutli-million dollar drug operation that involved the seizure of seventy five kilograms of cocaine, seven luxurious automobiles, three hundred and fifty thousand dollars in jewelry, a mansion, and two point one million dollars in cash."

Motion watches the scenery on the television as they place all his cars on a flatbed. Motion's mugshot appears on the screen again.

"Motion Hopson a.k.a 'The Black Godfather' is reported as the ringleader of the mutli-million dollar operation. Authorities believe that he his responsible for four murders that took place over the weekend on Milwakee's city Northside. So far the authorities have no evidence on the murders and all three of the men have refused to cooperate with the law enforcement. All three of the men are being held without bail. If charged, all three of the men could face ten years to life imprisonment and a $250,000.00 fine.

There you have it, today's top story. This is Glen Cavalli reporting to you live from Fox 4 News."

The tall, frail, young soldier stands in front of Motion gripping a shank that is made out of chicken bone.

"So, what you 'gon do, kill me with that?" Motion asked, speaking for the first time. Before the young soldier could answer, a voice interrupts them.

"Hold up Killa Cal," said an inmate, breaking through the threshold.

Motion looks over his shoulder locking eyes with a man that he had promised to murk on site. But at this moment Motion is glad to see him.

"That's family right there. Me and my man go way back. Let me handle this," he continued. All the young soldiers back away, respecting the man's call. All of the inmates are members of the G.D's (Gangster Disciples).

The man takes a seat beside Motion, gesturing for the other inmates to give them some space.

"Before you say anything let me explain first. I know you probably salty at a nigga for what happened in the past. I know you feel like I played you, but it ain't like that. I had to get rid of my phone. I found out the feds tapped my phone. I had to get little, the feds was looking for me. I was on the run for about six months. If you want me to, I'll have my girl drop six stacks on yo' books in the next hour," he explained.

"Check this out Shake. I appreciate you offering me the money you owe, but it's all good. One thing I learned is that in this game shit happens. Keepin' it real, yeah I wanted to put one in you. Shit, at the time that was the last little money I had. I charged that shit to the game. Right now that's the least of my worries. I got a lot of shit on my mind right now," Motion stated.

"I feel you baby. Believe me, I know the feds will stress a nigga out. Well, not that we have an understandin', I know you need a care package until you have somebody drop some loot off. I got some hyigene and food for you in my cell. They serving some garbage ass shit fo' dinner. I barely eat the food they serve here," Shake said.

"It can't be that bad."

"Shieeeet, you'll see."

Shake rises out of the seat. "Come to my cell with me for a minute."

Motion walks to Shake's two man cell. Shake tosses a stick of deordorant in a plastic bag, two bars of soap, toothpaste, toothbrush, four cups of noodles, two Snickers, and two Smooth Magazines.

"Here you go famm. That should hold you down until we go back to commissary."

"Good lookin'," Motion thanked.

"Man that was some bogus shit yo' guy Scotty did. I would've killed that nigga for deceiving me like that," Shake proclaimed, walking out of his cell. Motion gives him a puzzled look.

"Man how you know that muthafucka ratted on me?" Motion asked.

I haven't told Shake what happened.

"What, the nigga ratted on you. I 'ont know nothin' about that. I'm talkin' about that shit with Dirty Red," Shake clarified.

"What you mean?" Motion inquired with a crinkled face.

"That shit he did when he had Dirty Red kidnapped."

"Had Dirty Red kidnapped."

"Yeah, you ain't know? I seen him leavin' my man Ball's apartment one day. He was carrying a bag in his hand. It surprised me when I seen him leaving Ball's spot, because Ball and his man Thump was stick up kids. When I hollered at Ball, he told me they just hit a lick for half a ticket. That's when he told me about Scotty givin' him the four, one, one, on Dirty Red," Shake informed, looking at the evil expression on Motion's face.

"I knew it was an inside job. I just couldn't put my finger on it."

"I never knew yo' boy was grimey like that."

"That ain't my muthafuckin' boy."

The lights in the dayroom flashes. "Man it's time for us to lock down. I'ma holla at you when we come back out."

"Dayroom is now closed, lock down!" yelled the deputy, standing behind the booth.

"A'ight, I'll holla at you." Motion heads to his cell wishing he would've killed Scotty when he had the chance.

*   *   *

Marco leans back in his GMC 1500 pick up truck, peering through the window at on coming traffic. Lil Wink is seated in the passenger seat pressing buttons on his laptop, surfing through the wireless web. For the thrid time, Marco is meeting with Mr.Gibson from the City's Accessor's office. Mr.Gibson has been schooling Marco on the real estate industry. Marco purchased two duplexes on the Northside for less than $10,000.00. Mr.Gibson assisted him by using his resources at the City's Accessor's office. Marco, Lil Wink, and Poochie renovated the houses, bringing them up to code. After making a few modifications, the houses were appraised at $78,000.00 to $80,000.00 each.

Lately Marco has been maintaining a low profile. After witnessing the feds apprehend Toon, Motion, and Dirty Red, it has him nervous at times. He can't believe how Scotty deceived the team. Everyday Marco wonder is the feds going to pick him up next. He knows that the federal government plays a dirty game and that they can keep you under investigation for up to 5 years.

A mint green 69 Lincoln Continental bends the corner. Pulling up behind Marco's pick up truck. Marco gazes in the rearview mirror admiring the old school automobile. Marco's mouth drops open in surprise, as Mr.Gibson climbs out of the car wearing a Fedora, short sleeve button up, jeans, and a pair of snakeskin boots.

Marco jumps out of his pickup truck dressed in a blue Dickie suit with white paint stains smeared allover it.

"How you doing Mr. Gibson?" Marco greeted with his hand extended.

"I'm doing a'ight. What about you young man?" Mr. Gibson asked, shaking Marco's hand with a firm grip.

"I'm doing okay 'ol school. I like that clean Lincoln you got. I always wanted one of them. Is those all original parts?"

"Yeah, those all original. I had this car for fifteen years. The only time I bring it out is on Sundays. This car never even seen the winter."

Marco traces the hood of the car with his fingertips looking through the window at the impeccable interior. A short whistle pierces his lips.

"Whenever you decide to sell it let me know," Marco said.

"I'll never sell my baby. I'm passing it down to my son." Lil Wink hops out of the truck joining them.

"What's up Mr. Gibson?" Lil Wink greeted with a smile.

"Just enjoying this Sunday afternoon. Well, let me get down to business. I have to hurry back home to my wife. We have a family gathering to attend this evening.

First of all, I want y'all to look around and observe y'all surroundings."

Marco and Lil Wink glimpses around at the sabotaged neighborhood. "Three years from now the city plan to knock down all these old dilapidated houses. The city has a development plan. So that means that this is a good area to invest in. You have three elements to go by when you buy real estate. That's physical, investment, and legal. Also remember before you purchase a house ask the owner for the Schedule E form. The Schedule E form will tell you the true value of a house. The owner has to submit it to the government. They can get charge for perjury for lying on the form. A Schedule E form makes their property lower in value, to save and reduce on taxes. So ask for that price on Schedule E form. You can't look up a Schedule E form yourself because it is not public information. If the owner don't want to show it to you walk away."

"What's the purpose of fillin' out a Schedule E form?" Marco interrupted.

"That's how you save taxes. A Schedule E is a supplemental form that goes with your 1040. You put all of your tax deductibles on the Schedule E form. You can add in auto and travel deductible. Cleaning, maintence, management fees, mortgage interest, repair supplies, and other taxes." Mr.Gibson explained.

"A'ight I get it now," Marco said.

"It's a lot you need to know when it come to this real estate game. This is another thing you need to know. Whenever you buy a property that's occupied. Find out if the tenants are on a lease."

"Why is that?"

"Because that lease has to be respected or there can be major problems. Also, you can't increase the rent or none of that."

"I never knew that."

"Don't forget this either. I know you already bought a few properties. When you fix up a property and bring it up to progression. Make sure it's the same value as the surrounding houses.

Once you pass progression, you go into regression, which means, you start losing money.

I'm going to share a few more things with you before I go. Do you know anything about asset protection?" Mr. Gibson asked.

"Never heard of it."

"Well, let me break it down to you. Whenever you make investments you want to protect it. How many properties you have at this time?"

"Four duplexes," Marco answers.

"Do you have them in your name?"

"Yep."

"See that's your first mistake."

"Why you say that?"

"Because if one of your tenets get hurt on your property. That mean they can sue you for all your asset. Anything that you have in your name is in jeopardy. What you want to do is put your property under a limited liability company. The first move you need to make when organizing an,(LLC) is to prepare and file the Articles Of Incorporations. The Articles of Incorporations consist of the (LLC) name, purposes and power, name and address of resident, agent, manager or member managed, operating agreement, managers, restrictions, on transfer of interest, distribution to members, profits and losses, meetings, and charging order. A charging order procedure is a unique part of asset protection offered by limited partnerships and LLC's. If someone tries to sue you, they can only obtain a charging order. One of the biggest and most significant benefits of the limited liability company and the major reason for its existence, is the fact the IRS recognizes it as a pass through entity. All of the profits and losses of the company flow through the (LLC) without tax. They flow through to the business owner's tax return and are handled on a individual basis. With a C-Corporation, the profits are taxed at the corporate level and then taxed again when a dividend is paid to the shareholder. The only thing you can do is minimize the double taxation of a C-Corporation. A S-Corporation is also taxed twice. The only way to make a S-Corporation operate as a flow through entity is by filing a 2553 form within fourty five days of registering your S-Corporation. You have to establish a board of directors. The board of directors contains a Chief Executive Officer, President, Vice President, Corporate Secretary, Treasurer, General Manager, Controller, and Assist Officers. You can put yourself down as all the titles if you choose too," Mr. Gibson explains, as they stroll through the neighborhood on feet.

"So which is the best business structure to have?" Marco asks.

"To me, the best business structure is the C-Corporation, LLC, and the S-Corporation. Never use a Sole proprietorship that's a bad entity. When using a Sole proprietorship you and the business are one person. That also goes for the General partnership. They do not provide any asset protection at all. A Limited Liability Company is a separate entity. An LLC act as its own artificial person. If someone sues your company, it doesn't affect you as an individual."

"I like the sound of that. I'm not tryna lose what I worked hard for to some scandalous board on section eight," Marco states, walking towards their cars.

Just as Mr. Gibson chuckles, his cell phone chimes.

"Hold up for a second," he says, holding his indexfinger up. "Hello . . . Okay honey I'm on my way . . . I love you too . . . Bye, bye." Hanging up his cell phone, he says, "That was my wife. She told me to hurry up and come home."

"I guess we betta let you get going. I don't want to be responsible for your wife puttin' you on the couch tonight," Marco says jokingly.

"That might be true if an oldschool playa like myself didn't know how to stroke it to the East and stroke it to the West," Mr. Gibson sings. Marco and Lil Wink explode with laugther. Mr. Gibson emphasizes by humping the air in a playful manner.

"Old school you a fool," Lil Wink proclaims.

"Well, before I go let me share one more thing with you. Check into Nevada corporations. Nevada corporate laws protects the privacy of individuals. Nevada is the only state in the United States that does not share information on a corporations shareholders with the IRS. Nevada has no state corporate or personal income tax. The state has no corporate shares tax and no franchise tax. Businesses save hundreds to millions of dollars each year being incorporated in Nevada. Two or more corporations may payless in federal corporate taxes. If your one corporation makes one hundred thousand to three hundred and thirty five thousand dollars, your corporate tax rates is thirty nine percent. If you formulate three corporations your corporate tax rate will be twenty two thousand and five hundred dollars, saving you ninteen thousand, two hundred and fifty dollars. All you have to do is upstream the income on each corporation making them have a profit of one cent less than fifty thousand dollars. Also make sure you never commingle your business account with personal things. That can cause the IRS to penetrate your corporate veil. I guess it's for me to get out of here. You two young men make sure y'all be careful out here. I'll talk to y'all next weekend."

"A'ight Mr. Gibson. Take care of yourself," Marco says, jumping into his truck.

*   *   *

Motion lies on the concrete slab, staring at the ceiling with his hands interlaced behind his head in deep thoughts. *I should've killed that bitch ass nigga when I had the chance.* A distorted sound breaks his train of thought coming from the intercom.

"Inmate Hopson!" the deputy shrills over the intercom.

"Yeah," Motion answers.

"You have an attorney visit."

"A'ight," Motion says, sliding into his shower shoes. *Man I hope he got some good news for me.* He gazes into the cloudy looking mirror brushing his hair.

Pushing the button on the intercom, Motion alerts the deputy letting him know that he is ready. The door clicks open. He enters a small conference room that is located in the hallway, adjacent to many others. Motion extends his hand greeting the well groomed young black man. He has on a tailor made Canali suit and a pair of Gucci dress shoes. Motion inspects the man's attire. He knows that a person's appearance speaks a lot of words.

"How you doing Mr. Hopson? My name is David Landers. I take it that you hired me to represent you?" he states, shaking Motion's hand with a firm grip.

"I heard a lot about you Mr. Landers."

"Oh yeah, well, hopefully I'll be able to assist you with your delimma." Motion seats himself across the table from the man.

"I received a payment just this morning. Also, I meet your fiance. She seems to be a very nice lady. She is very concerned about you." Hearing the attorney speak highly of Ayesha makes him feel confident in their relationship.

"So how is everything lookin' for me?" Motion inquiries, waiting for some good news.

"I'm going to be honest with you Mr. Hopson. At this time it's too early to say. I did get a chance to scrutinize the indictment. Once I get your discovery packet I'll be able to give you an accurate analysis." Motion rises out of his chair in silence walking toward the wall with his back facing the attorney.

"Just be patient Mr. Hopson. Like I said, I just received your payment an hour ago and I didn't get a ch-" Motion cuts him off in mid-sentence and turns around with a look of frustration on his face.

"I just had my fiance drop you a hundred thousand cash. My fuckin' life is in the hands of the devil. So, I'm gon' let you know this out the gate. I'm not gon' be playin' any games with my life. I want you to find out how I can make this case disappear. Remember, I hired you. So that means you work for me now. And for the record, if you make this case disappear it's a very big bonus for you," Motion says, leaning against the table staring into Mr. Landers' eyes.

"Do we have an understandin?"

"Yes Mr. Hopson. I'll get right on it," Mr. Landers replies, thinking to himself how much he can't stand this man already. Motion pushes the button on the intercom letting the deputy know that his attorney visit is over.

CHAPTER TEN

A throng of automobiles are cruising up and down the streets of Minneapolis. The mundane sound of car horns blare from every direction. Becky hangs up the payphone ending her call. During her whole ride to Minneapolis, she thought about all the promises Scotty made to her. Becky adjusts her bifocals and kneels down, picking up the luggage that Scotty gave her. She stands in front of the glass doors, peering through them, watching multiple yellow cabs pull up to the Greyhound station.

A silver Infiniti QX 56 turns the corner, slowing down in front of the bus station. It's shiny, tall, chunky rims is gleaming under its frame. Becky exits the bus station prancing to the passenger side of the luxurious truck. A tall, husky, dark complexion man with leathery skin hops out of the truck.

"What's up Becky?" he greeted, opening the back door.

"Nothing. I'm just a little tired from that long bus ride. What about yourself?" Becky inquired.

"Ain't nothin' changed. It's the same ol' thang." Becky climbs into the truck, as he tosses the luggage in the back seat. His iced out Datlantis watch sparkles on his wrist, as he jumps into the truck pulling off. Before he could make it down the block an unmarked car jumps behind them. Whoop! Whoop! He looks into his rearview mirror startled. A group of unmarked cars speeds up on them from every direction.

"Bitch, you fuckin' set me up!" he snapped, reaching under his seat. Becky looks at the DEA agents that are surrounding them.

"I don't know what's going on, I swear," Becky exclaims in tears.

Knowing that he is a three time loser, he puts the chrome 357 Mag to her head. He squeezes the trigger at point blank range, painting the passenger window with her brains. Becky's lifeless body slumps over in the leather interior. Hearing the sound of gunfire and seeing a flash of light. The DEA agents open fire, riddling the truck with bullet holes. The man jumps out of the truck holding his bullet wounded chest, squeezing the trigger of his 357 Mag. squatting down behind propped open car doors, the DEA agents continue to fire. A shower of bullets from the agents high powered guns sends him staggering backwards, stomping his feet on the concrete. He topples to the ground with blood leaking out of his body. He is sprawled on the ground next to his gun, convulsing with blood pouring out of his mouth. Slowly his body becomes cold and his whole world is complete darkness.

*　　*　　*

"Baby, I told you I was gon' take you to the top. When my back was against the wall and I was down on my knuckles, you were there. You never gave up on our love. You always believed in me. You listened to me with your full attention as I shared my dreams with you. I'll never forget about all the things that you done for me. I know there is no amount of money that can amount to what you did for me. I want you to know that I love you to the fullest. To show you my appreciation I did somethin' very special for you my love." Vegas says, with heartfelt words. Elane relaxes in the leather interior, wondering what Vegas has up his sleeve. Vegas always seems to keep her in suspense.

*　　*　　*

Scotty bends the corner in his black Mercedes Benz S600 Brabus with limo tinted windows. The chrome mirrored rims chops under its frame as he moves about.

"Kanisha, I promise you if you come home I'll never hurt you again. You know I love you. All I'm a skin' for is one more chance," Scotty begs.

Engrossed in the phone conversation, he pays no attention to the stop sign.

A sandstone colored Bentley Brooklands coupe is crossing the intersection. Its 22inch chrome wheels sparkles hard, as the beaming sun strikes them.

"Baby, I'll do anyth-" Errrk! The Bentley Brooklands screeches to a stop, honking it's horn. Scotty smashes on his brakes swerving out of control. Scotty peers through his tinted windows at the couple seated inside the extravagant automobile. The angry mid-aged man driving the Bentley is making gestures with his hands. Reading his lips, Scotty can tell that he is saying, "Watch where the fuck you going." Scotty's face twists in anger, as he shifts his focus on the female passenger. The Bentley pulls off, dipping around the corner glistening like a fine piece of jewelry. Scotty cuts the steering wheel making a U-turn, lingering behind the Bentley. From a distance, he watches as the Bentley pulls in front of a commercial building. It parks beside a reserved sign that reads "H.B.I.C." The doors to the Bentley swings open.

*   *   *

"Oh my God baby. I can't believe you put this all together for me," Elane says, holding her chest in awe. She stares at the building admiring all of its modifications.

The entire beauty salon is made of glass. Multiple plasma screen televisions are over-looking each individual booth. A large custom made sign decorates the entrance reading 'Barber & Grill Beauty salon.'

"You deserve nothin' less than the best sweetheart," Vegas says, standing next to his Bentley in a tailor made Cesare Attolini suit.

His lavender silk Michael Newell tie is tied in a Windor knot. Stretching his arm, he bends his elbow, glancing at his diamond bezel De Beers watch.

"Let me show you around your new establishment."

Elane's four inch Jimmy Choo pumps clicks, as she prances beside Vegas. Reddish bronze lipstick surrounds her flawless white teeth. Elane has her lengthy hair pinned up into a french twist, with a few strands of hair hanging loose, framing her face. Her Daniel K diamond earrings dangle with the rhythm of her walk.

"I had a bar and grill put in here for when the customers are waiting to get their hair done, there will be a two drink minimum. Chicken wings will be served from mild, spicy, to hot. All the customers will receive an electronical device that will alert them by a flash of light and a beep. That will let them know that it's their turn to get their hair done. Also I had a game room put in for the kids."

"Whoa baby, how you come up with such a creative idea?" Elane inquired.

"It came from doing time and utilizing my time constructively," Vegas replies, showing her the rest of the shop.

*　　*　　*

Scotty leans back behind the tinted windows watching Elane and Vegas, as they walk around the shop. ***Bitch I got you faded. You want get away with settin' me up. I promise you I'll be back. This shit ain't over bitch.*** Scotty thinks to himself as he pulls off into the light traffic.

*　　*　　*

"Inmate Hopson you have a visit! Booth number three!" yells the female deputy. Motion stands in front of the tiny mirror inside of the one man cell, brushing his spiraling 360 wave pattern. There is enough waves in his hair to make all the inmates in his pod seasick.

Motion struts toward the visiting area in his orange Milwaukee County Jail jump suit.

For the last eight months, Ayesha has been coming to see him every weekend like clockwork. This is the only day that Motion has to look forward.

A letter from Ayesha has become one of the most important things in life. Mail call is one of the most significant things to all the inmates. Ayesha makes it her job to write and visit him religiously.

Stepping into the visiting booth, he gazes at Ayesha's doll like face. Ayesha picks up the phone that is attached to the wall. Joy jumps around in her, lap excitedly.

"Daddddy!" Joy shouts, snatching the phone out of Ayesha's hand. "Heyyy daddy!" she greets, cradling the phone in her tiny hands.

"Heyyy boo!" Motion says, greeting her with a smile.

"When you comin' home daddy? Me miss you." Motion studies his precious little daughter's face in silence.

"I'll be home real soon boo," Motion hopes, having no idea if he will ever come home again. Lately the bible has become his bestfriend.

On the streets he didn't acknowledge the bible. The thing he believed in was the almighty dollar.

"You promise?" Joy asks in her child like voice. Motion touches the two inch plexiglass that divdes them and traces an imaginary heart glass.

"Yes . . . I promise, cross my heart." He traces a smeary x in the center of the smeary heart. Joy touches the glass with her little hand, as if she can touch his.

"Swear to God?" she asks, looking at him waiting for an answer.

"Yeah . . . I—swear."

"And if you lie."

"God can stick a needle in my eye."

"Kay. Love you daddy. Here go mama." Joy hands Ayesha the phone.

"Hey baby," Ayesha greets in her soft voice.

"Hey my love. How you been holding up out there?"

"I'm doing my best baby. But it's hard without you at home. I just pray to God that you come back home." Motion can see nothing but pain etched in Ayesha's face. "This'll all be over with baby. We gon' move and start all over somewhere else. Did you check the lock boxes?"

"Yeah, I checked them. Everything still in there."

"Did you make sure you whatn't being followed like I told you?"

"Yes baby. I did exactly what you said. I even traded cars with my mother."

"Good." Motion says, feeling a little relief.

He never told anyone about the 8 million dollars and the raw diamonds he brought from Sierra Leone. He had Ayesha retrieve a hundred grand out of the lock boxes. Usually, he never puts Ayesha in his business, but she is the only person he can trust right now.

"Booth three it's time to terminate your visit," yells the female deputy in an authorative voice.

"It's time for me to go baby. I'll see you next weekend. I love you sweetheart and don't ever forget that."

"I love you more baby," Ayesha replies, blowing him a kiss through the glass. He blows her a kiss back and says, "Impossible."

"Bye daddy!" Joy says, waving her hand behind the glass.

"Bye boo. I love you!" Motion waves back at her, watching them until they are no longer in sight.

*   *   *

"Mmmm, hmmm," Titianna purrs in satisfaction. A cascade of moonlight spills into the darkened bedroom. Marco whispers in Titianna's ear, grazing it with his warm tender lips. Shadows are swimming along the walls to the movement of their acrobatic love making. Titianna digs into Marco's muscular shoulders with her french manicured nails. Marco rotates his hips in a circular motion at a slow pace. Their moans are simultaneous, as they fall into an orgasmic daze.

*   *   *

An unknown male eases through the darkness with a skull cap on his head. He removes a screw driver from his pants pocket. Standing behind a single family house, he glimpses around sneakily. A pair of black leather gloves covers his hands. He moves closer to the house like a panther stalking its prey.

*   *   *

Marco traces the side of Titianna's face in silence, studying her cocoa brown eyes. "Baby I love you so much," Marco says.

"I love you too baby," Titianna replies, looking into his eyes.

"I want you to know that you mean the world to me. I'm glad that God allowed you to come into my life. If it wasn't for you comin' into my life, I'll probably still be on those wicked streets or in jail with my guys. I pray for them every night. I know what they are going through. I tried to go visit them, but they want me to lay low for a while. Sometimes I blame myself for them gettin' caught up. If I was there with them none of this probably would've ever happened," Marco ventilates, sharing his thoughts with Titianna.

"Baby don't blame yourself, it's not your fault. All you can do is stick by their sides and pray for the best. It was all a part of their destiny," Titianna responds.

"I guess you right." Marco rises from the bed. Leaning over, he scoops her up in his arms. He carries her to the shower.

After climbing through the window of the single family residence, the unknown man pads over the carpeted floor. He moves through the livingroom meticulously. His eyes adjust to the darkness, as he scans the neatly arranged livingroom. His beady eyes bounce around, stopping on a framed picture of a beautiful woman. Walking over to the picture, he picks it up with a gloved hand. Several emotions begin to invade him, as he plasters his eyes on the photograph. "I told you I love you, but you had to leave me. Why you didn't just listen to me baby?" he whispers to the framed picture, reminiscing on the good old times they shared. The sizzling sound of the shower snaps him out of his trance.

*   *   *

Titianna admires Marco's peanut butter reflection being illuminated by candle light, on the glass shower doors. Warm streams of water is pounding against their naked bodies. Titianna's silky wet hair clings to her drenched vanilla skin tone. Marco's tongue traces down her cleavage, inching its way to her pierced navel. He peppers her smooth inner thighs with soft gentle kisses. His fingers roll through her silky mound, as he grazes her clit.

"Mmmm," she moans. Her palm is smearing the foggy glass on the shower door; as she rests her hand on it for support. Staring through his partially closed eyes, Marco notices a shadow against the shower door. His eyebrows raise in fear. He can see the silhouette of someone gripping a gun. Noticing the changes in Marco's movement, Titianna looks down at a startled Marco.

"Somebody's in the house," Marco whispers, blocking her with his frame.

"Oh my God, it's my ex-boyfriend," she panics, staring at the shadow.

Bullets penetrate the glass shower door, riddling Marco's chest as he stands in front of Titianna blocking her. Sheets of glass shatters, rainning on their bodies. Titianna screams loudly gripping Marco's bloody body. The burning candles falls into the wet surface of the tub dying out. The only light available is the fire that is discharging from the barrel of the gun. Titianna and Marco are lying on the ivory surface. The water on the floor of the tub turns red, as their blood leaks from their bodies. Slowly water and blood goes down the drian. Titianna's ex-boyfriend towers over their lifeless bodies gripping his gun. "I'm sorry my love, but you made me do it. If I can't have you to myself nobody can." He studies Titianna's grosequely sprawled body and leans over kissing her on the lips. Quietly he exits the house, not realizing that one of the neighbors caught a glimpse of his face.

*　　*　　*

"Fuck!" Motion says aloud, placing the phone back on its cradle. *I hope ain't nothin' wrong. This ain't like Ayesha not to answer the phone.* Stepping into the one man cell, he paces back and forth. For the first time during his incarceration, Ayesha haven't showed up. She usually comes to visit him every weekend. Motion has been calling her over and over all weekend. He even called his lawyer's office, but his secretary informed him that his attorney Mr. Landers will be out of his office for the rest of the week.

"Inmate Hopson," a voice crackles over the intercom in his cell.

"Yeah!" Motion answers.

"You have a family visit in booth two."

"A'ight," Motion responds, stepping out of the cell. *Somethin' must've came up yesterday and she decided to come today.* He strides to booth number two, seeing no one sitting there. Sometimes the inmates will beat their visitors to the booth. Motion's heart races with anticipation, as he sits in the empty booth staring aimlessly. He can't wait to show Ayesha the surprise that he has for her. Seeing someone's shadow shifting along the tiled floor causes Motion to look up. His eyebrows furrows, as he locks his eyes on a clean shaved man dressed in a double breasted suit. A smile spreads across his face as he seats himself. Motion's face registered a look of disappointment. His heart drops into his stomach, seeing that it isn't Ayesha. *What the hell he doing here?* Grabbing the phone Motion says, "What's up Poochie? What brings you here?" Out of all people in the world, Motion never expected to see Poochie.

"It's somethin' I need to tell you," Poochie replies with a serious look on his face.

"What's wrong Poochie?" Motion asks, hoping that nothing has happened to Ayesha or Joy.

"Somethin' real bad happened last night. I hate to be the one to break the bad news to you. But, Marco and his girlfriend Titianna was murdered last night." Motion drops his head like he just lost a championship game. His heart twists in agony.

"Damn this fucked up," he utters, swaying his head, gripping his forehead. "What happened?"

"They said Titianna's ex-boyfriend got jealous. He broke in her house while they were in the shower and shoot them. One of the neighbors caught him leaving the house and identified him. The police are still searchin' for him," Poochie informs. "But that's not the only reason why I came to see you. I have somethin' else that I need to tell you."

"I hope it ain't some more bad news," Motion says.

"Not really, but it ain't good either. I see you got Ayesha's name tatted on yo neck."

"Oh yeah. You know I have to represent for the wifey. She had my back since day one."

"Ain't nothin' wrong with that youngin'. The only woman I ever loved was taken away from me. Every since than my life was never the same. But I'm not gon' get into that right now. I know they only give you a thirty minute visit, so I'ma give it to you like this youngin'. The man that killed yo father back in the days was at Elliott's funeral."

"Say what!" Motion says in disbelief, staring at Poochie.

"How you know that?" Motion questions.

"Because I looked him in his face. The man Ricky Banks that we all called Slick Rick is a Pastor," Poochie informs.

"I can't believe this shit. You tellin' me the man that killed my father buried my little brother?"

"Yep."

"Man this is some fucked up shit," Motion snaps, shaking his head from side to side.

"The last thing that I heard was that he changed his life while in prison. That surprised the shit out of me when I laid my eyes on him."

Motion thinks back to the day of the funeral. *When once face with this similar situation I thought I was willing to pay.t. The long fourteen years of being away from my family, missing my children, denied of every conceivable freedom.* Pastor Banks' words fill Motion's head.

"So, that's Slick Rick . . . The man that killed my father," Motion says, as he starts to fume.

"That's him."

"Here it is he took my father's life and saved that rat mutha fucka Scotty's life. If it wasn't for him . . . Scotty would be a dead man right now," Motion states, regretting that he didn't pull the trigger on Scotty.

"He didn't only save Scotty's life, he saved yours too. Even though you would've taken Scotty out, those angry DEA agents was gon' take you out."

"You right about that. Right now I still have a chance. I would've been givin' up on Ayesha and my daughter. Man they really need me right now," Motion stresses, rubbing his dome.

"Don't worry Motion. You'll prevail in the long run. Trials and tribulations is all a part of growth and development. Look at all that I've been through. I haven't used drugs since the day Elliott got killed. I feel so much better. Also, I have a mission to accomplish and I can't do it with a clouded mind. Always remember the element of surprise is the best strategic way to handle your enemies."

"Inmate Hopson it's time to terminate your visit!"

"I guess I betta get going. It was nice seeing you Poochie."

"Use strategy Motion. A man can be strong, but strategy is more powerful than strength. Don't let these people break you. Don't think for a minute that circumstances make man. Man makes the circumstances. Through the law of attraction, all things come to him who believes in them, and every circumstance of your life is inevitably attracted to you your own beliefs. You are literally the product of your own thought. Don't ever forget that youngin'," Poochie hangs up the phone and struts away. His profound words are lingering in Motion's head. Motion never knew that Poochie was so deep and full of wisdom. Motion walks back to his cell with a lot on his mind.

*   *   *

Judge Mathis croons from the 60 inch plasma screen television. Malinda is lounging on the over stuffed leather sofa. David Landers climbs down the spiral staircase that leads to the livingroom. His number 7 red and black retro Jordans sinks into the thick carpet. He struts over to his wife of 6 years.

"Baby I have to go to the office for a minute and look over a case load. I have a big trial coming up soon. I want to make sure I'm properly armed when I step into that courtroom. My client is paying me top dollars to represent him to the fullest."

"But I thought you were spending the rest of the day with me?"

"Baby I promise I'll make it up to you," David promises, leaning over kissing her on the lips.

Malinda and David are high school sweethearts. Malinda's heritage is African and German.

"We'll see," Malinda says doubtful, watching him as he exits the front door.

David is one of the youngest and most powerful lawyers in the midwest. David grew up in the slums. His dream was to be a professional baseball player, but unfortunately he injuried his knee in a car accident. The accident ended up with him winning a $350,000.00 law suit, which contributed to him paying for his college tuition.

The door closes behind him. Malinda lets out a short breath of air, fluttering the long strands of hair in her face. She tucks her hair behind her ear. *He has been acting very strange lately. He don't even make love to me like he used too. I have to figure out a way to find out what's going on.* She picks up the remote to the television flicking through the channels. Stopping on channel 26, she comes up with an idea. Her eyes are focused on the television show 'Cheaters'.

*　　*　　*

Whoom! Whoom! . . . Whoom! Whoom! The loud earth shaking bass pounds against the paved streets, vibrating the windows on a single family residence. Lisa prances over to the window peering through the blinds. A winter white Range Rover whips into the driveway. Its large chrome wheels gleams like a huge diamond obscuring her vision. Lisa shields her eyes with her french manicured hand to get a better look. Multiple television screens shone from the interior of the truck. Recognizing the silhouette of her new found love, she struts to the front door exiting the house.

"Money and the power! Money and the power! I don't give a fuck! I got money and the power!" Scarface's classic song spits out of the powerful sound system.

Clump! Clump! Clump! Lisa's 4 inch stilettos bangs against the wooden paneled porch. Her round plump 43 inch ass pushes her Roberto Cavalli jeans to the limit.

Lisa is like many of the other women who were left behind to fend for themselves, after their high rolling lovers got caught up in the system or killed in the concrete jungle. Although Lisa has a lot of love for her incarcerated boyfriend, she knows that she have to continue on with her life. There is no way that she can wait on him and he's never coming back home. After long nights of crying and living in misery, she snapped back to reality. All that goes through her head is "He's never coming home." If he were facing anything less than ten years, she could stick it out with him. She thought about how her mother went through the same thing with her father.

Lisa settles into the passenger seat of the Range Rover, clutching her Hermes purse under her arm. Her pretty eyes glistens, accentuating her glossy full lips.

"Hey baby," David greets, turning the volume down on the sound system. He reaches into the glove compartment, pulling out a Glock 19. David tucks the gun under his thigh. From his experience of growing up in the hood, David knows that it is not safe to ride stylish without a gun. Being that he is an attorney and never been convicted of a felony. David has a permit to carry his gun. He has represented a lot of his clients who were a felon in possession of a firearm, but he never knocked them. He is no stranger to the streets.

David met Lisa at his office a few months ago. At first sight he just knew he had to have her. David slept with a lot of his clients girlfriends. He always uses his persuasive ways to get what he wants. But most of the time he prey on their lonely hearts. David manipulated Lisa by telling her that her boyfriend doesn't have a chance to beat his case and that he will end up behind bars for the rest of his life. On top of that, he even promised her that he will divorce his wife.

Lisa and David has been, spending a lot of time together. One of the things he like most about Lisa is that she never depend on him for money. She always manages to pay her own way. David bought the single family house for himself and Lisa. Malinda knows nothing about him purchasing the house.

"I've been missing you all day baby," Lisa says, studying his handsome features. A thin goatee frames his kissable lips.

"I've been missing you too sweetheart," David replies, slapping cologne on his cheeks. His diamond bezel presidential Rolex sparkles with a rainbow reflection. If a person was to see David on his days off, they would think that he was a big time drug dealer instead of a young powerful attorney. On many occasions David got pulled over by the police being mistaken for a drug dealer. After finding out who he is, law enforcement would apologize and let him go.

"You ready to wine and dine baby?" David asks, pulling out of the driveway.

"I've been ready for that all day," Lisa says, leaning back in the leather peanut-butter interior.

CHAPTER ELEVEN

A red pickup truck moves along the winding pathway, kicking up pebbles of rocks as it make its way down the graveled pavement. The truck comes to a complete stop. A cloud of dust lingers in the air, making it hard to read the writing on the side of the truck.

Grabbing his diploma out of the passenger seat, Lil Wink hops out of the truck. He walks across the manicured graveyard to visit Marco's gravesite. Lil Wink kneels down in front of the custom made tombstone in a prayers position, placing his diploma on top of the tombstone.

"Hey Marco," Lil Wink says, dusting off the tombstone so that he could look at Marco's face, which is engraved on the tombstone. "I come here today for several reasons. First I want you to know that I graduated from highschool." Lil Wink taps his diploma. "Second, I've been takin' real estate classes cause I believe that was your next plan for me. And last but not least." Lil Wink stands up dusting the dirt off his knees. Reaching into his pocket, he removes an envelope. "I couldn't open this without being in the presence of my business partner." Lil Wink rips the envelope open, removing a piece of paper from it. "This here is our sealed and dealed corporation papers Marco. We did it. We are the proud owners of M & W Rehab Services. See there, I even drove the company truck up here," Lil Wink says, pointing at the pick up truck. Lil Wink's eyes becomes glassy, as he share the good news with a deceased Marco. He is like the big brother that Lil Wink never had. "Marco . . . I just want you to know that I love you famm and I miss . . . you. Take care and I'll make sure I come and visit you in the future. I love you Marco man. See you at the crossroad." Lil Wink kisses his two fingers and places them on Marco's picture before leaving. Walking across the grave yard, Lil Wink feels a gust of wind pass by him.

"If you want somethin' you never had . . . You must do somethin' that you never did."

Lil Wink stops in his tracks and turns around. He could have sworn that he heard Marco's voice. Seeing that nobody is there, Lil Wink smiles and retreats back to the pick up truck. A trial of dust floats behind the truck as he exits the cemetery.

*　　*　　*

The tall street lamps are illuminating the streets in front· of Barber & Grill Beauty Salon. All the customers cleared out of the shop about an half hour ago. Vegas' Bentley Brooklands is gleaming under the streetlights parked in the reserved parking space.

Vegas and Elane sets the state of the art security system, securing the premises. Clack! Clack! Clack! Clack! Vegas' David Edens dances along the pavement. His Brooks Brothers blazer flops open from the midnight breeze. Elane clutches her Versace purse, sashaying behind Vegas. They climb inside the foreign whip, melting into the butter soft leather interior.

Vegas inserts the key into the ignition. He turns the key and the car does nothing. "What the fuck!" Vegas snaps in frustration. After turning the key again, he gets the same results. "What the fuck! Don't tell me I spent over three hundred and fifty grand on a trapper," Vegas snaps, smacking the steering-wheel. "I know the battery can't be dead already. Shit, I just bought this muthafucka!" he continues, stepping out of the car to check the battery. Standing in front of the car, he flings the hood open inspecting the battery cables. "What the hell. Somebody cut my fuckin' battery cables." Blocka! Blocka! Blocka! The sound of gunfire reverberates. Vegas can feel a burning sensation in his legs. Looking down at his leg, he notices blood leaking on his shoes. Becoming weak at the legs, he collapses on the ground grimacing in pain. Elane screams hysterically, as she watches a man climbing from under the Bentley. Elane looks into the angry man's eyes recognizing him instantly. He smacks the passenger's window out with the butt of his Sig & Sauer P226 9 millimeter, shattering the glass. Elane cringes covering her face with her arms, protecting herself from the rainning glass.

"Please don't kill me!" Elane cries, staring into the man's icy eyes.

"She don't have n-nothin' to do with this man! T-This is between me and you!" Vegas yells at the armed man.

"My fiance and my son didn't have shit to do with it either!" Blocka! Blocka! Blocka! He squeezes the trigger shooting Elane in the head three times. The barking sound of gunfire pierces the tranquil atmosphere. A trail of blood stains the pavement, as Vegas drags his body.

"Come on man. L-Lets talk about this! I'll give you anything you want! I'll give you enough money to last you for the rest of your life!" Vegas pleads.

"This ain't about no fuckin' money Vegas. This is about you destroying my life and killin' two people that I loved dearly. You took the only thing I had away from me. The only thing I had to live for."

"Come on Poochie let's talk! I promise you I'll make up for what did."

"You could never make up for what you did to my family. I treated you like a brother and you crossed me," Poochie replies, aiming at his head. Blocka! Blocka! Blocka! Blocka! Blocka! Blocka! Bloc ka! Blocka! Blocka! Blocka! Blocka! Click! Click! Click! Poochie empties the clip on Vegas. He is sprawled on the ground drenched in blood. Poochie kneels down over his lifeless body removing his diamond De Beers watch, diamond bracelet, and his platinum chain.

"I waited a long time for this day." Poochie spits on his corpse. "Game over you bitch muthafucka!" Poochie struts across the street with his gun tucked under his hoodie. Finally the day has come for him to revenge the death of his fiancé and son. Poochie makes a vow to never use drugs ever again.

* * *

"Lower middle!" the female deputy announces, standing behind the officer's station, calling one section at a time to line up for breakfast. Motion grabs his tray and two cartons of milk.

"Yo Motion!" Shake calls, gaining Motion's attention. "I got you a seat right here famm." The gold teeth in Shake's mouth flashes, reflecting off the light. Shake is seated at the table with an older man who just arrived to the pod yesterday. He has long lengthy braids and a neatly trimmed platinum colored bread. Across from the older man is a

246

younger man with a bald fade. Motion sits at the table for four joining them. "Motion this is Deck and old school right there, that's a legend. His name is Ali," Shake introduces the men.

"What up?" Motion greets, staring at Ali.

"You look real familiar old school. What they used to call you back in the days?" Motion questions. Ali takes a sip of his coffee before answering.

"Convertible Jones."

"Convertible Jones. Mannn I remember you. When I was a shorty I used to look up to you. I remember that mint green convertible Benz you would pull up in our driveway in. The next day you would pull up in a drop top Saab. You used to roll with my father back in the days before he got killed."

"What was yo father name?"

"Big Fifty."

"What! You mean to tell me that's yo father? Man, Big Fifty was like a brother to me. We used to ride around breakin' up every gamblin' spot in the city. Come to think about it, I remember when you was about this big," Ali says, holding his hand two feet from the ground. "Man you really grew up. I been gone for twenty one years. It seem like a lot has changed since I been gone. I heard ol' boy Slick Rick, who killed yo old man got out four years ago. They said he is a pastor now. Everybody say he changed his whole life around."

"That nigga bet' not ever let me catch 'em," Motion says, with an evil look on his face.

"I feel what you sayin' young brotha, but that's not the way to handle the situation. If it was ten years ago I would agree with you. You have to realize no matter what you do it won't bring him back."

"You just don't understand the pain I suffered as a kid, growin' up without a father. The abscence of my father wounded me forever. First I loss my father, now I loss my little brother. This shit is too much for me to handle," Motion expresses.

"Let me tell you somethin' young playa. I know exactly how it feels to grow up without a father. I came from the bottom of the barrel. Not only did I grow up without a father, I grew up without a mother. This is all a part of life that we never want to accept. We have to work with the hand that we are dealt and play it to the best of our ability. I got a life bid and I been down for twenty one years. By the grace of Allah I made it back on appeal. I served seventeen years in the feds and four years in the state. The state picked me up from the feds to serve a life sentence for a murder that I didn't even commit. Hopefully things will go in my favor and I'll get my freedom back. But right now I have to roll with the punches. I could've cooperated with the federal government and testified against my man and walked away a free man, but I chose not to. For twenty one years I've been livin' in this hell on earth. I never received a penny from my man. Not a letter, not a card, nothin' at all. It's been mind out of sight out of mind. I learned a valuable lesson that I had to pay for with blood, sweat, and tears."

"I feel you old school," Motion says.

"Man fuck the dumb shit. I'll kill that nigga for killin' my father. Shit, if you put me on I'll handle that business for you. All I got is a probation violation. I'll be out of here later next month. I'm tryna get back in the kitchen and cook me a quarter chicken. I'm ready to get paid. My palms been itchin' for a long time," Deck interrupts, rubbing his palms together.

"Come on Deck, I know you ain't for real," Ali says.

"What else I'm suppose to do? That's the only thing I know," Deck replies.

"Don't play yo' self like that young brotha. You must don't know nothin' about the feds? Let me explain somethin' to you. I'ma 'bout to keep it playa with you and drop some real jewels on you." Ali climbs out of his chair and struts to his cell. He returns to the table with a federal law book. Motion watches closely in curiosity. "Here it is. You see that chart right here?"

"Un huh. What is that?" Deck question, analyzing the numbers on the paper.

"I'ma show you what it is. First tell me how many felonies you have as an adult?"

"I got one felony for possesssion with intent to deliver."

"A'ight, now check this out. Less say you got caught with at least fifty grams of cocaine base (Crack). Without a criminal record you would face a minimum of ten years, and a maximum sentence of life. That would put you at a level thirty two and a criminal history category one. Now, let's add your prior drug offense. That would place you at a statutory minimum of twenty years to life. Your offense level would be a thirty two, criminal history category two, which would put you at

135-168 months. But having the twenty year statutory minimum there is only one way you can get under that and that is to cooperate with the government. Let's say you had two prior drug convictions under fifteen years old. Automatically you qualify for career criminal, which starts at thirty years to life. Let me ask you another question. Do you keep a gun on you when you out there handling yo business?"

"Hell yeah, that's a must."

"Well, check this out. With a 922G, or 924C, that will enhance you two more levels, placing you at thirty plus years. If they give you a statutory charge that can put you at fourty years for felon in possession of a firearm. That also disqualify you from gettin' the one year off for participating in the drug program, or in less you are in the ninth circuit. Fifty grams of cocaine base is in violation of 21 U.S.C.S 841 (B) (1) (A) and that alone will put you away for at least ten years. Three prior felony convictions is a mandatory life sentence without the possibility of parole. I'm tellin' you from experience young school, these feds ain't playin' no games with us. You think you a gangsta. Shit, the real gangstas in the white house."

Everybody at the table listens to Ali in silence. "How many of y'all think y'all made a million dollars or got a million dollars?" Ali questions, his eyeballs dancing from face to face as he waits for a response. Nobody replies to his question.

"Well, let's just say that one of you here at this table had a million dollars or got a million dollars," Ali says, jolting numbers on a piece of paper. "I'ma do some mathematics for y'all. Let's say that you was sentenced to thirty years in prison. How much do you think that come out to per day?" Ali looks at Deck waiting for an answer.

"I 'ont know," Deck says, shrugging his shoulders.

"That means you made less than a hundred dollars a day. You can work a job making thirteen dollars an hour and make more than that in thirty years. Now that is what you call hustlin' backwards."

"Damn, I never thought about it like that," Shake says aloud.

"All I'm tryna do is get y'all to see the light. Ain't nothin' wrong with hustlin'. You just have to find a legal hustle. You don't have to change your hustle, you have to change the product."

Motion sits back listening to the old head, as he fertilizes them with some true game. Everything that he is saying makes a lot of sense to Motion. "Bill Gates is a hustler, Robert Johnson is a hustler, Don King is a hustler, but in corporate America hustler is call entrepreneur. Just look around at all these faces that are surrounding us. I bet everybody in here got a dope case or a pistol case. This dope shit ain't about nothin'. You got computer nerds and hackers that embezzle millions of dollars in the matter of minutes and they only get a couple years. They take people hard earned money that they worked for all their life, causing them to commit suicide and get divorced. I'm not tyyna preach to y'all, but all I'm saying is think before you react," Ali says, tapping his temple with his indexfinger.

"Day room is now closed! Report back to your cells!" the deputy yells, flashing the lights. Slowly, all of the inmates gather their belongings and heads back to their assigned cells.

* * *

"Grandma, can I go outside and play with my doll?" Joy asks, holding her Dora The Explorer doll.

"Yes baby. You make sure you don't go near that street. Stay in the front yard," Ms. Hopson replies, standing over the stove with her apron wrapped around her waist.

"Kay grandma," Joy agrees, before going outside.

Ms. Hopson places a large spoon in a pot. The fresh smell of greens colonges the air. As she stirs up the greens, Ms. Hopson speaks to herself, "Hmm, these gon' be some good homestyle greens. Just like my mama used to make."

Hearing the chiming phone, Ms.Hopson places the lid over the pot. She wipes her hands off on her apron.

"Hello, the Hopson's residence."

"Hey Ms. Hopson, it's Bridget."

"I know who this is baby. You don't have to say your name every time you call here. Your my grandson's mother," Ms. Hopson says, joyfully. "Speaking of my grandson, how is my little peanut doing?"

"He in his baby crib sleep. He had me up all night," Bridget complains, sighing deeply.

"I know what you mean. Elliott was the same way. So, I guess he got it honestly. When you gon' bring my peanut back over here to see his granny?" Ms.Hopson asks, picking up the spoon.

"I'm going to bring him b-" Joy's ear piercing scream steals Ms. Hopson's full attention. She drops the phone immediately. It dangles by its coiling cord.

"Hello . . . Hello . . . Ms. Hopson are you there?" The faint sound of Bridget's voice escapes the receiver.

*   *   *

The clamoring of inmates fills the atmosphere. Two inmates are seated across from each other slamming dominoes against the table. "Get in the yard nigga!" Toon barks at the inmate that is challenging him.

"You know who run this shit! One bone jones!" Dirty Red barks back at Toon. Pop! The deputy seated in the officer's station opens the door, allowing three new inmates and a male deputy into the pod.

Toon and Dirty Red looks in their direction. The deputy who escorted the three inmates into the pod hands the deputy at the work station their face cards.

"Man, it looks like I know ol' boy from somewhere," Toon says, watching one of the inmates.

"Which one?" Dirty Red questions, scanning their faces. "The brown skinned one with the wavy hair."

"I know exactly where you know him from. It looks like he might be your new roommate." Toon and Dirty Red watches him closely, as he steps into Toon's two man cell with his bedroll.

"Where I know him from?"

"Man this gon' trip you out when I tell you this. That's the nigga that . . ."

*   *   *

A clamorous scream penetrates the atmosphere, embracing Poochie's attention. Poochie swivels his head looking in the direction of the outcry. He takes off bolting through the alley on foot. His Airmax slaps against the pavement, as he moves at top speed. Cutting between two houses, he spots Ms. Hopson swinging a broom, striking a red nose pitbull that is tossing Joy around like a rag doll. Seeing what is transpiring, Poochie reaches in his pants pocket pulling out a butterfly knife. He moves with swiftness diving on top of the pitbull. Foam is caked up in the corners of the pitbull's mouth. The pitbull has Joy's shoulder and neck in a powerful lock. It's sharp teeth is ripping through Joy's flesh. Blood dots the concrete, leaking out of Joy's frail body. Poochie twirls the butterfly knife like a professional Japanese chef, slicing open the pitbull's jugular vein. Blood oozes from it's neck.

"Oh my God!" Ms. Hopson frantically wails, dropping to her knees. The pitbull slowly releases it's grip, as it falls on it's stomach. Sirens are whining in the background.

"Please Jesus don't let my grand baby die on me," Ms. Hopson cries, cradling Joy's bloody body. Joy's pretty face has been disfigured. Her doll lies in the grass with blood on it. Lying in the warmth of her grandmother's arms, her tempature rises ten degrees. Poochie rips off his shirt, covering Joy's open wounds to slow down the bleeding.

"Be strong Ms. Hopson, she'll make it," Poochie hopes, trying to console Ms. Hopson. Poochie stands up slowly walking away from the scene. *It's time for me to get my life back together. I can't live like this.* Poochie struts to the bus stop with his hands in his pockets. After ten minutes of waiting, he hops on the bus headed to the rehab.

CHAPTER TWELVE

A convoy of automobiles veers through the thick traffic. A black sports utility vehicle is leading the group of motorists. They pull in front of a single family residence. A group of men pour out of the vehicles wearing plain clothes, toting various communication devices. Their feet shuffles across the manicured lawn like a stampede of horses, as they approach the house.

Malinda climbs out of the sports utility vehicle, accompanied by the host of the show 'Cheaters'. A camera man trails behind them with a digital camera. Malinda looks at her husband's winter white Range Rover sitting in the driveway. As they move closer to the front door, Malinda hears the faint sound of a woman screaming on the other side of the door. She brushes her fingers through her hair in frustration, fighting back her impending tears. The reality of her husband's infidelity sinks into her head. Her heart leaps into her throat. Tears trickles down her cheeks. Hurt is sitting in the windows of her eyes. Mentally tormented, she fishes through her purse with a trembling hand. She removes the keys that she had Lockmasters make for her, after she was informed by the private investigator about the house.

Slowly she twists the key opening the door. Malinda's heart beats painfully. Her mouth drops open along with the staff of Cheaters, as they stare at what lies before their eyes. Malinda buries her face in her hands in disbelief. In all her life she never witnessed anything like this before. The host seen a lot of things during his years of being a private investigator, but this scenery has him paralyzed. Staring at the naked woman he says aloud, "Holy shit."

*   *   *

"Inmate Hopson get dressed the nurse is here to see you," the deputy speaks through the intercom breaking his train of thought. All he keeps thinking about is Ayesha and why she haven't came to see him. Motion haven't ate in the last two days.

"I had my TB shot two weeks ago, why the nurse wanna see me?" Motion says, putting on his uniform. He strides across the pod staring at the overweight nurse, who has a smile on her face.

"Mr. Hopson right?" the nurse asks.

"Yeah that's me," Motion says, with a puzzled look on his face.

I'm sorry to break this bad news to you, b-"

"Don't tell me I got Aids," Motion says, cutting her off.

"No sir, you do not have Aids. I'm here because your daughter Joy Hopson was involved in a serious situation. She is at the Children's Hospital." Motion's heart drops to his stomach.

"What happened?" He questions, looking at the woman with genuine concern.

"She was attacked by a dog. Right now she is in critical condition. We need to know if you can give us some of your blood. We tried contacting the mother, but we haven't been able to locate her. I believe your mother tried giving some blood, but it can be dangerous for her because she is a diabetic. So if you are willing to give your blood, I will need for you to sign here. Then we can begin the process," she says, handing him a legal documentation and a black ink pen.

"Is my daughter gon' be okay?"

"Yes, as long as she get some blood."

"Well, let's do this than." Motion says, rolling up his sleeve.

* * *

Shasha travels down Bluemound Road in her black Benz truck, making her way to the Children's Hospital. She received a letter from Motion, telling her to go check on Joy. Every since Motion has been locked up, Shasha haven't been to visit him at his request. Motion doesn't want her involved with him during his trial. Although he would love to see her, Motion doesn't want to jeopardize Shasha's freedom.

Shasha misses Motion so much that she put a picture of him and her on the screen of her cellular phone. Lately Shasha has been thinking about writing Motion about something that she'd been keeping from him every since the first day they met.

Breaking from her hypnotic state, Shasha stares into the review mirror. A green sports utility vehicle lingers behind her three cars down. *Why is that truck following me? Maybe the Feds has been watching me. Scotty probably gave me up.* Shasha pushes the pedal to the medal zooming through traffic losing the truck.

*　　*　　*

Malinda prances into her lawyer's office clutching her designer purse. She has been up for days trying to fight her depression. Her red-rimmed eyes dance around the lobby, as she makes her way to the elevator. *I love my husband dearly, but I can't ever forgive him for what he did.* The scenery that she witnessed still has her mentally disturbed. The story made the front page of the newspapers. The media has been following Malinda allover.

Stepping off the elevator, she digs into her purse pulling out a business card that says Robert Stein divorce attorney. *I never thought I would be divorcing my husband.* Malinda thinks to herself with a sad look glued to her face.

*　　*　　*

Ali strides into the pod with a stack of legal papers in his hand. The look on his face says that his appeal did not turn out in his favor. He struts over to Motion with his head down. Like all of the other inmates in the pod, Motion is eager to find out the outcome of his situation.

"Man why you lookin' all down like that? What they do for you?" Motion asks, looking up at him from his seat.

"Man, I can't believe this," Ali says, swaying his head with a look of disappointment.

"Can't believe what Ali?"

"These people granted me . . . my . . . freedom," he says, with a tear flowing from his eyes. Motion jumps up hugging Ali with a brotherly hug.

"That's what I'm talkin' about old school. These people can't keep a real man down," Motion shouts with enthusiasm. All the inmates are surrounding Ali glad to hear the good news. Ali is like a father figure on the pod. After two decades his prayers are finally answered. For the last few weeks he has been even going over Motion's discovery packet trying to find a flaw in his case. Motion has two weeks before he goes to trial.

"Man Allah is good. I thought I was going to spend the rest of my life in this man made hell. I can't believe it, less than seventy two hours I will be a free man."

"Man I'm glad for you oldschool."

Shake walks over to Motion with a newspaper in his hand. "Aye Motion, don't you got that top flight attorney David Landers?" Shake asks, interrupting Ali and Motion's joyful moment.

"Yeah that's my attorney. Why you ask me that?"

"Because it look like your going to have to hire another attorney," Shake proclaims, tossing the newspapers on the table. Motion picks up the newspapers reading it.

ATTORNEY CAUGHT IN THE ACT

Attorney David Landers was apprehended Monday morning after being followed to a Westside single family residence that he purchased recently. His wife Malinda Landers hired the show Cheaters to conduct surveillance on her husband Mr. Landers after becoming suspicious. When entering the single family home to confront her husband about his infidelity, they found Mr. Landers standing over a mutilated body. Mr. Landers was detained by the staff of Cheaters, who are also licensed to carry firearms.

After receiving an autopsy report, the woman was later identified as Lisa Ayesha Abdullah. Approximately 8 million dollars in cash was found at the scene. The money is believed to be her former boyfriend's money, who's currently incarcerated for major drug charges. Authorities also found large barrels of acid that Mr. Landers intended to use to dispose of Ms. Abdullah's body. Mr. Landers and Ms. Abdullahs' love-affair began six months after meeting him at his office to drop off a detainer's fee for her boyfriend. At this time Mr. Landers wife of six years is filing for a divorce. If Mr.Landers is charged, he will face a mandatory life sentence.

Motion drops the newspapers on the table with his heart in deep pain. His whole body starts to feel numb, as he rises from his seat walking off.

"Motion what's wrong?" Shake asks, noticing pain written all over his face. "You look like you just loss yo best friend."

"I did," Motion says, turning around with a solemn expression on his face. He never thought in a million years that Ayesha would betray him. The only woman that he has ever let into his heart broke his heart. Day by day Motion is starting to feel an emptiness inside that is making him grow cold-hearted. Why *did Ayesha do this to me? All I ever did was love her to the fullest. Why you punishing me like this God? I've always been a good hearted person. It seem like the evil people always prevail. Why would she run off with my money like that and leave me with nothin'? I wonder what she did with the diamonds I had in the lock box. Maybe the police took them and didn't report them. Damn this fucked up. I don't have anything but two thousand dollars to my name. My daughter really needs me now. I have to figure out a way to get out of here.* Tears well up in Motion's eyes, as he sits on his bunk all alone.

*   *   *

Scotty weaves through the bustling downtown traffic in his convertible Jaguar. Periodically, he glimpses through the review mirror. He could've sworn he seen a green Tahoe trailing behind him. Heavy rain is pounding on the windshield. The windshield wipers dance from side to side, accommodating him with a clear view.

After bending a couple of corners, he no longer sees any signs of the truck. Every since he has been cooperating with law enforcement, he haven't been able to sleep. His paranoia has him suspicious of everything.

Scotty is disturbed by the information that he just received at his attorney visit. *I can't believe that bitch ass prosecutor still tryna give me ten years even after I cooperated with them. I can't do no fuckin' ten years in the hell hole. Hell naw, fuck that. I know how to solve this shit. I ain't doing no time.* Scotty thinks about the murder weapon that Motion gave him to destroy. It's the same gun that Motion used to kill Nisha and her brother with. Scotty stashed the gun in the woods for a rainy day. He never thought that he would be deceiving his childhood friend.

But like they say, "Pressure bust pipes."

Pulling into his driveway, Scotty shifts the steering wheel parking in the garage. Before, jumping out of the car, he snatches the Milwaukee Journal out of the passenger's seat. Lately he has been reading the newspapers keeping up with the status of their case.

Scotty steps into the spacious livingroom. His Rockports sinks into the soft, plush carpet. He falls back on the butter soft leather sofa partly buried in it. Flipping open the newspapers, his chin drops as he reads the dark bold letters on the front page. "Man that's crazy as hell," Scotty says aloud, carefully reading every line in the article. *What a waste of good pussy.* Scotty says to himself, massaging his dick through the fabric of his designer jeans. He thinks about how he fucked Ayesha, when Motion went out of town to meet Julio for the first time. Closing the newspapers, he says aloud, "Oh well. We all gotta go some day." He tosses the newspapers on the coffee-table. A muffled thump coming from the kitchen area collects his attention. Scotty springs to his feet, clutching his Sig & Sauer Mosquito semi-automatic hand gun that he produced from his waistband. He eases into the kitchen taking a fleeting view, checking for any signs of intruders. Hearing the whispering wind, he looks at the damped fluttering curtains and the open window. *Man I'm trippin'. I musta left the window open.* Scotty sits his gun on the marbled countertop and closes the window. He takes a bucket of left over chicken wings he bought from KFC and places it into the microwave. *I gotta stop eatin' all this fast food. I wish Kanisha was here to cook a home cooked meal.* Scotty flips open his cell phone calling Bodo.

"Hello. Who I'm speaking too?" Bodo answers.

"This Scotty."

"Hey buddy. What's going on?"

"I got somethin' for you."

"Oh yeah."

"Yeah, but I'm not givin' it up if you can't get me immunity."

"This must be something good."

"It is somethin' good. It's a triple homicide that Motion and Dirty Red did a while ago. Motion gave me the gun and I kept it."

"I tell you what. If you are telling me the truth, I'll see to it that you get immunity. So where you want to meet at?"

"I'll meet you at Lincoln Park in an hour."

"A'right. I'll see you then buddy." Click!

Scotty flips the cell phone closed and opens the stainless steel refrigerator. Reaching inside of it, he retrieves a bottled water. Scotty's low cut waves dances, as he tilts his head back satisfying his thirst. Scotty shuts the refrigerator door. The closed refrigerator door is replaced by the site of an angry Shasha, gripping a 9 millimeter Berretta with both hands. She stares at him sharply with a menacing look in her eyes. Scotty stands there paralyzed in his tracks.

*   *   *

Toon struts into the two map cell waking James up out of his sleep. "James, James, Wake up."

"What's up Toon?" James says, as he turns over.

"I hate to kick you out the room, but I gotta use the bathroom bad as a muthafucka," Toon proclaims, holding his stomach. "I don't know what the hell they put in that meatloaf."

"Yeah, that shit had my stomach kinda fucked up too," James says, stepping out of the room.

Every since Toon found out who James was, he took him under his wing. Toon even had someone put some money on his account. Whenever Toon ate, James ate. If it wasn't for who James was, Toon would have kicked him out of his cell the same day he moved in there.

Toon hangs a piece of paper in the window to let the other inmates know that the bathroom is in use. He sits on the toilet relieving himself, thinking about the upcoming trial.

*   *   *

Click! Ali hangs up the phone ending his call with his daughter. He made all of the proper arrangements for his release in the morning. Ali has scrutinized Motion's whole case still trying to find a loophole in his case. Realizing that Motion hasn't came out of his cell all day,

Ali decides to check on him. He knows about the bad news he has been receiving lately.

Knock! Knock! Knock! "Yeah, what's up?" Motion says, acknowledging the knock.

"Can I step in here for a minute and have a word with you?" Ali asks in a reapectful manner.

"Yeah, come on in old school." Ali sits on a concrete slab adjacent to Motion's bed.

"I know you been going through a lot lately and trust me I do understand your pain. Believe me, I been through a lot over the years. My daughter mother broke bad on me a long time ago. She got pregnant by two different men and got married on me. You have to understand this is all a part of the game. We can't expect people to share the same values that we have. If we expect that, we will be disappointed every time we turn around. It gets greater later. They shit on you, they piss on you, and act like you don't even exist. I've seen a lot of deception in my life time. We can't change the way other people act. We have no control over that. All we can do is control our own actions. Remember it's not about what lies behind us or what lies before us. It's about what lies within us. I know you love Ayesha with every beat of your heart, but you have to let it go. It may rain or snow hard tonight, but the sun will still shine tomorrow. Despite of all the clouds in my life, despite all the storms and the pain, we have to keep on pushin'. A lot of people don't understand that four letter word called love. Love without nothin' else can turn into disaster. We have to have trust, understanding, communication, dedication, commitment, and friendship. You can't bake a cake without all of the ingredients. Love and hate come like the wind. Feelings are so unpredictable. They will have you doing things you thought you would never do. I'm not going to preach to you all day. I'm going to leave you with these last words. You don't choose how your going to die or when. You can only decide how your going to live." Ali rises from the concrete slab, patting Motion on his back. He exits the cell in silence.

*   *   *

"Whoa mami," Scotty says, putting his hands in the air. "What's up with the gun?" he continues.

"What you mean what's up with the gun, you coward ass mutha fucka! You thought you was gon' get away with snitchin' on the family papi?" Shasha shouts angrily.

"What was I suppose to do mami? They had my back against the fuckin' wall! They was talkin' about plantin' me under the prison!" Scotty shouts back defensively in a high pitched voice.

"You was suppose to stand up like a man papi! That's what you was suppose to do! I promise you that you'll never get the chance to cross anybody else papi!"

A beeping sound steals her attention, causing her to glance over her shoulder at the microwave. Moving with swiftness, Scotty side steps to the left, slapping the gun out of her hand. The gun slides across the marble floor spinning in a circle. Shasha dives to the floor trying to recover the gun. Scotty strikes her brutally with a vicious jab, disheveling Shasha's hair. She staggers backwards from the impact of the punch, crashing against the wall, sliding down in a sitting position. She winces in pain, holding her swollen face. Shasha is dizzy. It seems as if the kitchen is doing a somersault.

Scotty kneels down scooping the gun off the floor, aiming it at an injured Shasha. A malicious grin spreads across his face.

"You came this close to killing me," Scotty admits, making a tiny space between his thumb and indexfinger. Shasha's eyes are ignited with hatred. Her nose is flaring and her lips are tightly pressed.

"This make you feel like a real man don't it papi? Crossing the people who had yo back from day one. The ones who reached out to you when you didn't have nobody else to turn to. I guess this is all a part of the game huh papi? Before you pull that trigger just remember . . . A coward die a thousand death and a solider die once."

Scotty watches her intently flexing his trigger finger, as if he is deliberating. "I never meant for things to end like this. You think I wanna take yo life mami?"

"You already took my life. You took my life the moment you deceived my family."

"Well, I don't know what more I can say. I still got love for you mami. One thing y'all fail to realize is that the game is dirty, but it's fair. And before I squeeze the trigger I want you to know that I'll be at your funeral to pay my respect. I'ma make sure you have a nice burial."

Scotty levels the gun with Shasha's head. "I guess I'll meet you at the cr-" The cold barrel of a Heckler & Koch P5 kisses Scotty's temple.

"Game over Scotty. Put the gun down."

*   *   *

A white Cadillac CTS turns the corner in the residential neighborhood. Moving at a slow pace, it proceeds down the block.

"Mommy are we going back home to live with daddy?"

"I don't know yet junior," Kanisha replies, as she pulls in front of her old home that she once shared with Scotty. All the long phone conversations with Scotty was enough to convince her to come back home. Scotty promised her that he will change his ways and marry her. Kanisha couldn't bear all the lonely nights without Scotty. The thought of him waking up to another woman was killing her emotionally.

Kanisha notices a strange man sitting in front of Scotty's house in a green Tahoe, talking on a communication device. Going with her instincts, Kanisha pulls off without him recognizing her.

*   *   *

A compassionate breeze presses against the towering trees forcing them to sway. The shimmering sun is bathing the tranquil neighborhood. Bodo shifts the Dodge Durango into the parking lot of Lincoln Park. Raking his fingers through his hair, he scans the area searching for Scotty's car.

Bodo is eager to get his hands on the murder weapons that were involed in a triple homicide. Bodo promised Scotty that he'll talk to the superior Federal pyosecutor about granting him immunity for his substantial assistance.

A large smile decorates Bodo's face, as he recognizes Scotty sitting in his champagne colored Jaguar. He pulls up behind Scotty's car and climbs out of his truck smoking a cigar. B.G. flows out of Scotty's car system. "Don't talk to me, don't talk me, don't talk to me, if you got life and doing three, don't talk to me, don't talk me. Don't talk to me, cause I don't wanna holla."

Bodo struts to the passenger side of Scotty's Jaguar opening the door. Climbing inside the car, he flops back in the leather interior.

"What's up budd-" Bodo stops in mid-speech, staring at Scotty with wide eyes. "Holy shit!" Bodo blurts, reaching for his police radio. Scotty is lying back in the driver's seat with a grotesque look froze on his face. Scotty's eyes are stretched open. Fresh blood leaks out of his neck. Looking at slit in Scotty's neck, Bodo can tell that it was classic mafia style murder. Scotty sits in the seat lifeless with a Colombian necktie. Bodo shuts the car system off and climbs out of the car inspecting the crime scene.

Milwaukee County Jail

A day later

Motion grips his breakfast tray, as he struts to the table that him and Ali sit at every morning. Today Motion notices something different. Ali is not sitting at the table drinking his coffee like he does every morning. Motion didn't even hear him do his salat this morning. *I know he didn't just up and leave on a nigga without saying bye.* Motion places his tray on the table and heads to Ali's cell.

Upon entering Ali's cell, Motion sees him lying on the bottom bunk with his discovery in his hand. *He must've been working on my case all night. Maybe he just tired.* Motion grabs his discovery out of Ali's hands. "Ali, wake up!" Motion says, shaking him around. "You act like you don't wanna go home today. Ali, wake up!" Motion's heart beats with trepidation, as he checks Ali's pulse. "Hey! Somebody get the deputy! Ali ain't breathing!" Motion shouts into the day room. "Come on old school you can't go out like this," Motion says aloud, holding his stiff hand. Hearing the sound of the deputies responding to the medical emergency, Motion steps out of the cell with his head down, clutching his discovery papers.

A group of deputies rushes into the cell. "Man what's going on?" Shake questions, walking up to Motion.

"Man it's old school. I think he died in his sleep."

"What?"

"Yeah man. He was workin' on my case when it happened. "Motion sits at the table with his head down.

"You dropped somethin' Motion," Shake informs, kneeling down picking up a piece of paper with Ali's handwriting on it. Motion reads the paper right away.

"I can't believe it. Ali found a loophole in my case. Look at what this say," Motion says, handing him the paper.

"Damn, that look good right there."

"We already filed a motion for ineffective counsel, removing my attorney from my case on numerous grounds. All this sounds good, but now I don't have nobody to help me with my case. I only got two thousand dollars to my name. I can't go in there with a public defender. Man I can't believe this. I went from being a self made millionaire to a broke nigga with the snap of a finger. I can't even afford to hire a lawyer to file my suppression motion," Motion utters in frustration, thinking about all of his money getting caught up when Ayesha got killed.

"Maybe you might need that sixty five hundred owe you," Shake says, gaining Motion's attention.

"That sure would come in handy right about now," Motion says. Finally he realizes that everything happens for a reason. If it wasn't for the bad dope that Shake sold him in the past, he would be in bad shape right now. "Well, I guess I betta get the show on the road," Motion says, rising out of his seat heading to the pay-phone.

CHAPTER THIRTEEN

T his court hereby commits you to the custody of the Brueau of Prisons for a term of life without the possibility of parole." Bang! Honorable Judge Studmiller hits the table with his gavel having no remorse for the defendant that is seated before him.

Toon stares at the pale faced judge with an expressionless face. He was already prepared for the inevitable. None of this is a surprise to Toon. He refused to break the code of the streets. No matter what it comes down to, Toon will never be disloyal to the game he lived. "I'm sorry that I couldn't do nothing to help you," Danny Marino apologizes to Toon.

"I'll be a'ight Mr. Marion. This is all part of the game. You don't have to feel sorry for me. Just make sure you put in for my appeal," Toon says, rising out of the swivel chair in his orange uniform.

Two U.S Marshals escorts Toon back to the bullpen. Walking down the long hallway in shackles, Toon takes short calculated steps. The rattling sound of his shackles breaks the silence, as they exit the elevator.

"Turn around for a second," one of the U.S Marshals instructs. Toon turns around, as the Marshal punches a code into the elevator. Making it to the bullpen, they remove the handcuffs off of him. They place him into the cell with Dirty Red.

"What they give you?" Dirty Red asks.

"Shit, the same thing they gave you . . . forever."

"Damn, they act like we killed somebody."

"You ain't lyin'."

"I'ma give 'em a reason for giving me all this time," Toon says.

An hour passes by and they are escorted from the Federal Courthouse back to the Milwaukee County Jail.

*   *   *

Toon and James sits on the lower bunk playing a game of Casino. The day room is closed for the night. It's 1:30am. Several inmates are talking out their doors to their neighbors. One of the inmates they call D-Smoove is banging a beat on his door spitting his poetic lyrics.

"Man I'm about to chill, you got this game. I can't even think straight. I can't believe these crackers gave me a life bid for a dope case," Toon stresses, tossing his cards on the bed.

"I feel you Toon. These people don't give a fuck about us. They probably gon' give me two life bids for what I did," James proclaims, raking up all the cards putting them up.

"These crackers ain't gon' give you no two life bids."

"Why you say that?"

"Trust me they ain't," Toon replies, grabbing a small box of letters from under the bed. He shuffles through them removing an old letter. Toon opens the letter with a serious look on his face. "Man, I can't believe my little homie is gone. This is the last letter that he wrote me. He was the only one that kept it one hundred with me and made sure I kept some money on my books. It seem like the good always die young. Here check this out. This is what you call a true friend," Toon says, handing him the letter.

James plasters his eyes on the letter, reading it carefully.

Dear Toon,

> **What's up with you family? I hope this letter finds you in great spirits. I'm sorry that things turned out the way they did. Myself, I'm doing alright. I really miss you all. I started my real estate classes last week. This dude I met a few month ago has been putting me up on some major game. I've been keeping myself busy. I have a lot of plans for the future. Besides that I'm just trying to make it out here. By the way, I hope you received that thousand dollars I put on your books. Oh yeah, one more thing I forgot to mention to you. Me and Titianna are about to get married. We have a baby on the way. I just found out that she is two weeks pregnant. I can't believe I'm about**

to be a father. Well, I'm going to holla at cha soon. You keep your head up in there. Death before dishonor.

Love family,
Marco Piage

James tilts his head looking Toon in the eye. "That was my man you killed nigga," Toon says in a raspy voice. Toon stabs James in the neck with a sharp pencil, breaking it inside his neck. Blood oozes from his neck. Toon grips James by the head, banging it against the steel toilet. James gags with blood leaking from his mouth. "You . . . bitch . . . ass . . . mutha . . . fucka . . . you . . . killed . . . my . . . man . . . and . . . his . . . girl!" Toon snaps banging his head against the toilet repeatedly in between his words. Toon goes into a zone. He knows that he has nothing to lose, after just being sentenced to life.

A deputy makes his rounds doing count. The deputy peers through the window, witnessing Toon beating the life out of James. The deputy presses the panic button on his radio. James' body convulses on the bloody floor. Toon pulls out his manhood and urinates all over James' lifeless body. A massive group of deputies pour into the pod. All of the inmates stand at their doors shouting, watching all of the commotion. Within five minutes Toon was restrained by the deputies and escorted out of the pod to Solitary Confinement.

*   *   *

"Mr. Hopson, are you already?"

"Yeah, I'm ready," Motion answers, tossing all of his beding in the blue hamper. A deputy stands at the exit holding Motion's face card. Motion heads toward the door.

"Mr. Hopson," the female deputy calls, stopping him in his tracks. He turns around facing her.

"Yeah, what's up?"

"I got some mail for you. They must've sent it to the wrong pod," she says, giving him the white envelope.

"Thanks." Motion takes the envelope without bothering to look at it. The only thing that is occupying his mind is getting the hell out of jail. The suppression motion that Ali put together for Motion was filed by his new attorney. All of the evidence was dismissed. Ali went over Motion's paperwork finding out that he breached the contract that he had with the storage company, which means that he wasn't authorized to be on the premises. His attorney argued that technically Motion was trespassing on private property. Motion's storage bill was a year overdue. The Federal judge dismissed all of the evidence that was found in the storage room. The Federal Government's only star witness was found dead in his car. Before leaving the courtroom, the angry prosecutor promised Motion that it isn't over with.

Motion unzips the blue mesh bag with his belonging in it. He removes the wrinkled up double breasted Ermenegildo Zegna suit that he was arrested in. Slipping into his clothes, Motion recognizes the keys to his Drophead Phantom that he once owned. Although the Federal Government seized all of his possessions, Motion still feels good all over. The deputy hands him an envelope containing a check for $983.00.

"Here Mr. Hopson. Sign right here saying that you received your property." Motion leans on the counter top signing his name on the legal documentation.

"Thank you sir. You can head out that door to your left," the deputy instructs, popping the door open, giving Motion access to his freedom.

Clack! Clack! Clack! Motion's hard bottom shoes smacks the pavement, echoing in the empty hallway. He has all of his worldy possession in a plastic bag. A slender built woman in a two piece business suit prance pass him carrying a briefcase. She flashes a smile at him, as she steps on the elevator.

Motion peers through the glass folding doors that awaits him up ahead. Seeing all of the life moving about brings him to reality. *I can't believe I'm a free man. Now it's time for me to go see my daughter. I know she really needs me. Joy is the only thing that I have left, but we gon' make it. I'ma take her some where far away and we gon' start all over.* Motion pushes the glass doors open being blinded by the beaming sun. Having been isolated from the world, Motion feels like a foreigner. He tilts his head skyward inhaling a fresh breath of air. "Thank you father," he says aloud, appreciating his freedom.

Car horns blare from every direction, bustling through the energetic traffic. Motion struts along the sidewalk in search of a pay-phone, so that he can call a ride to pick him up. Crossing the street, Motion doesn't notice the green Tahoe whipping around the corner on State street, driving recklessly. Motion jumps out of the way preventing himself from getting ran over. He locks eyes with the two men sitting in the truck. Looking at the man in the driver's seat causes Motion to become confused.

"Get in," the man in the passenger's seat orders, looking at a baffled Motion. He opens the rear door climbing into the truck. His body jerks back involuntarily, as they pull off.

"Man, what's going on Julio?" Motion questions.

"I need to talk to you for a minute Motion. First of all let me introduce you to my friend right here. His name is Jose. He is a private investigator that is a part of my team. I had him watching your whole circle from day one. I even had him follow you back to Milwaukee when I first met you. He was on the Greyhound bus with you. Don't take this as a sign of disrespect. In this game you can't trust no one. Not even yo own mama. I play the game by the rules. That's why I'm still out here. But I have to admit it, Eddie was right about you. It's very few people that know how to honor the code of the streets. I really respect yo gangsta. They don't make many men like you today," Julio proclaims, peering through the windshield, as they move about.

"I respect the game for what it is. I'll never go out like a coward," Motion says.

"I'm sure you know about what happened to Scotty."

"Yeah, I heard about it."

"Your friend Shasha is lucky that I had Jose on Scotty's trail. Cause if I didn't, she would be staring at the sky right now. Jose seen her climbing through Scotty's window. Once he informed me about what was going on, I made my way to Scotty's house. I wanted to get the satisfaction of killing him myself. I didn't kill 'em because of what he did to you Motion. I can care less. You was the one who got caught slippin'. I killed him because I don't like rats," Julio admits with an evil look glowing in his eyes. "Well, I'm not going to hold you up. I just wanted to have a few words with you. But once again, I wanna commend you for standing up like a true solider."

"No doubt."

"It's somebody waiting on you. She told me not to keep you too long, because she's dyin' to see you," Julio informs.

They pull into a parking lot in front of Jewels grocery store. A black Benz truck pulls up beside them. A smile stretches across Motion's face, as he makes eye contact with Shasha.

"Be careful out there Motion. Walk away while your ahead, because the Feds won't rest until they get you. Go get yo daughter and get out of here." Motion looks at Julio with a how you know about my daughter look. "Don't even bother to ask Motion. I've been playin' this game for a long time. Now get going, don't keep Shasha waiting."

Motion hops out of the truck feeling like a new man.

"Hey papi!" Shasha screams excitedly, embracing Motion with a tight hug. A warm sensation travels down Motion's spine. This is the first time he has ever felt like this in Shasha's presence. He always looked at her as a little sister.

"Heyy mami!" Motion greets, holding her warm frame up against his chest. They jump inside her truck pulling off.

"Papi I missed you so much. I wanted to come and see you so bad papi. I just didn't want to go against your wishes. Now that your in front of me, it's somethin' I been wanting to tell you for a long time papi."

"Oh yeah. What's that?" Motion questions, while reading his mail that he received from the deputy before getting released.

"I'm in love with you papi," Shasha confesses.

"Aww, man I can't believe this. Damn!" Motion mutters in frustration, dropping his head. Shasha looks at him in confusion.

"Papi what's wrong? I was only being honest with you." Shasha stares at Motion's misty eyes. Tears roll down his face, falling on the piece of paper that is in his hand. He hands the paper to Shasha with a trembling hand. Shasha cups her mouth with extended eyes, as she reads the letter.

*   *   *

Ding! Dong! The chiming sound of the doorbell seizes Ms. Hopson's attention. She rises off the sofa to answer the door. Peering through the peep-hole, she can't believe her eyes. Ms. Hopson opens the door in silence.

"How you doing mama?" Motion greets her with a sad look on his face. This is the first time he has seen or talked to his mother since he was arrested.

"I'm doing okay. Come . . . on in," Ms. Hopson says, ushering him into the house. Motion looks around as he steps inside the livingroom.

"I need to talk to you about Joy," Motion utters, with his head down.

"I already know Motion. I spoke with the doctor yesterday," she informs.

"Mama I don't . . . understand this. Here I was being a man mama. I did everything I could for that little girl. Now they send me a letter sayin' that Joy ain't my daughter. This ain't right mama. Why would Ayesha do me like this. I don't understand this shi-" Motion catches himself, remembering where he is at.

"Baby, I understand why you feel like that. You have a right to feel like that. Even though Joy is not your daughter you should do what's best for her. You are the only father she knows. Ayesha is gone now. It's not about you Motion. All I'm asking you to do is think about it."

"Mama I can't live a lie. I ain't takin' care of another man's baby. Naw, I can't do that mama."

"Motion please just think about it," Ms. Hopson pleads.

"I think it's time for me to go. I just need some time alone." Motion heads for the front door.

"Motion wait. I got some mail on top of the television for you." Ms. Hopson grabs the stack of mail. Scanning the letter on the top, Motion rips it open quickly.

"I need to get going mama. I'll talk to you some other time." Motion storms out of the door.

*   *   *

Motion stands behind a lock smith employee watching closely, as he sticks a utensil in the key hole of the lock box. *Man, pray to God that this bitch ain't took my damn diamonds out this fuckin' lock box. I wonder why the hell she didn't clear all of the lock boxes. It could only be two things, some money or my diamonds. I hope it's my diamonds. If it is, it's on like a muthafucka. Please God, let them diamonds be in there.* The lock smith employee removes the lock, allowing Motion into the lock box. Motion reaches into the lock box removing a small bulging black bag.

"Is there anything else that I can help you with sir?"

"Naw, that's it." Motion pulls out the remainder of his money that he has left, after paying all the late fees on the lockbox. He drops a fifty dollar tip in the man's hand. "I appreciate your services," Motion thanks him, making his way out of the train station with the black bag concealed under his suit jacket. He climbs back into the truck with Shasha. "Come on, lets go mami."

"Where we going?" Shasha questions, as she brings the engine to life.

"Just get on the highway, we out of here," Motion replies, looking in the black bag. He inspects the uncut diamonds.

"What's that papi?"

"Somethin' that's going to put us back on top." Shasha maneuvers through the traffic on 194, heading towards Chicago. "Get off on the next exit mami," Motion instructs.

"You sure papi? I thought you wanted to get out of here?"

"I do. I just want to say bye to somebody before we leave." Shasha whips the Benz truck on 43 West.

*   *   *

Motion exits the elevator on the fourth floor of the Children's Hospital. Slowly, he struts down the hallway to the intensive care unit. Motion eases pass the receptionist without being noticed. Quietly, Motion steps into Joy's room. The television croons in the background. Joy lies on the bed watching cartoons. Motion steps into her view.

"Dadddy," Joy greets with a weak voice.

"Heyy sweetheart." Motion looks at all of the bandages on her face. It was almost hard for him to recognize her. A sharp pain cuts into his heart, as he studies her in silence. Joy reaches for his hand, mustering all of her strength. She grips Motion's indexfinger.

"Daddy . . . you kept your promise," Joy reminds him.

"I told you I was comin' home soon. You know I wouldn't break my promise," he says. Motion glimpses around at the machine that she is hooked up to. Deep down inside, he hate that he have to leave and walk out on her. It will not be long before a nurse comes to check on Joy. "Baby I gotta go. Daddy has a long ride ahead of him."

"Daddy where . . . is mommy?" Joy asks, looking in the windows to Motion's soul.

"Mommy is gone to a better place."

"Will I ever see her again?"

"Yeah sweetheart, you'll see her again."

"When daddy?" Motion hesitates before answering.

"When you go to heaven. Now let daddy get going boo. Gon' and get you some beauty sleep." Kneeling over her bed, Motion plants a kiss on her lips. Reluctantly, he heads for the door feeling heartbroken.

"Daddy . . . please don't leave . . . me," Joy begs, with tears crawling out the corners of her baby brown eyes. Hearing her soft pleading voice, Motion turns around staring at her.

* * *

Shasha sits in her truck waiting patiently for Motion to return. She shuffles through her CD case, searching for her Mary J.Blige CD. Glancing out the passenger's window, Shasha spots Motion walking towards her, carrying something under a white blanket. He climbs into the passenger's seat.

"Lets go, hurry up," Motion instructs, leaning back in the interior.

"What are you doing papi?"

"I'm takin' my baby with us. I can't leave her here."

"It's whatever papi. You know I'ma ride with you 'til the end." They stare at each other in silence. Slowly their lips get closer and closer.

"I think we betta get out of here first and save this for later," Motion suggests.

"I think your right papi," Shasha agrees, stepping on the pedal. Motion peels back the blanket, exposing Joy's disfigured face.

"Where . . . we going daddy?"

"We're going to paradise baby." Shasha jumps on the highway. Motion peers through the windshield in deep thought. *It's time to take this shit to another level. I'ma get my baby the best plastic surgeon that money can buy. I can't believe all the shit I been through. I be damn if I go back to selling dope. That shit carry too much time. All the jewels, flashy cars, beautiful women, and designer clothes, they can have that shit if I have to sell dope to get it. It's a lot of other ways to make money. All this shit sound good, but I'm telling you, it ain't worth it in the long run. If you don't believe me . . . Turn to the next page and you do the math . . .*

THE END

Due to the changes of the Federal Guidelines there was no sense in placing them in here. Go to your local library and asks for the directions to the Law section. There you will find the up-date version of the drug laws.

Dream

CHAPTER 1

Cozac opens his cell phone and calls his rap artist Dro. The phone rings several times before being answered.

"Yo, what up Dro? That's cool. I want you to meet me at the studio at two o'clock instead of one. I have some business I need to handle so I'll holla at you then . . . A'ight, holla."

Cozac closes the phone and walks into his luxurious living room staring out the huge window. He glances at his diamond face Aqua Master watch with the rose gold band. "Damn, what's taking this bitch so long?" he muttered impatiently.

A blue taxi cab pulls up into his driveway behind his candy apple jolly rancher green convertible Jaguar XJS with the peanut butter interior. The cab driver honks the horn two times and a beautiful woman steps out of the cab wearing a two piece Baby Phat blue jean suit standing five foot three with a HalleBerry style haircut.

Cozac stands in the doorway watching her size seven-eight hourglass frame with admiration. They greet each other with a delightful smile and a warm passionate kiss. Cozac closes the door.

"I been waitin' for you Rhonda," Cozac said, smacking her on her firm voluptuous ass.

Rhonda leads the way up the spiral staircase heading to Cozac's bedroom. As Cozac climbs up the steps behind Rhonda he mischievously fondles her ass.

"Damn Rhonda, you wearin' the shit out of those jeans." Cozac's eyes burn with lust. She giggles at his remark.

"Boy, you so damn crazy," she said cheerfully.

They walk into the bedroom undressing hurriedly as if they are in a race. They climb on top of the queen size bed kissing each other wildly, while burning with intensive heat. Cozac puts his hand between her legs feeling the warm moisture flowing from her vagina.

*   *   *

Misha pulls up to her job in her 2003 Chevy Impala. Realizing that she forgot her employee identification card which gives her access into the facility, she mumbles, "Shit, I'm going to be late for work. I got to hurry back to the house and get my I.D. card. I knew I was forgetting about something before I left the house," while maneuvering the car making her way back home.

She feels her baby moving rapidly inside her stomach while driving back home. She speaks softly to the unborn child.

"I know you're hungry, momma going to get you something to eat baby." She rubs her belly, enjoying the experience of her first pregnancy.

Misha is deeply in love with her husband. He spoils her and buys her anything she wants.

She turns on 107.9, listening to the sounds of the latest R & B music. She rides through South Euclid, Ohio bobbing her head to the tunes.

She pulls into her driveway behind her husband's car. She turns the engine off climbing out of the car with a slight struggle because of her six month pregnancy. She approaches the front door while removing her keys from her purse. She unlocks the door walking into the house.

Upon entering the house she hears the sound of something knocking against the floor. Misha's curiosity causes her to quietly ease up the spiral staircase towards her bedroom. She hears a woman moaning with sexual gratification as she makes her way to the second floor approaching her bedroom.

Caught up in the throes of passion, Cozac and Rhonda do not notice Misha standing in the doorway. She stares in shock as she watches her husband penetrate deeply in and out of a woman who has her ankles wrapped behind her own neck, while holding her thighs. As much as the sight disgusts her, she can not seem to open her mouth or move her feet. With her heart in anguish, she is forced to watch as her husband makes love to another woman.

"Is it good to you baby?" Cozac inquired.

"Yeah daddy, yeah oooh give me that big ass dick. Hit this pussy baby. I want you to cum for me, ooh yeah, there you go."

Snapping out of her trance at hearing the woman's voice, she reaches into her purse and retrieves a small .25 caliber pistol that Cozac gave her to carry for protection.

"Damn Rhonda, this pussy good as a mutha fucka. Come here baby, I'm about to cum. Put this dick in yo' mouth. Swallow this for daddy."

Cozac pulls his dick out of her pussy and places it in Rhonda's mouth. In the middle of him ejaculating, he hears the cocking sound of a round being put into a chamber of a handgun.

"You dirty mutha fucker," Misha said angrily, aiming the gun at the two adulterous lovers who have betrayed her.

The sound of her voice startles them in the moment of ecstasy. With his face contorted in pleasure Cozac spins around nervously at the sound of his wife's voice, causing him to pull out of Rhonda's mouth, spilling the last of his semen on Rhonda's breast. Falling back beside Rhonda he tries to explain.

"Baby." Misha stops Cozac in mid sentence.

"Baby my mutha fuckin' ass. You in our bed fucking my best friend. I ought to kill both of you no good mutha fuckas." Tears stream uncontrollably down her cheeks as her heart knots up in excruciating pain.

"Mimi I'm sorry. You was always telling me how good Cozac was to you and he just came on to me while I was weak. I didn't mean for it to go this far," Rhonda explained in her defense.

"Bitch shut up! You just as much wrong as this nasty dick nigga here," Misha explained near hysterics.

Misha walks further into the room. Rhonda grabs the sheets to cover herself.

"Hold on baby, hold on. I fucked up, but it ain't like that, she was just a piece of ass baby, with you being pregnant you ain't wantin' to get down. She came at me. She been tryin' to throw the pussy at me for the longest, but I wouldn't get down with her. Come on baby, you know I love you. Please put the gun down and let's work this out," Cozac exclaimed.

"Fuck that shit; you're my mutha fuckin' husband. That bitch didn't make any vows to me," Misha scolded, still aiming the handgun at them.

"I promise you this won't ever happen again baby. I just made a mistake. Baby, I promise you I'm sorry," Cozac pleaded.

With a look of pure hatred in her eyes she said, "You're a sorry excuse for a husband and you're right, I don't have to ever worry about going through this shit ever again." She cried.

Sensing that he is not getting through to her Cozac decides to switch tactics.

"Misha look, I'm not playin' with yo' mutha fuckin' ass no more. Now I'm tellin' you to stop pointin' that damn gun at me," he demanded.

He jumps off the bed and lunges towards Misha. In fear and anger she pulls the trigger, shooting him in the groin. Rhonda screams hysterically. Cozac falls back onto the bed grimacing and groaning in pain, holding onto his genitals. He sat up and she fired another round directly to his forehead. Rhonda flinches as Cozac's blood and brain matter flew into her face. She looks down into Cozac's lifeless eyes.

"Bitch you got ten seconds to get the fuck out of my house before I kill you," Misha said, staring at Rhonda with ferocity in the depths of her eyes.

Rhonda hurriedly gathers her belongings. She runs out of the bedroom and down the stairs screaming, making her exit from the house naked and holding her clothes against her chest.

Misha sits on the floor crying with the gun in her lap, wondering if life is worth living. Her baby kicks, reminding her that there is life growing inside of her womb, giving her an incentive to carry on. In the distance she hears the approach of sirens.

"We are going to be okay baby. Mama got you," she whispered to her unborn child.

*   *   *

Dro is at Cozac's recording studio Big Mouth Records, waiting for Cozac to arrive so they can finish recording his album. Cozac has invested thousands of dollars into Dro's project.

Allante "Dro" Gardner is a local up and coming artist out of Cleveland, Ohio.

Dro sits in the studio sporting his crispy Iverson braids smoking on a blunt of marijuana. He grips his pad of paper rehearsing one of his latest raps he wrote.

Cozac's in-house producer Bounce sits in front of the 19 inch Apple flat screen monitor rolling the mouse around operating the pro tools as he prepares himself to records Dro's latest hit song, "Take It To The Head."

Dro served a couple of years as a juvenile in Glen Mills Schools in Concordville, PA for carjacking and reckless use of a firearm. He dropped out of school after the 11th grade so that he could raise his little sister Alexus. Dro's mother neglected him and his little sister as she chased her heroin addiction. Ever since they were taken by social services their alcoholic father obtained full custody of them. Since the age of six, Dro dreamed of being a major rap artist. His favorite rap artists are Tupac, Nas, Scarface, and Jay Z.

"What's takin' Cozac so long to get here? He told me he would be here at two o'clock; it's goin' on three thirty," Dro stated with frustration. He pulls his cell phone out of his pocket and dials Cozac's number. The phone rings continuously, connecting to Cozac's voice mail.

"Hello, you reached C.E.O. Cozac of Big Mouth Records, I'm not available at the moment, so can you please leave a message and I will get back to you at my earliest time." Dro hears a beep and leaves a message.

"Yo Cozac, I'm at the studio, what's up? Me and Bounce down here waitin' on you. Give me a call and let me know something. A'ight, peace." Dro presses five making the call urgent. He hangs up the phone and places it back into his pocket. "Yo Bounce, play that beat back for me one time," Dro requested.

Bounce plays the beat back and Dro bobs his head to the beat in good spirits, knowing that he is close to being finished with his project. Every time Dro is gone off that green marijuana he writes his best lyrics.

"Take it to the head, smoke somethin', smoke somethin', take it to the head, smoke somethin' wit' me, smokin' on that green leaf got a nigga blowed, makin' me forget that this world is so cold, a pound of that good got my eyes red, sittin' on cloud nine as I take it to the head."

Dro delivers his lyrics as he sits on the couch making gestures with his hand while holding on to a piece of paper. Bounce rocks his head to the bass line as Dro entertains him.

"Bounce dog, you laced the shit out of that beat baby, wait until Cozac hear this shit. He gon' flip," Dro excitedly stated, after finishing his short rehearsal.

Hours pass by quickly as Dro and Bounce impatiently wait for Cozac. "I hate to say this Dro, but I got to get out of here. I have things to do on the side," Bounce admitted.

"That's cool. I can't knock yo' hustle dawg. I know a nigga got to put bread on the table. I got to do the same thang. This shit ain't like Cozac when it comes down to takin' care of business."

"I know, he's usually on time. Somethin' gots to be wrong," Bounce added.

They head out of the studio after shutting everything down. Standing outside of the studio they dap fist.

"I'll holla at you tomorrow Bounce baby."

"A'ight, cool."

Bounce jumps into his Ford F-150 utility vehicle and pulls off. Dro hops into his eggshell white boxed Chevy Caprice. He pulls his black .357 revolver from his waistband and places it on his lap for easy access.

Living in the hood taught him to be on point at all times. He has a lot of enemies in the street because of his reckless lifestyle. His cell phone vibrates and he answers hoping that it's Cozac returning his call.

"Who dis?" Holding the phone to his ear, instantly his face contorts. "You bullshittin'." He continues to listen to the caller "Man that's fucked up. It seems like every time I try and make it happen somethin' goes wrong. We was on the verge of finishin' my CD. I can't afford to pay Bounce and promote my CD. I don't have that kind of money. Cozac let that jealous ass bitch of his take him out of the game. Man that's some bullshit. These hoes is crazy. Look man, we got to sit down and talk. We got to come up wit' somethin'. I'm too close to finishin' my CD. I can't let this just go down the drain. I tell you what, just meet me at my house in about twenty minutes, cool? . . . . A'ight, peace." Dro frustratedly hangs up the phone

Dro pulls up to his residence on 105th and St. Clair. He tucks his handgun back into his waistline and jumps out of the car. The neighborhood is buzzing with activity as usual. The traffic is flowing as dope boys, crack heads, and civilians mingle, making their daily runs. He throws his fist up to the corner hustlers in front of the store. He enters the building to the sound of loud rap music.

"That sounds like that nigga Soul new shit. Fuck, why you have to die on me Zac. We was this close to makin' this shit pop off," he mumbled to himself while putting his key into the door of the two bedroom apartment he shares with his 22 year old baby mother Tonya 'Tee-Tee' Sanders, his 7 year old son Andre 'Lil Dro' Gardner, his 17 year old sister Alexus Gardner, and his alcoholic father Charles 'Pops' Gardner.

He unlocks the door and crosses the threshold into the apartment.

"Lamont you big dummy." The 27inch T.V. sitting on the white entertainment center plays an old episode of Sanford and Son.

"Ha ha ha, Redd you a fool." Pops spoke to the deceased comedian in his raspy drunken slur.

"Pops what up?" Dro asked his father.

"Ain't nothin' son," he replied.

"Where everybody at?"

"I'm in here bae," Tonya yelled from around the corner in the kitchen.

Dro drops his keys on the glass brass table next to the door and heads to the kitchen. "Allante." Pops stops him in mid-stride, sitting up in the couch bed from where he lays.

"What's happenin' old man?" He responded.

"Here, take this and grab me that fresh fif' of Wild I out the freezer."

"I don't know what it's goin' take for you to leave this rut gut stuff alone."

"Rut gut, boy that's fine Irish wine."

"Yea, whateva," Dro said grabbing the empty bottle. He walks up behind Tonya who is standing at the stove cooking. He wraps his arms around her small waist and kisses her on the neck while grinding into her butt.

"Boy stop, you see me tryin' to cook," she said, pushing her nice round butt into his groin.

She turns her head to give him a peck on the lips. He leans over her shoulder and looks into the pan.

"Damn, them steaks smell good as hell. What you makin' with those?"

"Some steak fries and salad."

"Where Lil Dro?"

"You know where he at. He in there playin' that damn game."

"I'm a go back there and holla at him." He reaches into the freezer and grabs the fresh bottle of wine out for his father.

Walking through the living room he hands the wine to him. "Here Pops."

"Thank you son."

Dro walks down the short hallway to the bedroom his son and sister share. "What up lil man?" he asked, walking into the bedroom.

"Nuttin' much, just chillin' O.G. Just playin' the game," Lil Dro responded, putting the game on pause to look at his father from the edge of the bed.

"While you in here playin' this X Box I know yo homework done?"

"Yeah, ma already checked it."

"What you playin', Madden? Start it over. We can play a quick game while your mama finishes cookin'."

Alexus walks into the apartment carrying her book bag. She is a Junior at Glenville High School. Even though she has a dysfunctional family, she still continued to maintain a 3.5 grade point average in her ghetto environment.

She walks up to her father and gives him a kiss on the cheek. "Hey daddy."

"Hey Pumpkin, how was your day at school?"

"It was cool. Same old same old."

"Hey girl, you just in time to eat. Watch the last steak for me. I gotta pee," Tonya said, walking out of the kitchen and down the hall.

"Okay," Alexus agreed, sitting her book bag down and heading into the kitchen.

"Y'all come on out of there. Dinner is almost ready," Tonya said to Dro and Lil Dro while walking past the bedroom and into the bathroom.

"Alright, we almost done," Dro answered.

They finished the game with Lil Dro's Indianapolis Colts beating Dro's Cleveland Browns 27-20.

"I told you, you can't see me daddy."

"I only let you do that cause you my son."

"Uh huh."

"A'ight, you won fair and square. C'mon, let's eat," Dro said, grabbing his son in a head lock. They walk behind Tonya heading towards the dinning room.

"I know y'all about to go back there and wash y'all hands," she said, turning around glaring at them.

"Yeah, come on O.G." Lil Dro said, grabbing his father by the hand.

Dro leans down and whispers in his son's ear. "Dang yo mama mean."

They share a conspiratorial laugh.

"I heard that!" Tonya yelled, walking off to set the table.

After washing their hands the father and son joins the rest of the family at the dining room table to a meal prepared with love.

After finishing their meal Dro asks his sister, "So, what yo lil fast butt got up for this weekend?"

"Fast! Boy I ain't hardly fast. How many seventeen year old virgins you know?"

"Dro, leave that girl alone," Tonya added, clearing the table.

"What you mean leave . . ." Dro is cut off in mid-sentence by his cell phone ring. He answers the phone. "Yo, what up? . . . A'ight, cool, I'll be down in a minute." He hangs up the phone. "Baby, where's the case of apple Royal Blunts?" he asked Tonya.

"In the cabinet above the frigarator. Leave me some weed in the tray up there please," she responded.

Dro grabs three blunts and leaves a small amount of hydro in the tray for Tonya. "I'll be back later," he said, kissing Tonya on the lips. He gives his son some daps, who is standing beside Alexus helping her with the dishes. "Be cool Lil Dro," he said.

"Be cool O.G.," Lil Dro responded.

"A'ight baby sis," he said, mugging her in the back of the head.

"Gone, you play too much," she responded, flicking suds at his retreating back.

He walks through the living room and sees his father passed out on the couch bed. He grabs his keys off the table and heads out the door.

Dro jumps into the backseat of Tywan's white on white '96 Impala SS with grey interior on 20inch gold Daytons.

"Nigga where the fuck you get these shoes from?" Dro yelled after seeing the new rims on the car.

"Did the Kaine to a bitch ass nigga. Caught him slippin' in the drive thru," Tywan replied, pounding fist with Corey.

Tywan and Corey are Dro's best friends. They go back to kindergarten at Iowa Maple Elementary.

Corey cuts the music down by pressing the volume control button on the Panasonic face plate. "So what you need to holla at us about?" Corey asked, turning around to face Dro.

"Man listen, I feel fucked up that Cozac's dead. That was my man, but I can't let that stop me from gettin' this album done. We all know my money funny. It's been a minute since we hit a good lick."

"You bull shittin'," Tywan added.

"Look, we need a major pay day. I'm this close to blowin'. I feel it. Y'all already know what it is. I blow, we all blow. Who can we hit that's holdin' some heavy bread?" Dro continued.

"What about that nigga Banks from off ninety ninth?" Tywan suggested.

"Naw, I'm talkin' a six figure nigga," Dro said, shooting the idea down.

Corey sits in the passenger seat contemplating.

"Here, roll this up Ty," Dro said, tossing the three blunts and half ounce of hydro in Tywan's lap.

"A, I been thinkin' about this shit for a while. Y'all know my cousin Zo, right?" Corey asked.

"Nigga you know we know yo mutha fuckin' cousin," Tywan said, licking the flap of the first blunt.

"Nigga, do you eva shut the fuck up? Anyways, fam gettin' that major paper, but want to keep givin' me crumbs. Fuck that clown. He's been actin' real shady. I say we get his bitch ass."

"You fa' sho 'bout that?" Dro inquired.

"Hell yeah. It's the perfect time right now. That nigga off stuntin' in Florida somewhere. He left Block lil dumb ass handlin' shit while he gone," Corey confirmed.

"We goin' to get six figures fa sho fuckin' with that nigga. He holdin' M's," Tywan said, blowing out the smoke from the blunt. He passes the blunt to Corey who inhales deeply.

"I know where one of his safe houses at out in Beechwood," Corey further explained, exhaling.

"How many people?" Dro inquired.

"Should be empty. Run in, get the cash and dip," Corey responded.

Tywan finishes rolling up the other two blunts and passes them across the seat to Dro, who passes him the one already in rotation.

"Spin a few blocks Ty. Let's plan this shit out," Dro instructed.

Tywan starts the car and pulls off into the neighborhood.

*   *   *

Lorenzo and Soul pull up to the Big Toys exotic car lot in Miami, Florida. Seated in the back of the Silver Rolls Royce Phantom, Lorenzo glances at his gold faced diamond trimmed Versace watch.

"We made it right on time playboy. That flight wasn't to bad either," Lorenzo stated.

"Yeah, this was perfect timin'. We can go fuck with some hoes after this," Soul added.

Lorenzo steps out of the car. His six foot six, three hundred and thirteen pound bulky frame is adorned in a sky blue and white velour Enyce jogging suit. The sun beams on his cleanly shaven bald head. He is sporting two diamond studded platinum earrings, one in each earlobe. His freshly lined shadowed beard accentuates his caramel brown complexion.

Soul walks beside him, standing five foot ten, one hundred and ninety five pounds solid. He has on a black and red Jordan jogging suit and a pair of black and red retro four's on. His long custom made platinum necklace dangles from around his neck with a spinning diamond mic medallion attached to the end of it that deciphers the name 'Rock The Mic Records'.

He scrolls through his e-mail on his cell phone. Big Toys exotic car lot is owned by their Miami connect Carlos. Numerous of exotic vehicles are displayed. Lorenzo studies all of the luxurious cars and a silver SLR Maclaren Mercedes Benz with Lamborghini doors captivates his attention. He rubs his fingers along the hood of the car.

"Damn, this mutha fucka tough right here. I gotta cop me one of these shits."

"What's the ticket on one of those?" Soul asked.

"I don't know, but I gotta have this mutha fucka," Lorenzo said surely.

"If you flip one of those you gon shit on the whole city."

They walk into the front entrance of the car lot. Upon making their entry, a dark complexioned Cuban greets them with a friendly smile welcoming the two men.

"What's up papi?" He extends his hand giving them both a firm handshake. The men are very familiar with each other from their three year business relationship. "It's good to see you, Carlos. It's been a minute," Lorenzo said.

Carlos is a major cocaine distributor and entrepreneur out of Miami. He sells nothing less than 50 kilograms of cocaine. His legitimate business Big Toys consists of a connecting exotic car lots, an exclusive jewelry stores, and a boat yard that carries speedboats, yachts, and jet skis.

"Come on, let's go step into my office," Carlos suggested.

Lorenzo and Soul follow behind Carlos. As they pass the receptionist desk, Soul notices the beautiful Dominican woman sitting behind the desk answering the phones. As she takes a call she makes eye contact with him and gives him a flirtatious smile.

"A dawg, you see that?" Soul said, tapping Lorenzo on the shoulder.

"What?" Lorenzo inquired.

"Ole girl at the receptionist desk with the white dude standing by her reckless eye ballin' a nigga."

Lorenzo looks over his shoulder and scans the showroom floor seeing the many employees and customers milling about.

"Yeah, she is bad."

"I'mma get at ma."

They make their way to the rear of the building, stepping into Carlos' exquisitely furnished office.

"Would you guys like somethin' to drink?" Carlos asked, approaching the mini bar.

"Yeah, why not," Lorenzo answered, sitting in the Italian leather chair facing Carlos' mahogany desk. Soul sits next to him in an adjacent chair.

"What would you like?"

"Let me get a double shot of yac," Soul replied.

"I'll take the same thang."

He pours his guests their drink and hands them to them. He walks around his desk and has a seat.

"So, how much you want for that Maclaren that's sittin' out there on the lot? I gotta have one of those," Lorenzo asked.

"So, you like the Maclaren huh? That is a beautiful piece of art. I tell you what, after we handle our business I'll let you use it for the weekend, and if you still like it we'll discuss the price then."

"That's good lookin' Carlos, I really appreciate that."

"So, will you be purchasing your usual?"

"Naw, I don't think I'll be gettin' the usual. I wanna double up so I can bubble up papi." The men share a laugh at Lorenzo's witticism.

"I'll make the proper arrangements," Carlos stated.

"Take yo time, Carlos. We not in a rush. We got a lot of kickin' it to do," Soul said, with enthusiasm.

Carlos opens his desk drawer and pulls out the keys to the SLR Maclaren Mercedes Benz.

"Here, catch these." He tosses the keys to Lorenzo who makes a perfect catch.

"Yeah, this is what I'm talkin' 'bout. I'm ready to roll." Lorenzo reveals a grin that extends from ear to ear.

"Well let's do this then," Soul added.

Lorenzo and Soul pull up in front of Stallions gentlemen's club. A parking attendant notices the extravagant vehicle and makes his approach. The doors to the Maclaren Mercedes Benz pop up in the air exposing the cherry red interior. The automobile captures the attention of the employees and the many customers mingling outside because of the extraordinary look. The parking lot attendant hands them a ticket before pulling off to park the car.

The two men stride towards the main entrance of the strip club. Two bouncers positioned at the door scan the two men with portable metal detectors, upon making their entry. Soul is dressed in a pink and white polo shirt, pink and white Cleveland Browns fitted cap, a pair of white khaki polo shorts, and a pair of white and pink retro number ten Jordans. His platinum jewelry glistens as the fluorescent light shines on him.

Lorenzo walks right beside him wearing a purple two piece silk Versace short set, a purple alligator skin visor, and a pair of purple alligator skin sandals that coordinate with his attire.

They scrutinize the scenery, observing a cluster of beautiful exotic female dancers. As they make their way to the bar the bartender awaits their approach. The music reverberates throughout the club, shaking the floor. Lorenzo leans over the bar.

"Bartender, let me get two triple shots of Hennesy straight up on the rocks," Lorenzo requested.

"Comin' right up," said the bartender.

They sit patiently waiting for the bartender to return with their drinks. As they sit at the bar a well dressed gentleman approaches them asking, "Would you gentlemen be interested in our V.I.P. section?"

"Let's do dis," Lorenzo replied smoothly.

The bartender returns with the drinks.

"That'll be forty dollars." Lorenzo reaches into his pocket and pulls out a wad of crispy hundred dollar bills.

While attempting to pay for his drinks the well dressed manager puts his hand up signaling the bartender, "Never mind Ricardo, this one on the house."

A beautiful unblemished coffee complexion exotic dancer stares at the wad of money as Lorenzo places it back into his pocket.

"Let me escort you men to the V.I.P. section," the manager suggested, leading them to the V.I.P. section.

The dancer focuses on them with a look of greed burning in the depths of her eyes.

"Man it's goin' down in here," Soul proclaimed.

"Like the twin towers," Lorenzo retorted.

They are seated at a private booth equipped with a wide screen monitor that displays the numerous performances that are occurring inside the club. They place their drinks on the table in front of them. The booth is situated with a box of Zino platinum cigars.

"You guys have a good time. If you need anything, please feel free to ask. Just press that button right there and somebody will be here to assist you. By the way, my name is Santana and I run this place. Enjoy the festivities."

"Good looking out Santana, we appreciate it," Lorenzo said, kindly.

Santana walks away, vanishing into the crowd to attend to other duties.

Soul opens the box of Zino cigars and grabs one. He lights the cigar and inhales. He instantly starts coughing. Lorenzo bursts out in laughter and says, "That's what yo' dumb ass get. You know you don't smoke cigars." Soul places the cigar in the ash tray while choking on the cigar smoke.

"Man . . . Fuck . . . You, I don't see why niggas smoke this shit anyways!" he replied.

"Man we gotta take us some freaks back to the telly tonight," Lorenzo stated.

"I'm wit' dat playboy, that sounds good to me. I'm 'bout to get twisted."

In the middle of them conversing the dancer that was eyeing Lorenzo's money eases behind them, tapping them on their shoulders, garnering their attention.

"How did y'all like my show?" she inquired.

"Baby, I ain't seen no show yet, but it would be nice to see one," Soul replied. Soul reaches into his pocket pulling out a small roll of five dollar bills. He tucks a five dollar bill into her G-string, she smiles flirtatiously as she teases the two men by shaking her firm apple bottom ass. Lorenzo smacks her round ass.

"Damn baby, that ass bigger than Ki Toy's. How much it's gonna cost for a nigga to hit that tonight? I know you got a couple of friends to bring along?" Lorenzo coerced.

"Baby, we might be a little to expensive for y'all," she replied.

"Baby, money ain't a thang," Soul said with confidence. He reaches into his pocket and pulls out a fist full of large denominations. Greed flashes across her face once again at the sight of big money. She leans over Soul and presses her firm naked breast into his face.

"Damn baby, you ain't lyin', money ain't a thang," she said, with seduction in her eyes and voice. "Look, I get off at three. Meet me in the front."

"So, what they call you around here shortie?" Soul asked. She turns around with her back facing him, exposing a tattoo on her ass that reads 'Juicy'.

"You can call me Juicy," she replied.

"Well Juicy, why don't you head out to the floor and grab the three finest girls in the club next to you and y'all come on back here and get this money," Lorenzo suggested, flashing his large wad of bills.

"Yeah, I can do that. I'll go grab a few of my girls. We'll show y'all out of town boys a good time now, and a greater time later on," Juicy replied, sexily.

As she strolls towards the exit of the V.I.P. room Lorenzo and Soul watches her ass wiggle with every step in her stiletto heels.

"We goin' have some fun with her thick ass tonight," Soul stated, lustfully.

As Juicy steps back out onto the main dance floor she is approached by Santana.

"So, what's up with those two guys who pulled up in the Maclaren?" he inquired.

"They got some paper they tryin' to spend with the girls. They asked me to bring a few girls back to their section."

"You do that. As long as they tippin' you girls are strippin'. Understand?"

"Yeah, I got you."

"Good."

As Santana walks away, Juicy whispers, "Dickhead."

Lorenzo and Soul relax in the V.I.P. awaiting Juicy's return. A pretty petite young Hispanic waitress approaches them.

"Is there anything I can get for you gentlemen?" she asked in her heavy Cuban accent.

"Yeah, let us get four bottles of Cristal, and let me get five hundred dollars worth of singles too," Soul added.

"Right away, sir," she stated, walking off to fill their order. As she walks away two beautiful light skin women enter the V.I.P. area.

"Damn, look at them hoes. Looking like two twin Lisa Rayes," Soul said, enthusiastically.

The two women approach Lorenzo and Soul. "How you playas doin'? I'm Erotic and this here is my twin sister Exotic. Juicy sent us back here to entertain two bosses such as yourselves," Erotic stated, stroking their egos.

"How y'all doing?" a voice asked, catching the attention of the foursome. "I'm Hypnotic and this here my girl Hennesy. Would you fellas like some dances?" Hypnotic continued.

"Hold the fuck up, y'all goin' just stroll y'all asses over here like y'all don't see us?" Exotic said, angrily.

"Chill out baby girl. I got this. We appreciate the offer ma, but we good," Lorenzo informed Hypnotic, letting her down easy.

"Well, just call for us if y'all change y'all minds," Hennesy stated.

The four women look at each other venomously with clearly apparent bad blood between them. Hypnotic and Hennesy walk off rolling their eyes at the twins.

"Anyways, like I was saying, what can we do to entertain y'all?" Erotic asked, biting down on her peach bottom flavored lip.

"Why don't y'all have a seat and we can discuss that," Lorenzo suggested.

The waitress returns to the table carrying a tray with four ice buckets with chilled bottles of Cristal, two stacks of five hundred dollars in singles, and two Champagne flutes. "Here are your orders," she said, placing the items on the table.

"We need like three mo' glasses," Soul said, reaching into his pocket to pay for the order.

"Make that four. Juicy bringing another one of our girlfriends back wit' her," Exotic informed the waitress.

"It's cool homie. I got this. How much?" Lorenzo stated, stopping Soul from paying the bill.

"Twenty-two hundred," the waitress responded. Lorenzo counts out twenty-three crispy hundred dollar bills and hands them to the waitress.

"It's a tip in there for you," he informed her.

"Thank you. Just holler if you need anything else. I'll be right back with those glasses." She walks away and is summoned by Hennesy who along with Hypnotic is surrounded by a group of men. Seeing the hundred dollar tip Lorenzo so generously gave away and the large stacks of singles, the twins know tonight is going to be a big night for them.

"Since the club on you, the tel on me tonight," Soul said, popping the cork off one of the bottles of champagne like a true pro, not spilling one drop. He pours the flutes and offers one to Exotic.

"Naw, let us dance for y'all first," she said, declining his offer as 'Shake it like a salt shaker' blares from the club's surround sound system.

Exotic stands up grabbing Erotic's hand. They turn their backs to Lorenzo and Soul and proceed to do just as the song says. Their round juicy ass cheeks clap together as their thick cream colored thighs wiggle.

"That's what I'm talkin' 'bout baby!" Soul shouted, excitedly pounding fist with Lorenzo.

Distracted by the twins, neither one of them notices Juicy approaching them until she is up on them with the thickest woman either one of them has ever seen. Asia stands in front of them in a silver thong with some silver lace up heels. Her 40DD-32-46 frame glistens with baby oil and glitter. "Pussy Poppin" by Ludacris comes on.

"Let's show them how we do this in the M.I.A," Juicy instructed, clearly the leader of the group.

The four women lay on the plushly carpeted floor placing their hands in the small of their backs, using their elbows to lift their apple bottoms from the floor. As the gyrate their hips to the beat of the music, Lorenzo and Soul slide their thongs to the side, taking a glimpse at their well maintained neatly shaven pussies. They stand over them showering them with singles. The women look into the men's faces seeing the intense lust that their writhing bodies stimulate.

After a couple of hours, four bottles of Cristal, and several lap and table dances, Lorenzo is in the corner of the booth playing with Juicy's clit.

"So what's it goin' cost us to get y'all four back to the telly for the night?" he asked.

"Seeing how y'all been tippin' us real good tonight, I'll say like two G's."

"Y'all got that comin'. Me and my man goin' step out for a minute, but we'll meet y'all outside at three."

Asia, the thickest of the four dancers has her hand in Soul's short fondling his dick. He stares into her slanted eyes. She says, "I'm goin' have fun with this big boy tonight." Soul is mesmerized by her beauty.

She softly kisses him on the cheek. "I'm looking forward to this tonight baby." She walks off flirtatiously smiling.

*　　*　　*

Soul and Lorenzo sit back in the extravagant sports car waiting patiently. As Soul sits in the passenger seat writing a rap on his SideKick II, a mustard yellow Honda Civic pulls behind them. The headlights to the car shine on their rear end. Lorenzo gazes into the rear view mirror.

"I hope that's them hoes. I'm ready to down them twin bitches," Lorenzo proclaimed. The passenger door of the Honda opens. Asia steps out of the car dressed in a Baby Phat halter top, a denim Baby Phat shirt, and a pair of leather buckle pumps carrying a leather printed crocodile purse. She strolls toward the Maclaren Mercedes Benz with a soft bounce in every step. Soul stares into the door mirror admiring the angelic looking woman making her approach.

"Damn Exotic, them niggas rolling hard," said Juicy.

"I'm goin' break these niggas," Exotic added.

"I'm goin' fuck the shit out of them sexy ass niggas. I haven't had no dick in a minute. All my man do is give me a five minute fuck, bust his nut, roll over and fall asleep on a bitch," Erotic stated.

"Girl, me and that nigga would have a problem. I hate that when a nigga nut, he feels like it's over with. It's hard to find some bomb dick out here. That's why I keep my vibrator with me. This pussy stays wet," Juicy admitted.

"Girl, you so crazy." The women fall into a short burst of laughter.

"I'm just speaking the truth. You know how these niggas is." They pull off trailing the trio.

"Damn baby, where you get all that ass from? You gotta be mixed with some African genetics with an ass like this," Soul stated.

Asia sits in his lap giggling. **I'm going to get in his pockets by the time I leave the hotel. This trick ass nigga going to pay the down payment on that new Toyota Avalon I'm trying to get.** Asia said to herself while teasing him.

They pull into the parking lot of the Marriott Hotel. Lorenzo and Soul rented the room strictly for the purpose of tricking. They have another suite at the Four Seasons Hotel and Tower. Lorenzo calculates his every move to stay a step ahead of the game. He knows that in the game of life a bitch can be a man's quickiest downfall.

The six of them walk into the hotel room, closing the door behind them. "Y'all sure y'all ready for this Cleveland dick?" Lorenzo asked.

"I'm ready for whatever baby. The question is are you ready for some Miami pussy," Juicy responded, sexily.

"Let me show you girls how ready I am." Lorenzo opens the drawer to the dresser and pulls out a tiny suitcase. The women are curious, wondering what is inside. Lorenzo unzips the suitcase and dumps out a variety of sex toys.

"Damn baby that's how y'all get down in Cleveland?" Exotic inquired, anticipating a good time. She recognizes the Jack Rabbit Vibrator which is her favorite toy. **He can't be an amateur at this.**

"Let's get this party started," Asia said loudly, in her beautiful sexy monotone. She slides her skirt down slowly in a teasing manner, exposing her long, well defined legs. Her hour glass frame stands five foot ten in her high heel pumps. Soul appraises the beautiful creature who looks as if she was molded by God himself.

Soul walks in her direction burning in lust. Asia stands completely naked. **Now that's what you call eye candy. I'ma fuck the shit out of her pretty ass.** Juicy breaks Soul's train of thought.

"Ain't you forgettin' about somethin' baby?" Juicy asked, stopping Soul in his tracks.

"What you talkin' 'bout shortie?" Soul asked. Juicy puts her hand up in a motion emulating as if she is counting money by rubbing her fingers together.

"That bread baby. Before a nigga play, a nigga gotta pay," she reminded him.

"Aww, my bad ma. I feel you," Soul replied. He stands face to face with Juicy reaching into his pocket. He shuffles through his thick wad of money while she stares greedily, with her hand out.

This nigga holding heavy. I'ma trim this sucka when he go to sleep. As this dishonest thought travels through her mind, he hands her two thousand dollars. "It's all about you now daddy," she said, after counting the money.

Seeing the large amount of money exchange hands, the women prepare themselves to put on the best performance ever. Each woman thinks of how they are going to spend their share of the money. Asia sits on the edge of the queen size bed.

"C'mon daddy, show me what you working with," she said to Soul, seductively. She unfastens his shorts, grasping at the size of his thick dick. "Shit daddy, your dick is big as hell. You're going to have to take your time with this pussy."

Juicy goes to accompany Soul and Asia as she plots her deceptive act. "Damn baby that's too much dick for one man. God showed you too much love." Soul chuckled at Juicy's remark. He receives the same response from all the women he engages in sexual activities with.

Asia leans forward, placing his dick into her mouth. Juicy joins the sexual activity by dropping to her knees softly licking on his nut sack. His shorts drop to his ankles. He kicks his shorts underneath the bed.

"Oh shit, suck this mutha fucka. There you go ma," Soul moans softly, as he closes his eyes.

Lorenzo is enjoying the company of Exotic and Erotic. His fantasizing has him feeling as if he is being sexed by twin Lisa Rayes.

Exotic and Erotic are sharing a double headed dildo. The two women ride the dildo with one end of it in each of their wet pussies. Lorenzo stands in between the women kneeling down in a position with Erotic's head in his hands, grinding against her face as she sucks his dick. Exotic spreads Lorenzo's ass cheeks apart. She gently flicks the tip of her tongue across the outer rim of his ass. She pushes her tongue against his asshole then removes it as if she was ringing a doorbell with her tongue. She uses the full width of her tongue to completely lick his ass crack. A tingling sensation races up his spine

"Damn you suckin' this dick like a pro," Lorenzo complemented Erotic on her excellent head game.

Soul grips the head of Juicy as if he is palming a basketball. Asia lays back on the bed horny, welcoming him. She fondles with her clit.

"C'mon papi, give me that big dick," Asia begged, as she entices him.

Juicy is still trying to figure out a way to clip him for his money.

Asia spreads her legs wide open, making a watery sound with her pussy as she plays with her clit. Soul remembers that he has no condoms at hand.

Fuck wearing a rubber this bitch fine as hell. I'm hittin' all pussy. Soul thought, looking at the extremely beautiful woman. With her sex appeal Soul feels that she is worth taking a chance on. He climbs on top of her struggling to penetrate her tight wet pussy. She grimaces as his dick slowly sinks inside of her. The pain reminds her of when she lost her virginity.

"Ooooooh papi take it easy," she cried. Juicy licks Asia's hard honey brown nipples.

Lorenzo activates the battery operated Jack Rabbit vibrator. Penetrating inside of Erotic from behind, he spreads her ass cheeks open, seeing the wet moisture on his dick. Exotic licks on Lorenzo's balls from behind. Lorenzo reaches around Erotic's waistline with the Jack Rabbit vibrator placing it against her clit. She cums right away and the creamy juices from her pussy warm his dick. He smacks her on the ass as she goes wild fucking him back. Her big round ass wobbles as she throws it, bucking against his pelvis.

"Fuck me daddy. Ohh, that dick feel good as hell. Ooh, oooh, oooh, I'm cumming again, what you doing to me?" Erotic cried. Moans of sexual enjoyment travel across the room along with the clapping sound of flesh.

Asia is lying on her back with her legs spread wide open as Juicy eats her wet loose pussy. Juicy is in the doggy style position getting banged out from behind. Soul places two fingers inside of Juicy's asshole. Juicy reaches around her back, trying to push his hands away.

"What's wrong, you can't handle this dick baby? You never had a nigga bang this shit like this before?" Soul inquired, while stroking deep inside of her.

"Ooh shit baby, ooh, ooh, oh yea . . . yeah I can handle it," Juicy replied.

Asia is lying on her back shaking slightly in the middle of an orgasm. Soul pulls out of Juicy spreading her ass open, making an attempt to fuck her in the ass. She lowers her hips, resisting.

"Hold on baby don't nobody go up in there."

Soul holds his dick in his hand as the woman rejects him. Knowing he has more money, she makes another proposition. She knows that when a man is eager for a nut he is vulnerable.

"It's going to cost you anotha five hundred to hit this asshole with that big mutha fucka in yo' hand. Shit, you done stretched the shit out of my girl pussy."

Soul knows that the stripper is nothing but a money hungry bitch trying to get another dollar.

"Five hundred more huh? I tell you what; I'll give you a thousand dollars if you think you can handle this dick?" Soul exposes a friendly smile knowing that money is not an issue. "I suppose you want the money up front?"

"That's right baby. If the money is not on the wood it's not no good," Juicy responded, displaying her experience in dealing with tricks.

Growing up in a whorehouse, she was molded by her mother at an early age.

Soul climbs off the bed hearing all the moaning behind him. He reaches underneath the bed for his shorts and counts out another thousand dollars.

"Here you go shortie." Dollar signs flash in her eyes as she recounts the money. Soul cracks a smile as the stripper stashes her money in her purse.

Lorenzo inserts the vibrator half way inside of Erotic's pussy, licking on her clit at the same time. Erotic moves wildly as he eats her pussy from the back. He smacks her thick ass while Exotic is lying underneath Lorenzo sucking his dick.

Asia spreads Juicy's ass cheeks as Soul slowly slides into her asshole with force.

"Ooooooh shit it hurt, hurry up," Juicy screams loudly, pounding her fist against the pillow. Asia licks the other half of Soul's dick that is still forcing its way inside of Juicy's ass. She grimaces from the excruciating pain. Her moan pierces the atmosphere. Asia smacks Juicy on the ass causing her to become irritated. "Bitch stop smacking, this . . . shi . . . shit hurt."

Soul lets out a chuckle, enjoying the moment. Juicy has one thing on her mind and that's money. She knows if her plan succeeds she will be able to get that brand new Lexus she's been looking at. She feels his large dick damaging her insides. But for another dollar she knows a hoe gotta do what she gotta do.

Urban Tales Publications, Inc
Ordering List

You Said Forever By: Sparkle Douglas (Coming Soon)
Dead Or Indicted By: Troy Smith (Coming Soon)
Dream By: Maurice Hawthorne & Jason D. Brantley (Order Ready)
Change The Game Part 1 & 2 By: Jason D. Brantley & Maurice Hawthorne (Coming Soon)
Dutchess Part 1 By: Dutchess (Order Ready)
Dutchess Part 2 By: Dutchess (Coming Soon)
Dutchess Part 3 By: Dutchess (Coming Soon)

<u>Urban Tales Publications, Inc information</u>
Phone # (414) 627-7800
E-Mail: utp_inc@yahoo.com
Web-Site Add: www.urbantalespublications.net
Mailing Add: Urban Tales Publications, Inc
              P.O. Box 250293
              Milwaukee, WI 53225

Money & The Power

Author Biographies

JASON D. BRANTLEY

My name is Jason D. (Jay) Brantley. I'm a 30 year old felon with 5 children. I reside in Milwaukee, WI. Currently I'm going to school for my BA in Business. I'm homeless and I feel great to be alive . . .

MAURICE HAWTHORNE

Maurice Hawthorne is a 33 year old Milwaukee native who developed the passion for writing in his early teens after winning every poetry contest at John Muir Middle School. Being a young man growing up in the poverty stricken streets of Milwaukee, he became infatuated with the fast money. After going from a small time hustler, he found himself heavy in the drug game. His flashy lifestyle made him the target for the stick up kids, which led him to being shot four times in cold blood and his 18 month old son being murdered right in front of his eyes. Two years later he was indicted by the Federal Government and once again he was battling for his life. Facing a life sentence for drug charges, he thought it was over. Having a mistrial, he was later charged with a lesser offense, giving him another chance at life. During his period of incarceration, he picked up the pen and decided to bring his dream to fruition. He incorporated all of his street experiences and trials and tribulations into his writing skills and penned 7 powerful novels with his co-author Jason D. Brantley.

To write Maurice Hawthorne or Jason D. Brantley, please send fan mail to:

Urban Tales Publications, Inc
P.O. Box 250293
Milwaukee, WI 53225

Money & The Power